THE GORBACHEV VERSION

THE GORBACHEV VERSION

RICHARD HUGO

ZEBRA BOOKS
KENSINGTON PUBLISHING CORP.

ZEBRA BOOKS

are published by

Kensington Publishing Corp.
475 Park Avenue South
New York, NY 10016

Library of Congress Catalog Card Number: 90-062888

ISBN 0-8217-3288-9

First British Edition: 1989

First Zebra Books hardcover printing: March, 1991

Printed in the United States of America

Acknowledgments

I would like to thank Alan Fox for his help and support; Clive Carrington for his knowledge of diamonds; and B.K., for reasons B.K. knows best.

Prologue

Our childhood is like our dreams, fractured in our memory, intense but unreal. I remember the Secret Policeman, my father, bending over my truckle bed smiling his affectionate Secret Policeman's smile. I do not remember his face (though I have photographs, the two that survived the search of our apartment) but his uniform remains: my fingers used to run over the braid and pips of the shoulder boards and touch the collar tabs of an NKVD general; my nose recalls the wax of his gleaming boots. And what else? He spoke to my mother while I was in the room. A day to remember because something good had happened. He was smiling and full of a policeman's obscure joy. He said: "Lavrenti told me that everything is going to be OK" — the only words he spoke that I remember. Lavrenti was referred to as *Uncle* Lavrenti, with a degree of emphasis that meant he was not my uncle but that a good boy should be gifted with such an uncle. One of my photographs includes him. The other is of my father at school, but which of all the faces is his I never could tell. Uncle Lavrenti stands arm in arm with my father, both beaming at the camera. My father is in uniform, Uncle Lavrenti is in white ducks and shirtsleeves and wears a straw panama; and behind them the sun casts long shadows of palm fronds or perhaps ferns: they were at Sochi or some other Black Sea resort. Lavrenti had another name — Beria. He was Stalin's last police chief after Yagoda and Yezhov had vanished into the execution cellars. Beria himself did not long survive the death of the Great Leader: Khrushchev and the rest had him killed to secure their own positions. But that was later. First, in 1953, Uncle Lavrenti had my father shot.

1

The Brezhnev Version

"In our country, rich in resources of all kinds, there could not have been and cannot be a situation in which a shortage of any product should exist . . . It is now clear why there are interruptions of supplies here and there, why, with our riches and abundance of products, there is a shortage first of one thing then of another. It is these traitors who are responsible for it."

Vishinsky at the trial of Bukharin

1

There are investigations that begin with a bang. There are others that begin with an unregarded event and ease their way along a path of trivia and routine to expire of boredom. The Sokolskoye Incident was an example of the first. The Great Jewish Antibiotics Ring appeared to be a case of the second, and would have remained so if the MVD Anti-Corruption Squad had not decided to arrest Viktor Gusev.

It was difficult to say when the investigation into the Great Jewish Antibiotics Ring started. For years the shortage of pharmaceutical drugs had been a scandal and there was a common opinion that something ought to be done about it. It might, of course, have been possible to produce more drugs; but that raised difficult questions of the performance of the relevant enterprises and ministries, not to mention the broader issue of the priority of antibiotics production within the current economic plan and the drain on the available resources by the army. On balance it seemed easier and preferable to delve into the black market that had sprung up on the back of the shortage, to break up the rackets and arrest the racketeers — Viktor Gusev, for example.

Within the Second Chief Directorate of the KGB the investigation struggled for a place and was shuttled between the 12th Department, the 10th Direction and the Industrial Security Directorate, all of whom might plausibly be interested in the subject but claimed to be short of resources. The problem was of competition with more glamorous topics such as the meat racket operating out of Kiev and the public scandal of the Moscow housing shortage, which could be discussed now that new blood had taken over the Moscow Party machine.

Colonel Pyotr Andreevitch Kirov became involved in the Great Jewish Antibiotics Ring when his superior, General Rodion Mikhailovitch Grishin summoned him to his office. This was in the aftermath of KGB's investigation into the Sokolskoye Incident, when Grishin was still relishing his promotion and KGB itself seemed bright with change, if only because the painters were in the building in Dzerzhinsky Square, partition walls were going up and down, the place smelled of paint instead of tobacco, and in a world where that could happen anything was possible. So Grishin laid the file on his desk, which was covered with debris for the occasion of the move into the new office that went with the promotion.

"It's really a Fraud Squad case," he elaborated casually. He fingered two of his favorite talismans, a water carafe with a Ricard label that he had lifted from a café in Paris, and a photograph of his wife and mother — my spouse and my parent, as he called them with a notional tear in his eye. Grishin often gave the appearance of being an emotional, even a sentimental man. "Tread gently," he suggested. "Let the Public Prosecutor's Office and the boys from Petrovka take the lead."

Kirov asked whether he was authorized to intervene in the course of the investigation.

"Intervene? No, not intervene. This is a regular police matter. Consider your job as liaison."

"Keep an eye on them."

"If you like," Grishin mused in a forgiving way as if Kirov were resisting his intentions. Then he smiled again, cheerful and innocent.

The day that Viktor Gusev was arrested, Kirov slept badly. His dreams were troubled by recollections of his father, about whom he had not consciously thought in years. The day before, he had received a message that an old family friend was sick, perhaps dying. Old friends, old memories; he put the dream down to that. Its echoes were still there when the telephone by his bedside rang and he found Bogdanov on the line, saying: "The Great Jewish Antibiotics Ring. It's going live. Bakradze is about to make an arrest."

Bakradze was an investigator with the Public Prosecutor's Office, a young, eager lawyer. Bogdanov hated all indirectness and loathed him. But he gave the appearance of being honest and cooperative and so far Kirov had taken him at face value. It was even possible to like him.

"Where are you?" he asked Bogdanov.

"At the Centre. I got a call from my man at Pushkin Street, who swears he saw our friend himself there at four in the morning, finalizing his arrangements with Petrovka for a CID squad to do a dawn raid and pick up some character name of Gusev."

Kirov did not recognize the name.

"I'm not surprised. I'm asking myself the same question: how is it that after months of silence we find ourselves with a Gusev? You've never heard of one; I've never heard of one. Only Bakradze, who's supposed to tell us about these things, has heard of one." After a pause, which used up the remains of his exasperation, Bogdanov asked: "What do you want to do?"

"Drive here. Collect me and we'll pay them a visit."

Twenty minutes later Bogdanov was at the door, lounging against the jamb, thin and lugubrious, in a worn fur cap and leather greatcoat, rubbing his finger against his nose in one of the petty-criminal gestures he had acquired from the rubbish end of the business. He slipped through the open door and took a position by the coffee jug, batting his arms against his sides and throwing off a cold lopsided grin. "Bloody freezing, huh? What a morning for a raid! Who needs it, huh?" Misery made him cheerful. "Sod them all, what do you say?"

"Coffee?" Kirov poured the coffee. Bogdanov stared sourly at the cassette player.

"Do we have to have Mozart at breakfast?"

Kirov turned the music off. Mozart was his addiction. He wondered sometimes when music would lose its charms like all addictions. Bogdanov was a fan of horse racing and football.

"Why do you want me along? Why don't we leave this one to the Fraud Squad and wait for the report?" Kirov offered a chair. Bogdanov's natural intrusiveness frayed him.

"Bad night?"

"I couldn't sleep." He accepted a cigarette, and without looking for sympathy added: "My uncle Kolya is sick."

"General Prylubin? I thought he was dead a long time ago. I'm sorry." Having disposed of that subject Bogdanov wiped his lips and nudged his spectacles back into the groove worn into his nose. The spectacles were an old pair with wire frames mended with tape and gave him the air of a seedy bookkeeper. He reverted to the other topic: "Trust your uncle Bog. Something odd is going on."

They drove in Bogdanov's car. During the night it had snowed. An early fall and not the real thing. At this time of year the snow came and went and taxed the nerves. The true onset of winter was always a release.

"Gusev?" Kirov prodded mechanically while his attention strayed to the window and the view of snow in gray lumps or melting from the roofs along Kalinin Prospekt and running into the gutters. Empty streets except for a few dull trucks, the militia prowl cars and the early buses. The Okytabr Cinema advertised a new film, *Iron Harvest,* and a gang of women was being organized outside the Arbat restaurant ready for snow clearing.

"*Gusev,*" Bogdanov intoned monotonously between efforts of concentration on the road. "Viktor Maximovitch. An official with the city water authority or a right ponce, depending on which way you want to look at it. He has one of those do-nothing jobs, pushes paper and gets his subordinates to do all the real work. Probably trades on the side: cement, pipes, construction equipment — he must get a lot of opportunity in that line. Still, you can't chase them all, am I right? But antibiotics? Bakradze says yes, I say maybe — and you?"

"I don't know. How did Bakradze get on to him?"

"He doesn't say. Officially we don't even know that he *is* on to Gusev. That's the point!" He glanced at Kirov. "You feeling OK? Have you read the reports, the ones from Antipov and all the girls in Sadovo-Sukharevskaya Street?"

Kirov tried to cast his mind back to the reports he had received from the MVD Anti-Corruption Squad. Bogdanov anticipated him. "Any mention of Gusev?"

"No."

"No! See? For months this investigation has been chasing its tail, catching nobody but a few crooked pharmacists selling off stock and some wide boys with brains enough only to trade in the street. Now suddenly we have Viktor Gusev the Antibiotics King — that's Bakradze's story according to my man at Pushkin Street. He says that Gusev is going to take the fall — that Gusev is the mastermind behind the Great Jewish Antibiotics Ring."

"Perhaps he is." Kirov stared wearily at the snow vanishing as it hit the waters of the river. Why did I dream of my father? It's not important: I must dream of something.

8

"Then why don't we hear about him? Why aren't we invited to the party?"

They parked on the Frunze Embankment. The street leading from it was being roped off by a gang of *druzhnikki;* some of the early cars were slowing for a look, but the special constables, self-important in their red armbands, waved the traffic on. "See what I mean?" said Bogdanov, jabbing a thumb in the direction of the *druzhnikki* as they slopped through the melting snow. "Look at them. Civilians! I bet Bakradze has got everybody here except the Red Army choir. This is a Hollywood production."

The special constables allowed the two men through the barrier. There were vehicles in the street, half a dozen militia cars, a truck with a canvas roof, which had brought the *druzhnikki* and the stuff for the barrier, and Bakradze's modest Zhiguli looking bright and cared for. A Black Raven was parked against one of the buildings to carry away the accused; the engine was running and the driver was strolling round it kicking the tires.

"Who is the photographer?"

A figure stood across the street; Kirov examined him — a kid, not police, not KGB.

"I'll ask him." Bogdanov trudged in the stranger's direction, his tall spindly frame hunched forward. Kirov waited and occupied himself in detached study of the police cars as they stood, beautiful in the moist dawn light and the snow. Bogdanov dragged his way back with the stranger in tow. The younger man was flashing a red *Komsomolskaya Pravda* press card. Bogdanov had a hand on his shoulder and said gloomily: "Aleksandr Mikhailovitch — Pyotr Andreevitch, and vice versa. OK, Sasha, just repeat the story. Get this, boss, you'll love it. I love it. This is America we're living in." The photographer looked sheepish. Encumbered by camera straps and the rest of his gear he struggled to put away his press card.

"Well."

"I'm here to photograph the arrest."

"Photograph — publicity — get it?" said Bogdanov. "Go on, kid, tell him."

"There's always a first time, isn't there?" Aleksandr Mikhailovitch said uncertainly.

In his tiredness Kirov was impatient with such innocence. He asked: "When did you get the request? There was a request, wasn't there?"

9

"Yesterday."

"Yesterday?"

"Maybe five o'clock."

"When we were still in the office," Bogdanov commented pointedly. "My phone was working, was your phone working, boss?"

"Who called you?"

"The Public Prosecutor's Office."

"Investigator Bakradze?"

"I think that was the name."

"Personally?"

"Yes — well, not me personally but my chief."

"Of course. But it was Bakradze on the phone?"

"Yes — I mean I think so — that's what I was told."

By now Bogdanov was looking away in annoyance. He had never got wholly out of the habit of breaking heads, a relic from his police past. He acted sometimes as if he thought words were a barrier between himself and the truth. Ignoring the photographer he asked: "Does any of this make sense to you, boss? He tells the press but doesn't bother to inform us."

One problem at a time. Kirov was distracted by curiosity why Aleksandr Mikhailovitch's editor had sent a youngster. So that he could put the incident down to misunderstanding and inexperience if questions were raised later? He glanced at Bogdanov for his thoughts but the latter, bored with frustration, was scraping the snow from his rubber overshoes, the ends of his trousers tucked into the tops of his ragged socks against mud spatters.

Kirov shared a relaxed smile with the photographer like a cigarette. He pulled out a pack and offered one. Bogdanov supplied a match. Aleksandr Mikhailovitch was appreciative and opened up in return.

"It's the new style, isn't it?"

"Is it?" Kirov said sympathetically.

"Drag corruption out into the open air after all these years. Show these crooks to the people for the scum they are."

"Yes, of course," Kirov agreed, which appeared to encourage the other man to more of the same eager moralizing until Bogdanov stopped him tetchily with, "Christ, we've got ourselves a Communist!" and slapped the photographer on the back. "OK, Sasha, pop along now and take your snaps." To Kirov he said: "What do you think now? Glad you came? Is this a circus or is this a circus?"

They walked over to the apartment house. Kirov checked his

10

watch; seven o'clock and the day turning to a faint glimmer in a sky banked with gray cloud and underfoot a crust of ice on the snow. He showed his badge to the militiaman at the door. "How long have you been here?"

"Half an hour, comrade Colonel."

Bogdanov stuffed a hand into his pocket and came up with a piece of dry bread and some cheese wrapped in newspaper. He offered it to Kirov. "You had breakfast? I hate these early jobs. Still, seven o'clock is almost civilized."

There was a cage elevator but it was locked. They took the stairs, showing their badges to the guards on the landings. Outside Gusev's apartment Bogdanov took the guard aside. "How's it going? Any shots? Screams? Breaking glass?"

"They're talking," the guard said blankly.

"Talking — cozy. Gusev in there?"

"Yes."

"How many with him?"

"Two of them, Antipov and some big chief from the Public Prosecutor's Office."

Bogdanov grunted and bit into his cheese. "All this muscle and yet they go in there on their own. Wonderful!" He slipped his spare hand over the handle and tried a gentle turn. "It's unlocked," he observed quietly to Kirov. "Looks like they're not expecting to be disturbed." He wiped his hands on the scrap of wrapping paper and dropped it down the well of the stairs. He scrutinized the door panels then Kirov, who was examining the skylight with its art-deco glasswork.

"Nice place, boss? How many rooms, do you think — two — three? It's incredible the way some people can afford to live! Did I tell you he was a bachelor?"

"No." Kirov turned from his own thoughts. He was used to Bogdanov moralizing before they made an arrest. "Let's go in."

They passed through the door silently. A short hallway lay in front and two more doors. They picked the second from where the voices were coming; Bogdanov turned the handle and shouldered the door sharply open so that it banged against the wall. Three men stared with varying degrees of surprise in the direction of the intrusion.

"Good morning, comrades." Kirov entered the room, glanced at the occupants and took in the scene. Gusev was living well if tastelessly. The walls of the room were papered in a deep red flock, the chairs were upholstered in a burgundy moquette and the carpet was Chinese. Pink and indigo chintz covered the windows; the curtains

11

were open and the window gave a view of the street. In one corner stood a cocktail bar, and next to it a number of small boxes piled on the floor with cotton wool and tissue paper spilling out of them.

"Come in, come in." Bakradze was on his feet and, after a second of hesitation, looking puppy-dog pleased, an expression that came to him easily since his face was naturally open and bore a surprised look as if he had been awarded a prize. Today he was looking as clean and fresh as his car and wearing a suit for the occasion. With small deft movements he offered a chair and continued eagerly: "Come in, close the door. At this stage we're just asking a few questions. This is our subject—is the word 'subject'?—Viktor Gusev. Viktor Maximovitch, may I introduce comrade Colonel Kirov, who is from another organ of law enforcement. Comrade Colonel, this is Viktor Maximovitch Gusev who is assisting us with our enquiries."

Kirov let his attention drift from Bakradze to the owner of the apartment, Viktor Gusev. How old? Fifty or so. Handsome in a studied way, with gray eyebrows and black hair; large-featured in a fashion that a filmmaker might favor, reminding Kirov of—the image fled him. The point was in any case inconsequential; he stored the impression until later, and in the meantime noted the calm hands folded across each other with well-clipped nails and a ring in heavy gold set with a single sapphire. The look of an impresario—was that it? Gusev was wearing tan slacks and a cotton shirt and had had time to shave. Meanwhile Bakradze was saying: "We're about finished here. CID will do the search. We can complete the interrogation at Petrovka. By the way, do you know Antipov?"

Kirov knew Antipov; in a way the detective was Bakradze's opposite, no ambition or innocence, and accidentally sinister from bad health, bad habits and too much time associating with criminals. Lots of policemen got to look like Antipov as they faced retirement, and their appearance didn't particularly signify. Bakradze explained: "We're working together," meaning the Public Prosecutor's Office and the Anti-Corruption Squad.

Kirov nodded to Antipov and returned his attention to Gusev's hands. You could learn a lot from hands, and about Gusev's there was a disturbing and unruffled calm that was inappropriate to his situation. No doubt it would explain itself.

"Why wasn't I told about this arrest?"

"Oh, didn't you get the message? I assumed you must have—I mean, here you are, yes? In any case," Bakradze suggested, "the actual arrests are not KGB's concern—not as such, are they? I thought that your people had only a watching brief, or so we were told. It was in the coordination procedure, *a watching brief,* I believe those were the words, but you can check for yourself." He had identified conciliation as appropriate. "I hope you're not dissatisfied?" He was looking at Antipov. "We would have sent you a transcript of the interrogation." Antipov grunted in support. "Can I say fairer than that?"

A clattering came from the next room. Bogdanov emerged from the kitchen with a piece of ham stuffed in his fist. He went to the bar, helped himself to some cigarettes from a bark box that stood with the glasses, and disappeared again into the bedroom. Kirov used the distraction to ask: "The arrest — what was the basis?"

"A source," answered Bakradze, trying to follow Bogdanov's noisy wanderings with one ear. "Look," he urged, "this isn't the time and place to go into that." The suspect was sitting upright, alert for cues. Yet aloof, Kirov thought. The owner of the apartment had the face of a manipulator: what he didn't control didn't happen. No — it was too early to reach conclusions. Kirov filed the impression and confined himself to watching Gusev ask casually for a cigarette. Antipov passed him the bark box. Bakradze continued: "In any case, who cares how we got on to him? The evidence is all here. We don't need anything else." He waved a finger at the pile of boxes. Kirov picked one up. Antipov got up from his seat, coughing. He was a heavily built, grizzled man, yellow-skinned and yellow-eyed, the type who stands too near and whose clothes smell of tobacco smoke. He looked like someone not long for the world, and Kirov wondered if he knew. As the detective moved, his damp black overcoat fell open and briefly revealed a gun tucked into a holster, which in turn was worn over a woollen cardigan. Kirov resumed his examination of the boxes.

The first contained vials of liquid with labels on the cartons, package codes and expiry dates. A second held packs of tablets. The producer's name in both cases was Bulpharma. The instructions were printed in Bulgarian and badly translated into Russian on a cheap gummed sticker. Meaning? Kirov held a bottle up to the light and saw the other men through the glass: Bakradze, neat, young and bland; Antipov, tired and indifferent; and the enigmatic Viktor Gusev who reminded Kirov of a stranger met somewhere. He replaced the bottle and picked up another box. Inside was a collection of small denomination bills, mostly American dollars, a few Deutschmarks, some English bank notes and a wad of certificate rubles tied with a rubber band.

"The wages of sin," Bakradze quipped in a friendly fashion.

13

". . . is death." Kirov dropped the currency back into the box. "That's how the quotation goes. No mention of dollars."

Gusev stretched his legs. Kirov watched him, thinking: a man too relaxed. He had a passing impression of inverted order: racketeer, MVD, KGB—not the way it was supposed to be, but perhaps the idea was just an effect of tiredness. Gusev said: "Well? Are you going to get on with it? Arrest me?" It was the first time he had spoken; he had a soft tenor voice, attractive in its way. Antipov told him sharply to shut up.

"Do you want me to send you a copy of the report?" Bakradze inquired in the same cooperative vein. "We have our man. The rest is all routine." He suggested delicately that Kirov would be free to involve himself in the further prosecution of the matter as much or as little as he wished.

"I'll let you know," Kirov answered noncommittally. He had lost interest in the lawyer and was watching Gusev and noting the changes. He had an idea that the other man was also conscious of a discrepancy in the atmosphere, something wrong, but maybe not the same thing. Returning to Bakradze, he said: "On reflection I'll come with you now and sit in on the interrogation."

Kirov expected a reaction, but what he didn't expect was Gusev's hand diving to his seat then moving to his mouth and cramming something between his lips. Bogdanov leapt toward him. Antipov was already reaching into his coat and producing his gun. "No!" Kirov shouted and his arm swept up to catch the detective's arm. But the weapon had fired and Gusev was jerked out of his chair and pitched onto his back.

"I thought he had a gun," Antipov explained dully. He studied his handiwork and replaced the gun in its holster. Gusev lay on the floor with blood leaking over his shirt and Bakradze was backing away because this sort of thing wasn't supposed to happen when lawyers were around. Kirov knelt by the body. He saw an object let fall by Gusev's limp hand and scooped it up before anyone else could see it.

It was a black velvet bag closed by a drawstring but now lying open. It looked too small to hold anything of importance.

2

"You know Scherbatsky? Works the American desk — sometimes acts as bagman for the Washington Residency when Yatsin wants someone to carry his dirty underwear to Moscow."

"No." Kirov didn't know Scherbatsky, but Yatsin was his fat sidekick from his days in America. Nowadays Yatsin was the head of the Washington Residency, worried about his health and his pension and eating macrobiotic food. And Kirov had a colonelcy as a consolation prize for solving the problems of the nuclear plant at Sokolskoye, and made a living investigating petty crooks involved in rackets like the Great Jewish Antibiotics Ring.

"Scherbatsky? No? Well, the name doesn't matter." Bogdanov drove one-handedly and smoked Gusev's cigarettes while talking. "This Scherbatsky, he's a cheapskate. He fiddles his expenses, deals in black-market dollars and cheats on his wife. To salve his conscience he decides to buy her a watch. So, on his last trip, he goes through all the cheap jewelers' shops in New York. He buys her a fifty-dollar Rolex — get it, a fifty-dollar Rolex?"

"I understand."

"Sure. So, the watch fails. Scherbatsky sends the watch and the guarantee card to Switzerland or wherever they make Rolexes. He tells them to send him a new watch, to Captain Y. S. Scherbatsky, Committee of State Security, number two Dzerzhinsky Square, Moscow. You understand, this is going to impress them."

"And?"

"Rolex reply. Sorry, this is not our watch. Made in Taiwan!" Bogdanov laughed. "Those Chinese will fake anything!" He let his face fall into tiredness. "What the hell, maybe the story is a fake too."

In the traffic their car failed. Bogdanov blew the horn in case that helped, got out and stared at the tires. He returned and asked whether Kirov wanted to wait until he could call up a replacement or continue on foot; they were close to Kropotkinskaya metro station.

As they walked, Kirov said: "According to Bakradze his office notified us that Gusev was about to be arrested."

"Not me," Bogadnov answered.

"Perhaps the message took its time to arrive."

"If Bakradze wanted it that way, he could be sure the message took its time. I still say we weren't intended to be there."

"Perhaps." Kirov changed the subject. "What time did Gusev wake up?"

"How should I know?"

"You went into his bedroom."

"OK, so I was testing you. I checked his alarm clock. Are you a mind reader? The alarm showed six o'clock, and the clock was lying face down as if it had been knocked over when the alarm was switched off. So I say he got up at six. Probably before Antipov sent in the scouts to stake the apartment out, and for certain before Bakradze arrived."

A crowd was milling around the entrance to the metro station, churning up the snow. Bogdanov searched in his pockets for a coin for the trip. Kirov watched the crowd, but his mind was still on Viktor Gusev, dapper and relaxed, living in a different world from the crowds struggling on the subway trains, another Moscow.

"He washed, shaved, went into the living room and opened the curtains." Meaning what? Kirov tried to slot the facts into his memory of the apartment. Something in the timing troubled him.

"Are we still talking about friend Viktor?" Bogdanov asked. "One of Antipov's men could have opened the curtains."

"No. Antipov would have closed them — to keep out prying eyes."

"Maybe. But so what?"

Kirov tried again to imagine the apartment: Gusev in the white cotton bathrobe found hanging behind the door, Gusev splashing his pampered body with the lotion found in the cabinet next to the woman's razor (whose was it?); perhaps Viktor had done some exercises, he had a flat-bellied look and suits cut to match. Then the man's body on the floor, the door open and Antipov yelling to the militiamen to get an ambulance.

"He was finished in the bathroom by six fifteen — six twenty at the latest."

"Bakradze arrived at six thirty."

"But the MVD squad must have been there already, they were packing the street like an army review. When Gusev opened the curtains he had to see them." Gusev was in his vision again, standing at the window with the street light falling on his lean face, watching with curiosity as the militia gathered on the pavement. There was the oddity. "Why didn't he hide the drugs and the money?"

"Maybe he did. Maybe Antipov found them. We weren't there. We don't know what went on." Bogdanov disliked speculation, and instead nurtured a faith in confession — like a priest, Kirov sometimes thought.

"When we arrived Bakradze and Antipov were the only ones who'd been in the apartment. There was no sign that they'd searched the place, but the boxes were already on the floor. Gusev didn't try to hide anything."

"He knew the game was up."

"No." Kirov could read Gusev's studiously relaxed expression and knew the answer, if not the explanation. "He didn't care."

Back at the office there was a message to see Grishin, but, when he tried, the General was tied up with Radek. Radek was back from smashing the meat wholesale racket in the Ukraine. The gang had been operating for ten years until Radek and his team shook out the local KGB, harassed the Kiev Fraud Squad and broke the operation in six weeks. The story had made its way into *Pravda* and Radek had even figured in a TV news story for *Vremya* which was unheard of. The last time Radek was in Moscow he had suggested that the two of them share some beers in the bar in Stoleshnikov Lane. Radek was overcome with his own success. He drank a few too many and became confiding. "What's going on, Petya, I mean *really* going on? This push against the black market as if it were something new. For fifteen years we could only attack the fringes, but now — *whoosh!* — " he swung an arm and knocked a bottle off the table. Then he closed up and breathed beer into Kirov's face. "I tell you, before I die, I shall have my picture in the papers. Ace crimebuster Radek!"

Kirov thought that perhaps he would. Bakradze had brought the press along for the arrest of Viktor Gusev, if that wasn't incredible enough.

"Radek had asked about Kirov's case.

"No progress, eh? The Great Jewish Antibiotics Ring — whoops —

pardon—too much beer. Why—" he asked affectionately, "why *Jewish?* Where is it getting you except for pulling a few small dealers in?"

Kirov suggested they finish their drinks, but Radek wasn't finished. He had a flash of inspiration: "Perhaps the small dealers are all that there is to it. Here and there, all over the place. Little guys pocketing a few tablets and selling them. Perhaps—have you ever thought that the Great Jewish Antibiotics Ring doesn't exist? Maybe it's just something we invented."

"Let's go."

"Yes? Oh? OK. Let me pay." Radek reached for his wallet, and knocked over another beer spilling it over his clothes. "Shit!" He stood up and Kirov noted a change that had come over him since the Brezhnev days when Radek kept his head down and looked as gray as the walls. He was wearing his coat slung over his shoulders like a film star.

Radek came out of Grishin's office and spotted Kirov in the corridor. "How goes it, Petya?" he said cheerfully. Behind him the door to the outer office was open and Grishin's secretary was watching them meditatively. "How are you getting on with your drugs case?" He didn't wait for an answer. Kirov watched his back disappear down the corridor, then Grishin's secretary was inviting him in.

Grishin had finished refurbishing his office. The rest of his possessions had come out to join the Ricard water jug. On the desk a Gauloise ashtray, another with the Shell logo on it, and a set of Sheraton hotel pens. Grishin was sitting behind his souvenirs, wearing his Rumpelstiltskin look, outwardly cheerful but with a hint of malice. As a small man he had probably decided years before that he had to unsettle people in other ways than by physical presence. On the surface he was always and everywhere all affability. As sincere as an adult telling stories to children.

"You wanted to see me, Rodion Mikhailovitch?"

"Did I? Oh, it was nothing important." Grishin was fussing distractedly with the desktop ornaments. "I thought a status report on your antibiotics affair might be in order." He looked up. "Perhaps I can help?"

So Kirov gave him the account of Viktor Gusev's arrest. Grishin listened and had his secretary bring tea. Meanwhile he lounged in his chair, his face full of warm concern. Like my father, Kirov thought, for no other reason than a half-forgotten dream. He put the idea away: he had no idea how his father would have looked.

"What are you trying to suggest?" Grishin asked. "Some form of

18

collusion with this Gusev? Who is involved? MVD, the Public Prosecutor's Office, or both?"

"I don't know."

"You don't know?" Grishin repeated, not unsympathetically. He gave the matter some thought. "Bakradze was making a public show?"

"Yes." Kirov agreed though he knew what was coming next.

"Then he must have been serious about Gusev's arrest — you follow me, it doesn't sound like much of a deal for Gusev."

"He could have arrested Gusev for show and released him later."

"Not after getting authority to publicize the arrest. Men who are publicly arrested don't get released."

"Gusev was in no position to know about the publicity."

"Gusev was shot," Grishin reminded him. And again: "It doesn't sound like much of a deal."

"No, it doesn't," Kirov admitted. He felt the mystery and the explanation slipping away.

"Where is he now?" Grishin asked.

"In the prison hospital at the Butyrka. The wound isn't too serious. He's in police custody but I have men baby-sitting him."

"Do you?" Grishin replied gnomically.

Kirov waited for some request or instruction, then said: "Bakradze has a strong case against Gusev: there were antibiotics all over the apartment. We could withdraw our interest and leave Petrovka to get on with the prosecution and conviction. Is that what you want?"

Grishin looked up. "No."

"What *do* you want?"

"You make it sound as if there is something personal in the matter." After the slight flicker of concern, Grishin withdrew into piety: "The shortage of medicinal drugs is a matter of public interest. It's our job to make sure that the Anti-Corruption Squad investigates these cases properly. In this particular instance I should ask you: are there really grounds for suspicion?" He reverted to sympathy. "Perhaps I should also ask what you are looking for. Glamour? Do you want to take over the Ukrainian meat case? Turn over a few meat distributors — after all everyone knows that there isn't one that isn't shot through with corruption. It's a popular cause and you could hardly fail — why do you think I gave it to Radek? It's just about his level." When Kirov didn't reply, Grishin let his eyes fall on the photograph of his family and changing the subject he said: "You look tired, Pyotr Andreevitch. Why don't you relax this weekend, come to my *dacha*, meet

19

my spouse and my parent. You can bring your girlfriend, Larissa Arkadyevna."

"Thanks. I'll think about it." He didn't mention that Lara had cleared out of his apartment. It wasn't important. Women came and went and he didn't own them. "I may have other things to do. One of my relatives is ill. I may have . . ." For the first time the idea of Uncle Kolya dying seemed sharp and credible.

"Anyone I know? Someone in the service?"

"General Nikolai Konstantinovitch Prylubin. Do you know him?"

"A fine man," Grishin answered solemnly.

Kirov returned to his office. He remembered the black velvet bag he had recovered from Viktor Gusev and took it out of his pocket. On reexamination it appeared insignificant, a scrap of cloth. He summoned Tumanov and told him to put the bag through analysis. Tumanov was a jaunty youngster. He asked skeptically what the lab was supposed to go looking for. Anything. Anything? All right, whatever you say.

Next Bogdanov called from the Butyrka to report on the prisoner's condition. "They've removed the bullet and he's OK."

Kirov asked whether blood tests had been done to discover what it was that Gusev had swallowed.

"Yes. But they came up negative. It wasn't a drug. And there's no point in asking Gusev. He just lies in bed and smiles," Bogdanov said sourly. Then: "Let him smile. I'm waiting here with a bedpan, and when he shits then we'll know."

He drove out to Babushkino and turned up on the doorstep of Uncle Kolya's *dacha* in time to meet the doctor leaving. She was a small, pretty woman with a serious face that perked up in a smile when anyone spoke to her.

"How is he?" Kirov asked. He caught a glimpse of the fat housekeeper, Tatiana Yurievna, peering through the window to see who the visitor was.

"General Prylubin is an old man," the doctor said. "He drinks too much and smokes too much and he doesn't take advice. His chest is bad and I don't think he could survive a case of pneumonia. I'd like to take him into hospital, but he won't agree." She looked sad, and Kirov suspected she was fond of the old man. As who wouldn't be?

He could not remember a time without Uncle Kolya. He was there from the beginning, more clear than his father in Kirov's recollection.

He too wore the varnished boots and the NKVD collar patches on his uniform. When Kirov's father disappeared, Uncle Kolya came to the apartment. His face was flushed with exertion and emotion. He stood in the doorway silhouetted against the dull light of the landing, his greatcoat swinging from one shoulder like a hussar's pelisse so that he came into the room in appearance a romantic hero and said one breathless word, "Anya!" to Kirov's mother. Had it really been like that?

When Kirov was fourteen Uncle Kolya took him on holiday to Riga and the Baltic coast. They stood on the gritty shore, faces into the wind that blew across the cold sea and he told the boy the things that men should know. He used that coy expression. There on the beach with the sand filling their shoes, he wore a blue suit with baggy trousers, a snap-brimmed hat and a shirt with the collar undone because they were on holiday; and he handed the boy an orange, which Kirov thought a miracle. By then he was acquiring a paunch; he had a broad, friendly smile and teeth that were discolored from chain-smoking *papirossi*. At that time he was a colonel, as Kirov was now.

"Nikolai Konstantinovitch?" Kirov prodded the General softly with words. Tatiana Yurievna stood at his shoulder telling him that he mustn't get the old man excited and sounding annoyed, which meant she was pleased he had come.

"Who is it?" the patient said faintly. He raised one leathery eyelid and a cunning eye peeped out. "Ah, it's you, you young bugger. Come to see your old uncle?" His fingers tapped painfully on the bed-clothes. Kirov accepted the invitation and sat on the edge of the bed.

"It's dark in here." The window was shuttered and the atmosphere close.

"That's the Old Woman's doing. Peasant! She doesn't believe in light and fresh air. She'd have a priest in here if I let her. Got a smoke on you?"

"The doctor says you shouldn't be smoking."

"Bugger the doctor!" the old man retorted, but he was too weak to press the point. Kirov took his hand. It was mottled and shivering. Kirov held it and sat like that for half an hour, during which they did not speak.

It was evening. Kirov found he had dozed. His apartment was in darkness. He struggled with the discomfort of the chair and his right hand touched a soft piece of cloth. He unfolded a pair of silk camiknickers he had bought for Lara on his last foreign trip. He remembered discovering them under a cushion. In her haste to quit the flat, Lara had left them. They were not to be had in Moscow and so were a measure of her urgency after their last quarrel. He threw them onto the floor and went to make himself some coffee.

From the kitchen he heard the phone ring and went to answer it. It was Neville Lucas on a social call.

"Peter?" Lucas used the English form of his name. After twenty-odd years in Moscow the Englishman's Russian was still heavily accented and he spoke his own language whenever possible.

"Neville?"

"Are you there or have we got a bad line?"

"I was asleep."

"Ah, sleep of the innocent. Wish I could. My trouble is I'm not innocent. Just an old whore. Fancy a drink?"

Lucas's voice was full of sad humor. Kirov had never fathomed the source of that sadness. When he suggested from time to time that the Englishman regretted his life in Russia, the robust reply was: "Rubbish! The Soviet Union is the finest country in the world! God's own people!" The sadness was left as an echo. England on the other hand was "not the place it used to be." But Lucas had defected from the place it used to be, taking with him such paltry secrets as he could lay his hands on.

"I thought a few jars in the *Mezh* would be in order," Lucas said. Lucas liked to drink in the Mezhdunarodnaya or any of the other international hotels where he could speak English and be entertained by the visiting businessmen on the lookout for Moscow color. Nowadays, apart from his nominal rank in the KGB, he spent his time at the Writers' Union translating textbooks into English for the Indian market. "Not the real thing," would say of his efforts. "Like writing in code. English was meant to be spoken — declaimed, as witness old Will Thingummy, the Great Bard." Now he said, "How about wetting your whistle?"

"Not tonight, I've got something on," Kirov answered.

"Not something wicked, I hope."

"I have a case on."

"Enough said."

Kirov put down the phone. Almost immediately it rang again. Bogdanov was on the line. "Where are you?" Kirov asked.

"The Butyrka. Can you come here quick?"

"What's wrong?"

"Gusev—he's taken a turn for the worse. They've moved him into surgery."

It was ten o'clock, the snow was gone, the streets were wet, and a slow melancholy train of clanking green carriages gave a wail as it entered Byelorussia Station. Some marshals from the Party were supervising volunteers as they struggled to hang a banner from the station façade, and in Lesnaya Street a line of trucks held placards for the next day's rally. The demonstration was against war and in favor of peace. Since the pro-war anti-peace party wasn't numerous, no one was expecting trouble, but the Sluzhba had been kept hopping, checking the papers of nonresidents and packing off dissidents for a few days' unpaid holiday out of the city. Kirov supposed that the exercise was to warm up the population for the next round of the Geneva arms-control talks, which Gorbachev himself was scheduled to attend.

He parked the car in Lesnaya Street and walked the remaining distance to the Butyrka, counting the paces between the ancient turrets along the long penitential wall, gathering his thoughts in the monotony of movement. Bogdanov was waiting for him in the empty stone courtyard, smoking a cigarette in the doorway of the parcels reception office. He stubbed it and approached Kirov with an urgency in his step.

"Bakradze has beaten you to it," he said. "He turned up inside fifteen minutes with six heavies from Petrovka and a police medic; young Tumanov is keeping an eye on them. Bakradze is making calls, smoking his head off and walking the corridors as if he's expecting a baby. Gusev is unconscious."

"Why is he still here? Why hasn't he been moved to a proper hospital?"

"He's too sick to move—I believe them. An hour ago he suddenly started throwing up blood. It has nothing to do with his wound but he was puking blood as if he'd never run out of the stuff. He looked as if he was dying."

"Call one of our surgeons in."

"Do you know how hard that is at this time of night? Sorry, I'm tired. I was at home when Tumanov called me." Bogdanov avoided Kirov's inquiring eyes. He looked beyond Kirov's shoulder as if addressing his concerns to an invisible stranger. "I managed to find a surgeon. I had to drag him from a lecture at the Sklifasovsky First Aid Institute. He's on his way now." He checked his watch. "Fomin — do you know him?"

"No." Kirov glanced at his own watch, though time meant nothing to him. How long was a fatal delay?

They went inside and made their way to the operating theater. The door was barred and Bakradze and a brace of detectives from Petrovka were waiting outside, watched by a nervous Tumanov. Bogdanov had exaggerated Bakradze's concern. The lawyer seemed relieved.

"Pyotr Andreevitch! I'm glad you're here."

"Why?"

Bakradze looked hurt. He hesitated and for want of anything better took out a pack of cigarettes and passed them around the detectives. When he returned to speech, his manner was confidential even apologetic: "This morning I thought we didn't exactly hit it off. Partly my fault, I suppose. You took me by surprise when you suggested that I was trying to do something behind your back."

"I didn't say that."

"Didn't you? Oh — well, 'implied' may be a better word than 'suggested.' At all events I thought there was an atmosphere between us. Not what I wanted, Pyotr Andreevitch, believe me."

"I believe you."

"It's just that this cooperation thing is a bit tricky at the best of times," Bakradze said, and as if it had just occurred to him he proposed that they should have a drink sometime and talk matters over.

"Maybe," Kirov agreed.

There was a viewing window in the door. Kirov glanced through it into the room beyond. Gusev was laid out invisible under an operating gown and a team of doctors was working on him. The equipment looked second rate, relegated from one of the civilian hospitals. Watching the surgeons, he heard Antipov wheezing his way along the corridor on flat feet.

"How did you get on to Gusev?"

Antipov looked to Bakradze and back. "You talking to me? It was a stroke of luck really. We arrested one of our friend's distributors, a pharmacist called Zelenev — you should have a note of the arrest."

"No."

"No? Must be lost in the post, you know how it is. Anyway, this Zelenev kept a diary with a note of his meetings with Gusev. He couldn't explain what the connection was. I mean, why should he be meeting all the time with a Moscow city *apparatchik?* We figured that Gusev had to be his supplier."

"Or customer," Kirov answered distractedly. Looking at Gusev he had an idea that the man's vanity would be wounded by the scars left behind by the operation.

"No customer would want antibiotics in that quantity, not so that they needed to go once a fortnight, not unless the customer was a hospital, which Gusev wasn't. He had to be a supplier."

"Has Zelenev confessed?"

"No."

"Where is he now?"

"Dead," interrupted Bakradze with more than a hint of sorrow.

Antipov waited, silently plucking a fragment of ash from between the hairs on the back of his left hand.

"Well?"

"He's dead," Antipov confirmed. "We had him in custody for two days when he was killed by another prisoner. What can I say? It happens."

"You had him alive for two days," Kirov said neutrally. "And he didn't confess?"

Bogdanov intervened sharply: "What the hell were you doing with him?" It was Bakradze who answered, still striving for civility.

"We live in changing times. We don't beat up suspects any more. It's called Socialist Legality."

"Since when?" asked Bogdanov.

"Go on," Kirov prompted.

"There was a practical reason as well," Antopov stumbled over the reply. "Zelenev was no gangster: he was just a man making money on the side the way everybody does. I guessed that once we raided Gusev's place and got some more evidence, Zelenev would realize he was finished and cooperate voluntarily. That way we would get more out of him than if we'd knocked him around. In any case," he added as if this were new to everybody, "the rough stuff is old-fashioned. Maybe it'll come back or maybe it won't, but look around you. Ever since Mr. Clean took up home in the Kremlin we've all got a dose of morality. Take this antibiotics business. Under Brezhnev and Chernenko, who would have cared?"

While this was going on the KGB surgeon arrived. He came striding down the corridor, a tall erect man in a smart suit with his lecture notes stuck in one pocket and a table napkin in the other. "Are you

Kirov?" he asked, and glancing aside into the theater added: "Christ, what a dump!"

"I'm Kirov."

Fomin eyed the other man and put away the casually assumed arrogance. "I gather our patient is vomiting blood."

Kirov nodded.

"Hmm. Ulcers." Fomin studied the corridor uncomfortably. Gray-painted walls and small trays of rat bait where they met the floor. A pervasive smell of cabbage and disinfectant. He lit a cigarette and invited the others to join him. "I really don't know why I do this part of the job," he said easily. "I hate these places. By the way I pulled Gusev's medical records, which is why it has taken me so long to get here. They confirm that he has a stomach ulcer. Now, if Gusev were living in America — but it doesn't matter whether the Americans have drugs for controlling these things, does it?"

"You think the ulcer explains his symptoms?"

"It would explain the puking. What do they feed them on in here?"

"I think that Gusev has been eating something special."

Kirov left the newcomer washing up to go into the theater and the police team hanging about the corridor. He ignored Bakradze's curiosity.

Bogdanov followed him into the ward. "What are we searching for, boss?"

Beds lined each wall, lockers stood by the beds and the windows were barred. An orderly in a dirty white coat slouched in the space between the beds and a dozen or so patients in prison-issue pajamas lay in the beds or sat on them waiting for something to happen. The room was pervaded by a sullen silence.

Kirov asked where Gusev had been.

"Over there." Bogdanov pointed. "You still haven't told me what we're looking for."

"Gusev's last meal." Kirov reached into his pocket for the black velvet bag but remembered it was still being analyzed. What had been in it? He approached Gusev's bed and sensed a dull curiosity in the other patients.

"Come to clean up?" said a voice. "About bloody time!"

Bogdanov went over to the speaker and cracked him a sharp blow in the face. He ignored any risk of reaction and ambled back to Kirov murmuring: "Socialist Legality, my arse!"

A screen had been placed around Gusev's bed when the vomiting fit started, before he had been moved to the theater. The orderly came over and removed it without being asked. The bed was a mess of bloody sheets. The smell was foul. Kirov paced a slow circuit of the bed and noted the details. The iron frame showed signs of rust, the bedclothes were gray and patched, the door on the locker had lost one hinge and hung at a crazy angle. In his imagination Kirov could see Gusev feeling the burning in his guts and the onset of nausea. He had turned onto his side to lean out of the right-hand side of the bed and vomit on the floor. Then there had been the main rush of blood and Gusev had collapsed back onto his pillow and the blood had poured off him and onto the sheets.

Kirov turned to the orderly. "I want this bed stripped down one sheet at a time so that I can inspect them."

The man was dimly astonished. "What, me? There's blood on them."

"Do it!" Kirov commanded. The orderly yanked one of the convalescent patients out of his bed and the two men set about the business.

"Do you seriously expect to find something?" Bogdanov asked.

"Gusev didn't swallow drugs or they would have showed up in the blood test. Whatever he swallowed must have been solid enough to irritate his ulcer."

The orderly and the patient held the first blanket top and bottom and shook it but nothing fell out. They stretched it so that Kirov could inspect it. The blood showed as large stained patches reminding Kirov of the blot tests used by psychologists. They held the same ambiguity. You could read into them what you wished.

"Try another one." He moved to the window. It overlooked an inner yard, floodlit and bare. Sleet was falling gently and was caught in the beams of light. In the stillness of the ward the lights went out except for that by Gusev's bed, which burned like an altar lamp. In the yard someone was rolling a trash can from one place to another.

The second blanket held nothing. Neither did any of the other items on the bed. They revealed only that Gusev had shit himself in his distress, which explained the smell. The orderly waited for more instructions. The prisoner-patient stood dumbly, his pajamas streaked with blood and ordure. Kirov moved to the right-hand side of the bed and regarded the blood-slimed porridge of bile and food that Gusev had ejected onto the floor in his initial agony. The prisoner looked down on it. "Oh, Christ," he said softly and for the first time attracted Kirov's attention. He had the bitten lips and feral eyes that Kirov had seen before. He wore rimless spectacles that now hung loosely about his face as if his head too had shrunk in measure with

27

his spirits. He glanced at Kirov and Kirov felt a sense of recognition. But it went and Kirov's attention faded before the task in hand.

"You can do this one," said the orderly. The prisoner shrugged.

"Got a brush or a stick I can poke this lot with?"

"Use your hands!" Bogdanov snapped impatiently.

The man knelt in a posture of prayer and his fingers began to pick delicately in the mess of vomit.

Kirov interrogated the orderly but the man had nothing to say about Gusev, had hardly had time to recognize him before this business happened and he was rushed to the theater.

"Try harder," Bogdanov prompted him. "Didn't anyone come to see Gusev? Ask to see him? Bring him anything?" Kirov let his eyes drift again to the prisoner, seeing the stubble of the man's scalp and the gritty lines of his neck. He was barefooted and with his soles upturned the horny skin was visible. Kirov watched him neutrally, aware of his own indifference. Like inspecting a dog, he thought. A small collection of objects accumulated at the man's side.

"Bring me some cloth."

The orderly appeared with a thin cotton towel. Kirov bent down and, using the towel, picked up the fragments of — what? They were slime covered and looked like gravel.

"Water."

The orderly directed Kirov to a sluice-room. Kirov kicked the mops and buckets aside, tied the ends of the towel to form an enclosed bundle and put it under a jet from the tap. He returned to the ward, told the orderly to lay out a clean sheet on the floor, and emptied the contents of the wet parcel onto the sheet. He stared at them. The other men stared with him but without knowledge saw nothing. The prisoner wiped his hands on his filthy pajamas and as Kirov turned to search out Bogdanov he saw tears rising in the prisoner's eyes.

"What about me?" said the prisoner. "Who gives a damn about me?"

Kirov returned to the sheet. Lying in the middle, in a patch of dampness, was a handful of diamonds.

3

The Malachite Cask jewelers' store stands in Kalinin Prospekt next to the old church of St. Simeon Stylites. This is the busier end of the street; opposite the jewelry store is a bar and a metro station, and next door is the city's largest bookshop. The bookshop also sells stamps, and all day long outside the Malachite Cask book buyers and stamp collectors bump into the wives of Party officials buying jewelry.

Kirov knew Proskurov, the director. He had met him once at a party in the days of Lara and parties. Brezhnev's daughter and one of her dubious boyfriends had turned up unannounced. Galina Brezhneva had a taste for diamonds and acquired them when she could, and this night she wore a necklace, an old Tsarist piece of spectacular beauty. Proskurov was in her entourage. He told everyone about the diamonds while his client smiled and nodded as if they had only just become real. The other guests talked about cars and the delights of their trips to the West.

Proskurov wore spectacles and had brown wavy hair and a schoolboy face. His nervous voice varied in pitch and it squeaked when he invited Kirov to his office and offered him a seat and refreshment. He expressed hope that this was a social call and nothing to do with his business, which was run in a perfectly upright manner though he couldn't speak for every detail in the lives of his staff as he was sure Kirov — *Pyotr Andreevitch* — would understand.

Kirov took an envelope from his pocket and emptied its contents onto the other man's desk. The stones glittered in the daylight. "What can you tell me about these?" he asked.

The stones lay between them. Kirov hadn't looked at them too closely before. They were beautiful and neutral and as mysterious as Viktor Gusev. Proskurov regarded them blankly, then with a sharp movement of one hand turned on a small ultraviolet lamp and focused it on the stones, which fluoresced. Proskurov switched the lamp off and sat back in his chair.

"They're the real thing," he said. "Diamonds."

"You weren't sure?"

"For a second." He watched Kirov closely. "Where did you get them from?"

"I can't say. I was hoping you would help me."

"Ah."

For a moment there was silence, then the expression on Proskurov's face changed from caution to curiosity. With the same sharp movements he divided the diamonds into two parts, then took a series of stones and weighed them individually on a small set of balances. Next he took an eyeglass, screwed it to his eye and examined the same stones.

"Fine white — second pique — three carats. Commercial white — very small inclusion — five carats. Finest fine white — very small inclusion — two carats . . . I can't imagine . . . You say you don't know their origin?"

"No."

The jeweler put down his pen and replaced the stones. He was cautious again.

"I can tell you they're not from a single source, or, at all events, not from a single piece or set. The stones are individually quite excellent, but they don't match. The differences of weight, color and clarity — I can't see how one would mount them together."

"And the rest?" Kirov indicated the unexamined portion.

"Rubbish. They have no relationship to the others. Cape and silver cape in color; clarity is third pique, spotted or worse. Strictly for the masses." Proskurov scooped them up indifferently and put them back into the bag. He paused briefly to ask: "Could they be from a foreign source?"

"Can't you tell?"

The other man shook his head. "Not from the stones themselves. But, now that you've asked about them, these," he glanced in the direction of the bag containing the rejected stones, "make me curious. This is the sort of stuff that gets cut in India — pure junk for the Western market. In this country there's no demand. We would apply them to industrial use."

Kirov had no answer to that suggestion. Viktor — Viktor — what were you doing? "I believe they came from this country," he said.

"In that case," Proskurov said thoughtfully, "my guess is that they're black-market stones. Not stolen, you understand: the variety doesn't suggest that a burglar has taken them from a set. Smuggled production, perhaps. Straight out of the mines to an illegal cutting operation. It happens. And in that case I could see someone cutting the poorer stones. They could be given away as part of the larger deal. A commission, if you like, for the dealer."

"And what is the whole packet worth?" Kirov asked.

Proskurov stared back long enough for the seconds to be counted. Kirov waited and then an ironic laugh escaped him which shook the other man out of his hesitation.

"A hundred thousand American dollars," Proskurov said slowly.

He wasn't sure whether Kirov was buying or selling.

When Kirov returned to the office there were two notes on his desk. The first was from Anya Dimitrievna, his sluggish but motherly secretary: Neville Lucas had telephoned; would Peter return his call? The second was a scrawl from Bogdanov on a torn paper bag. It said: "I've taken Tumanov and gone to G's place. B and his boys may not have found everything. Latest news from the hospital: G on the critical list — may not make it."

Kirov asked Anya Dimitrievna to find Lucas's number and put a call through. He checked his diary and remembered that Radek had organized a seminar to explain how he had broken the Ukrainian wholesale meat racket. Tapes of the interrogations were promised, and slides.

Neville Lucas came on the phone. "How about that drink?" he asked. "You can't sit at home brooding about Lara," he added, missing the point — that it wasn't Lara that disturbed his dreams but something else.

"OK," Kirov agreed. "Tonight — eight o'clock."

He went to Radek's seminar. Radek had commandeered a lecture theater in the new building in Kalinin Prospekt and sat at the front with his team in their suntans and satisfied looks. Kirov caught Grishin's eye. The General had an indulgent smile on his face; he took the rostrum and gave a brief introduction. He said that he had asked Colonel Radek to make this presentation so that others could learn how to conduct what was a new style of operation. He quoted Gorbachev on the need to root out corruption and Chebrikov's dictum on the necessity for KGB to act in accordance with Soviet law. He waxed lyrical on "the new spirit of our times."

This last remark caught Kirov's wandering attention. It stirred a memory of having heard something similar before. He tried to remember and had a vision of Chestyakov saying the same thing to a class of candidates, God knew how many years before, when for a span KGB's foreign service had tried to clean up its act. Chestyakov spoke of the need for both sophistication and humanity. He had a wheezy whistle to his voice as a badge of his own brief spell in the camps. Yes, Kirov knew about the spirit of the times. It ebbed and flowed, and people who caught the spirit became beached as it retreated. The cadres of KGB were layered like fossils. Last year he had attended Chestyakov's retirement party. By then the years had passed since Kirov's own training. Last year what Chestyakov recalled were his days of digging holes in the ice and slipping the bodies underneath. The old man had a nostalgia for the "real Cheka," the way it used to be, a band of good-hearted buddies. Two months later Chestyakov was dead. Out of respect Kirov had attended the funeral, and now, watching Radek, he had a feeling that he too was buried in one of the shallow graves of the past.

Radek, however, was not. When Grishin was finished he got to his feet and was now working through a series of flip charts which described the organization of his task force and the methodology of his operation. He threw off acronyms and buzzwords as he went along in a way that Kirov hadn't heard since his time in Washington. Then, the preliminaries over, he dealt with the investigation itself, the leads, the clues and not forgetting the interrogations — "a subject about which there has been some popular misunderstanding," as he put it with a neatness that he never used to have; and he added a smile for those who still misunderstood. Under the new dispensation you could even joke about these things. And to prove his point he had some shots of the prisoners, not a mark on them, as spruced up and disreputable as guests at a wedding.

"We live in changing times," Grishin repeated wryly when afterwards he and Kirov found themselves together in the elevator.

"Security with a human face," Kirov answered simply. Grishin caught the meaning.

"Ah, yes. Some of us have been there before." He didn't mention Washington and the Ouspensky Case, which had broken Kirov's career until the business of the nuclear plant at Sokolskoye revived it. What had Yatsin said about Ouspensky? "Fuck your mother, Petya, even I didn't know whether he was defecting to us or you were defecting to them!"

"It was a matter of timing," Grishin cooed. "Like telling jokes. Back then — in the seventies — when there were only a few of you — you were out of harmony. But now we're in an era of mass-market liberalism. You should be pleased." He gave a charitable look, even saintly.

Back at the office the phone was ringing. Bogdanov's deputy, Tumanov, was on the line, breathless and excited. "We're at Gusev's place," he said. "Uncle Bog is tied up with something — he'll tell you himself when he sees you. Can you come here?"

"I'm on my way."

He got one of the drivers out of the Sluzhba pool to drive him to Gusev's apartment on the Frunze Embankment. There was a militia guard on the door swapping small talk and cigarettes with one of Uncle Bog's legmen. The KGB man snapped to attention and let Kirov in. Tumanov had heard the noise and was waiting at the door. He said: "Uncle Bog didn't want to say too much on the phone." He gave a worldly smile: you know how it is. Kirov knew how it was — and had been. How old was Tumanov? Twenty-five and looking like a Komsomol class leader and eager to learn. He had picked up the habit of calling Bogdanov "Uncle" — probably from me, Kirov thought. Then: I am — state a number, any number, like a magician calling for cards — years old. The operative word is "old" — when did I become old? Tumanov wore a leather tank jacket with a zip front. Like an American cop.

There were voices in the next room. Behind him Tumanov was saying: "She doesn't know who we are. Uncle Bog told her we were from the Public Prosecutor's Office."

Kirov opened the door.

Gusev's apartment was as he remembered it, full of tawdry luxury. Only the pile of boxes was gone, and the militia had helped themselves to the drink and the cigarettes and taken a portable radio and an onyx lighter. Bogdanov was sitting in one of the chairs and the woman in another.

He put her in her twenties, not particularly good looking but knowledgeable enough to make the best of herself. Her makeup was stylish; her hair had been lightened not with the usual crude

33

bleach but with something imported; the simple blue dress fitted over her figure without the bumps or straps that came from Soviet underwear. She had access to foreign goods but nothing too fancy.

As Kirov entered the room she turned in his direction. Her eyes were an indifferent blue but intelligent; her nose was on the snub side, set between high cheekbones. Neville Lucas would have called them "Slavonic looks"; they didn't appeal to the English. She highlighted the cheeks with makeup and wore a dull crimson lipstick.

Bogdanov gave a lazy, "Hi, boss," and returned to the woman, taking up casually some point he had left off.

"So you work for Aeroflot."

"Yes."

"Internal flights."

"Yes."

"Never abroad?"

"No, never."

"Meet Nadezhda Aleksandrovna Mazurova," he said to Kirov. "But you can call her 'Nadia' since we're all friends. So," he addressed her, "where does all this stuff come from?" He indicated her dress with his bony finger.

"You can get these things in Moscow, if you know where to look—though I don't suppose you do look, do you?" The last statement was made without any obvious irony. Bogdanov got out of his chair, stretched his legs, touched his toes and gave an animal grunt.

"Our friend Viktor's tart," he said to Kirov. "She breezed in while Tumanov and I were turning this place over." He reached to the table and picked up her bag. "Nice," he murmured and turned it open onto the floor. With his toe he kicked the litter of objects apart and picked out a key.

"For my locker—at the place where I live."

"She also has a key for you-know-where." Bogdanov spun it on its ring.

"Viktor gave it to me."

"And another key . . ."

"It's just a key. People collect keys. I forget what it's for."

"She forgets what it's for." Bogdanov's style of interrogation included a large measure of sarcasm. He could annoy people into confessing. Ignoring her he leafed through her internal passport and workbook. "A Moscow resident's permit." He threw the pa-

34

pers onto the table and from the contents of the bag selected a bottle.

"Aspirin," she said. Kirov detected curiosity not fear, and that made him curious in turn.

"No drugs? Antibiotics?"

"I don't need them."

"But Viktor had them, didn't he? Stocked like a pharmacy."

She shrugged her shoulders. "I never saw —"

"But you should have seen, shouldn't you? That's the point! You're Viktor's woman."

"No." She didn't bother to elaborate.

Bogdanov turned to Tumanov. "Take her into the bedroom." He saw a flicker of alarm cross her face and paused, seeming almost to hold that expression, then he continued: "Keep her safe, that's all." He threw her a withered smile. She followed Tumanov.

"Well? Question her? Hand her over to Bakradze? Throw her out into the street? What do you want to do, boss?" He stared into the empty cigarette box. "The bastards stole all the smokes. Well, what do you want to do?"

"Why is she here?"

"Came in today on a flight from Erevan and thought she'd stay with good old Viktor. Officially she lives in a women's hostel at Lyublino. Unofficially she lives here as Viktor's woman."

"She says not."

"So what? She has a key to the apartment — what does that mean? Man, woman, shared apartment — do two plus two still make four these days or have we changed all that?"

"Why does she say she isn't Gusev's mistress when she knows no one is going to believe her?"

"Search me. She's crazy? She doesn't want her mother to find out?"

"Maybe." Kirov dropped the point. He noticed that the television set was switched on. It showed peace demonstrators in Sokolniki Park. Peace was breaking out everywhere.

"Do you think he'll succeed?" Bogdanov caught Kirov's mood of distraction. "Gorbachev, disarmament talks, are they going to succeed? I can see the Army loving that — watching their appropriations vanish!"

"Things change," Kirov murmured, echoing Grishin and Radek. "Why wasn't she tipped off that Gusev had been arrested? He can't have been working alone and Petrovka have hardly been making a secret of the arrest. Someone must have known. Why wasn't she warned off coming here?"

"She was staying in a crummy hotel. The telephones were out of order. She said she tried to phone Gusev last night but couldn't get a line. Also she wasn't in her scheduled hotel; someone screwed up, the place was overbooked and the flight crew moved out. No one knew where she was." Bogdanov let his eyes wander to the television again. Kirov followed and saw in close-up the uplifted faces following the speaker's words. The speaker would be mouthing the Party line and yet the crowd was hanging on to every sentence. The faces expressed hope—sincerity. Maybe they even believed. Grishin was right. Things changed.

Bogdanov switched topics. "They found nothing in Gusev's guts. Fomin called me and told me the result of the operation. Viktor must have puked the lot up. I got the same story from Antipov, minus the bit about the diamonds, which he doesn't know about, though it makes you wonder why he was at the Butyrka with his team."

"He called you?"

"He thought we'd like to know. Bakradze told him to call me. Spirit of cooperation—that's the new line. Antipov shoved it at me like he was going to invite me to his daughter's wedding. We're all on the same side—official. What he didn't tell me was why Bakradze and the police team turned up at the Butyrka. What were they expecting? The diamonds? There's no obvious connection between diamonds and the antibiotics thing so why should Bakradze be looking for diamonds? Conclusion?"

"He saw Gusev swallow something. He wants to know what."

"So simple curiosity drags him mob-handed to the Butyrka? OK, if you say so, I'll buy that."

"Bring her back," Kirov said, and while Bogdanov rapped on the bedroom door he tried for a moment to picture the woman here in Gusev's apartment. But for now the material for his imagination was too thin.

Tumanov opened the door and let the woman through. He looked embarrassed. Five minutes of small talk had exhausted his resources; it wasn't in the training manual. But the way things were going maybe some day it would be. Nadia Mazurova maintained the same cool distance. She took a seat and faced Kirov.

"How long have you known Gusev?" he asked.

36

She waited long before answering, but it was not a hesitation; rather an appraisal. Kirov remembered that flash of fear before Tumanov had removed her from the room. He played with the choice of continuing as now or recreating that fear. He speculated over its cause. She was saying: "I've known Viktor two, perhaps three years. We met at a party."

"And how long have you been his mistress?"

"I'm not his mistress."

Kirov offered her a cigarette but she refused. "I don't smoke." Bogdanov took one. He moved behind her chair and leaned to rest his arms on the chair back so that she could feel his weight and sense his presence.

"You lived here," Kirov contradicted her. "I found some of your things in the bathroom."

"The apartment is more convenient, more pleasant than the hostel. Viktor lets me use it."

"Why should he do that?"

"He likes my company." She thought over that reply. "You know Viktor. He likes to live well—have the best of everything. It suits him to be seen with a . . ." her voice fell.

"A beautiful woman?" Beautiful was the wrong word, but Kirov could see the appeal of that composure, particularly for Gusev. The apartment, the gold jewelry, the perfume to pamper his body—he had a feeling that Viktor liked objects. "There was nothing sexual?"

"He held no attraction for me."

"Because of his age?"

"Not particularly."

"Because . . . ?"

"Because he held no attraction for me. It isn't necessary always to have explanations—is it?" She smiled for the first time. Good teeth, perhaps too large. The smile gave life and drama to her face so that Kirov had a picture of Gusev arrested by that smile, valuing it like the contents of his apartment. She shut the smile off sharply.

The chair creaked as Bogdanov put his weight on it. He shuffled his hands so that they were on either side of her neck, the fingertips hanging down to touch her shoulders.

"Tell us about Viktor's business," he said. "No! No, don't look at me, look at my friend." His leaning posture caused his breath to blow through her hair. Her body stiffened but her face was surprised into a sudden shift of emotion. Kirov registered the fact but could not identify it. The change swept and retreated like the sea through pebbles.

"I don't know about Viktor's business."

"Balls to that. Tell the nice man the truth."

"He had business interests, but I paid no attention."

"No attention?" Bogdanov said venomously. *"No attention?* You couldn't walk about this place without falling over the bloody stuff! Boxes of drugs and antibiotics, booze, cigarettes. And"—he sighed—"we ask ourselves where does it all come from, don't we, darling?"

"No," she answered simply. Bogdanov let go the chair so that the upright snapped back and she was jerked with it. He moved to her side, pulled up another chair, sat down and took hold of her left hand. He squeezed it hard then relaxed his grip and let it rest in his own. With his free hand he stroked the backs of her fingers.

"Now then, come on, tell your uncle Bog. Who were Viktor's mates?" He grinned and pushed his face forward until it intruded into her focus. Her eyes retreated and shot a glance at Kirov.

"Don't you talk anymore?" she asked.

"The nice man can't hear you," Bogdanov answered. "He only talks to people who cooperate. Look at him—go on, look at him—can't you tell he's deaf?" She was looking beyond him at Kirov's impassive face. *Knowing what I'm thinking—no—no more than I know what she is thinking: that's the object of the exercise.* He lit another cigarette and returned her gaze through the flame of the lighter. Tumanov stepped to the television and turned the volume to maximum. The crowds cheered. She turned to the noise, distracted in her defence.

"Terrible noise," Tumanov shouted. "You could commit murder in here and no one would know." He looked to Bogdanov for approval.

Bogdanov said: "You look like a girl who's used to violence. I know Viktor's type. He's the kind who beats up his women—am I right? Is that why he doesn't attract you? Or maybe he does attract you? No sex! You must have driven him wild. Bit of a prick teaser, are you?" He gave her hand a vigorous rub. Kirov watched as the skin grew red. She remained silent but her eyes were fixed on his. Pain was in them. But also curiosity. Bogdanov she could understand—but *him?*

No—I don't know what she thinks.

"Do you intend to hit me?" she asked at last, turning limply.

Bogdanov stopped.

"Hit you?" He signaled to Tumanov to switch off the set. He bent over her again, still holding her hand, and said softly: "I've shown you nothing but affection." He let his lips move toward her ear and whispered something.

"That's enough," Kirov said quietly. "Let her go."

Bogdanov glanced at him with a sharp caution, but Kirov was looking at the woman. The room was silent. The television flickered. Tumanov played with his knuckles like a set of dominoes. There was no evidence of tangible violence.

Yet the look of fear on Nadia Mazurova's face appalled him.

Bogdanov checked his watch. "Another day!" he said cheerfully. To Tumanov he said: "OK, get your coat on." He explained to Kirov: "I promised my old lady I'd be home on time."

Kirov was still sitting in the same chair from which he had interviewed the woman. The television continued to flicker silently in the growing darkness. The heating system thumped meditatively. Strains of music came from an adjoining apartment.

Bogdanov put on his coat and wrapped a muffler around his scrawny neck. He studied Kirov thoughtfully. "You know, boss," he said mildly, "you should have let me carry on. It was going fine. She knows Gusev's contacts, I'll bet on it. A bit more sugar from you, a bit more shit from me, and she would have given us names."

"Except," said Kirov, stirring from his seat, "that we don't do things like that anymore."

"Don't we? Oh, yeah, sure — I'd forgotten." Bogdanov turned to Tumanov and ordered him to see to the car. He returned to Kirov. "Leaving aside the rough stuff, why don't we take her in?"

"Because she belongs to Petrovka — to Bakradze — at least until Grishin says otherwise." Kirov stood up. He turned the television set off. Now it was dark and the rain made a steady drum against the window pane. He could hear Bogdanov panting as he struggled to put on his rubber overshoes. He noticed for the first time a sour smell hanging in the air.

"Someone turned the power off," Bogdanov told him. The smell was from the kitchen. A piece of meat was rotting in the refrigerator and dribbling its stinking juices onto the kitchen floor. There were still a couple of beers hidden behind the meat. Bogdanov opened them, returned to the main room, passed one to Kirov and

39

took a seat opposite him. "What's wrong, boss?" he asked.

Kirov had asked himself the same question. From somewhere he was dogged by a leaden lassitude.

"I'm not sleeping well."

"No? Still worried about Uncle Kolya?" Bogdanov paused and took a pull on his bottle. Then, almost gently, he urged: "Get yourself another woman. If not Larissa Arkadyevna then someone else."

"What did you say to her?" Kirov asked.

"To who? Lara? Oh, you mean the other one, Nadia Whatsherface." Bogdanov leaned forward, close enough for his features to be clear in the darkness. His mouth was set in the lopsided angle that passed for one of his smiles. "It was a guess—a hunch—a reading of her character, isn't that what they call it, the way they teach it?" He seemed to insist on an answer. An answer from Kirov who knew the right words.

"Yes—reading character."

Bogdanov wiped his lips after taking another drink.

"I told her that once you had left, young Tumanov was going to rape her." He belched softly, begged Kirov's pardon, and, placing the bottle on the floor, said: "I wasn't serious. Would I do a thing like that? If it wasn't for hanging around a crook like Gusev, she'd probably be a decent enough kid.

4

At the Mezhdunarodnaya the door staff were turning away the locals. Sometimes they did and sometimes they didn't; getting access to the international hotels could be hit and miss, if you didn't have a pass. Kirov had indicated to Neville Lucas that he would meet him at about eight; and now it was a quarter past and outside the rain had stopped, it was starting to freeze, the Moskva had a scum of frost on the water, and across the river the Ukraina was piled up like a black wedding cake.

Kirov had no trouble at the door. In the foyer the usual hotel crowd was milling under the great golden egg in the style of Fabergé which passed for a clock. He recognized a couple of journalists, the *Reuter*'s representative and the *Guardian*'s man in Moscow, away from his office in Gruzinsky Perulok. It was unlikely that either was expecting to meet any Soviet citizens other than the few public Russians of whom the KGB approved. The other sort were met in parks and apartments and not in good hotels, though lately that was changing and you couldn't tell where it would end. Kirov also spotted Archibald Lansdowne, the British Commercial Counselor, with his thinly acidic wife, Fiona. They were tied up with a party in Western suits, and some connection with the journalists seemed plausible. Whatever the case, the matter was none of Kirov's business. He searched out Neville Lucas in the ground-floor bar and found him holding court from a stool.

The first impression of Neville Lucas was of a slow and peculiar good nature, a combination of his soft wandering eyes and the slouch he adopted to bring his head down to that of ordinary humanity so that his head had a retractable appearance and hung out

41

of his overcoat like that of a family tortoise. The overcoat was a peculiar English garment, a gray duffel coat fastened with wooden toggles. When the visiting English saw it, it provoked a "Good God, I haven't seen one of those since . . ." followed by a wistful look that tried to fix the date.

There were plenty of visiting English. Several evenings a week Lucas made the rounds of the hard-currency hotel bars, trawling for businessmen. In his pocket he carried a plastic bag with a Marlboro logo, and he tried to fill it in the course of the night with cigarettes, duty-free Scotch, disposable lighters and the other bric-à-brac of travel. Not that he either needed or lacked access to these things: "But because they're *authentic*," he explained obscurely to anyone who asked.

Kirov was intrigued by the Englishman's whimsy and difficult sadness. Normally Lucas stuck to the company of a fellow Briton called Jack Melchior. The latter was an elderly man, the local representative of several British firms, who lived permanently in Moscow to avoid domestic complications caused by an illegal excess of wives. Melchior acted as impresario, introducing his clients to the traitor, displaying Neville Lucas as if he were the star turn in a cabaret. Lucas accepted the introductions with tolerant good humor in return for the cigarettes and the rest, and he would sit at the bar with Melchior on his right hand, answer questions and make easy promises. Lucas looked big and gray like a beached hulk, and Melchior hovered around him with quick, nimble movements like a tug. Jack Melchior was a small man who wore another sort of Englishness, a black blazer and light gray trousers with immaculate creases.

When Kirov entered the bar of the Mezhdunarodnaya, Lucas rolled his head in his direction and waved to a seat. He turned from his company, ordered a drink from the barman, and addressed the newcomer. "Hello, Peter — s'cuse me, Fred — how are you?" His English had a northeastern lilt that Kirov could never capture.

Jack Melchior put his hand on the shoulder of the third member of their group and said: "How about getting the stuff now, Fred, while Neville and Peter have a chat?"

Fred looked doubtful but finally agreed and promised to return in five minutes. "You'll still be here, won't you?"

"Of course we shall," Melchior hustled him and to his departing back muttered: *"Pillock."* To the others he said: "How does he expect to do business in this place? By the way, Peter, what's your poison? Ah, I see Neville's got you one in—one for me too, Neville, if you're in the chair. Hey ho, bottoms up!" He sat back cheerily and straightened the handkerchief that was neatly displayed in his breast pocket, the same pocket that bore a regimental badge which Kirov suspected was as genuine as Scherbatsky's Chinese Rolex.

"What are you expecting this time?" Kirov asked.

Lucas shrugged indifferently. "From Fred? I relieved him of his cigarettes last night—Dunhills. Fancy some? No? He's just gone to get the little medical pack that his firm supplies him with. Not that it's much use. Mostly laxatives and the other things, the ones that make you stop. I prefer the French packs; I like the liver salts even if they do cause cancer, so they say. Still, there could be a few antibiotics."

"You need antibiotics?"

"Not particularly. But a few extra always come in handy. You know how difficult they are to get, and you can always trade them for something useful. And you, how are you?"

"I'm OK."

"You don't look it." Lucas's melancholy eyes passed over Kirov's face.

"Anyone fancy another?" said Jack Melchior. "Set them up again, Boris, *spasibo* and chop-chop."

"I'm not sleeping well."

"No? I'm sure that Fred's got something for that in his little medical pack. That or a nice warm woman. What is it, can't sleep or bad dreams? Guilty conscience?"

"It's not important."

"Probably not." Lucas assented to be agreeable and he put his lips to his drink thoughtfully.

A man came into the bar and approached Kirov directly. He was forty or so and looked embarrassed in a sweatshirt and jeans that were more relaxed than he was. Kirov guessed at one of the hotel's MVD operatives. The man said there was a call for Kirov in the lobby.

Kirov excused himself and went to take the call. It was on a phone in the office behind the reception desk, which had been cleared but for a cup of coffee and a smoldering cigarette left by the ghosts. Bogdanov was on the line. He was brief.

"Gusev just died. Antipov called me—the guy's on his best behavior. I've sent Tumanov and a couple of the boys to watch the stiff and asked Fomin to get around to the Butyrka and do the autopsy. Are you listening, boss?"

"I'm listening." Kirov was thinking of Gusev: Viktor was finished with his apartment and all his toys, finished with his diamonds for whatever reason he had them. Finished with the woman. He told Bogdanov to keep him posted on the autopsy and returned to the bar.

He found Neville Lucas with his arm around Fred and his free hand holding the Englishman's medical pack. Both were grinning and Jack Melchior was skipping around in front of them, taking a photograph with Fred's camera.

"Something to tell your grandchildren about. How I met a famous spy! Come on, Fred, give us a flash of your dentures."

Afterwards Fred repossessed the camera. He told Kirov confidingly: "The truth is they're too young to have heard of Neville. My son would remember Neville—at least I think he'd remember him—but not his kids." He looked now as if he wished he hadn't bothered. He studied the camera then slipped the strap over his shoulder. He turned to Lucas and still with the air of having done something slightly foolish offered his hand. "Well . . . must hit the sack. Nice meeting you, Neville. Yes . . . well . . . see you again sometime."

"Again?" Lucas repeated compassionately. "Oh, indubitably!" He pressed the other man's hand and added: "Be good." Then he turned away leaving Fred to become gradually aware of his own nonexistence. The visitor stood silent for a few long seconds and then left the bar.

Suddenly Lucas was bright. "Bugger off, Jack, will you?" he said pleasantly to Jack Melchior. "Peter and I have some things to talk about." Melchior nodded, winked at Kirov and strolled off leaving the tab unpaid.

Kirov placed some money on the bar. "What's the special occasion for inviting me here?" he asked.

"Oh, nothing special," Lucas answered. Then: "Got a car with you?"

"Yes. Why?"

"I thought we could go to a party. I was feeling tired and a bit in the dumps, so I called my old pal, Peter. Then I remembered that I'd been asked to a party. So why don't we both go?"

"You could have asked Jack."

"Jack—ah, yes—Jack. But the truth is that if you take the old

44

lad to a party he always ends up getting pissed, which wouldn't be so bad if he didn't start cornering people and telling them about the time he was in the Palestine Police after the war, and before you know where you are he's doing Trimphone impressions. Now I'm scarcely in a position to throw stones — in fact treachery has given me a very forgiving nature — but *nobody* is that bloody tolerant!"

They drove in Kirov's blue Volga. Lucas chatted from the passenger seat and ate boiled sweets from a bag he kept in the pocket of his duffel coat.

"Heard of Yelena Akhmerova, have you?" he asked.

"The film star?"

"The very same. She played the female lead in *Iron Harvest*. That's the reason for the party," Lucas said. *"Iron Harvest* is entered for the Cannes Film Festival. The critics say it has a chance of picking up a prize, if you believe them."

"Perhaps it will."

For a while they drove in silence. Kirov watched the traffic, the pedestrians, the restaurant queues. Lucas, when he was drunk — "Drunk to the point of wisdom, Peter!" — had once tried to explain to him that there was another Moscow. It had something to do with night and snow, the silences behind words and the meanings behind songs such as "Moscow Nights," which was played every night in the hard-currency bars to the lonely Westerners in their long and melancholy waiting for business. Kirov sometimes tried to make Moscow appear strange to himself, the way that it appeared to Lucas, but couldn't succeed. Beyond the window glass some soldiers out on a spree gathered in the gray light of a shop to light their cigarettes and barter with a spiv; a group of working girls with heavy boots and fresh complexions giggled and watched a restaurant for famous faces bypassing the queue. *I don't see it, Neville. What is "Moscow Nights"?*

"By the way," said Lucas, "forgot to mention it, but tonight's 'do' is an all-English affair, which is to say that we all have to speak English."

"Why is that?"

"Good question. The fashion, I suppose; the Akhmerova regards it as sophisticated — also she wants to deliver a pretty speech in English when she collects her pot at Cannes. Why do you think I've been invited to the party? The famous have always considered it chic to associate with low life; and what could be more seamy

45

than an elderly English traitor?" Lucas paused and his tongue sucked wistfully at his false teeth. "I don't care," he said finally. "The drink's free and you never know your luck. With my advancing years and doubtful past, I'm cultivating a shady sex appeal. Who knows, eh, Peter?"

"Who knows?"

Yelena Borisovna Akhmerova occupied an apartment at the Visotny Dom among the generals and the Party stars. There was music from the interior and the door was opened by a lackey in a white ducktail who took their coats and introduced them to the waiter who attended to their orders. From the visible bottles Kirov noted a dreary preoccupation with imported Jack Daniels, Cutty Sark and Gordon's gin. The music was a bland Swedish rock band singing English songs. Kirov was reminded again of Scherbatsky's watch.

"Yelena Borisovna, may I introduce my friend, Pyotr Andreevitch Kirov." Lucas's voice fell as his natural shyness came out. Stripped of his duffel coat, he revealed an old tweed jacket and a green cardigan with football buttons.

"Helena," his hostess corrected him and her cool eyes appraised Kirov. "I'm pleased you could come to my little soirée, Peter — or should I call you 'Pete'?"

"Peter." Kirov returned the stare, penetrating the translucent glaze of her makeup. The brilliant green eyes had an unnatural offset look — contact lenses he supposed. Her face was locked immobile in its beautiful structure, so perfect that it might have shared the designer label of her shimmering blue-green dress.

"Peter it is," she agreed and then quickly passed him into the crowd, leaving Neville Lucas standing in the shadows by the door with a grin of idiocy pasted to his face.

Kirov took a glass of pepper vodka and found a place where he could detach himself and survey the company. The apartment suffered like Viktor Gusev's from a surfeit of random wealth. Even at the level of Yelena Akhmerova the acquisition of goods was an affair of chance, different from the struggle of ordinary citizens only in the value of goods obtained. So an icon of the Kiev school hung uncomfortably on the wall next to a lithograph of a strange sunlit house from which the people had disappeared, and the antique mahogany furniture jostled for space with the tubular-framed chairs.

Except in one quarter the conversation was in a hubbub of bad

English. A man with a bushy Old Believer beard, a peasant blouse and soft-topped boots clung obstinately to Russian and talked about Soloukhin and Vasili Belov and the "Slav Soul." Lucas identified him as the poet Valentinov. He was speaking to a film director whom Kirov knew from the days when Lara had made a point of attending the best parties, where members of KGB foreign departments were fashionable for their cosmopolitan, even liberal manners, a taste shared by certain Washington parties where the presence of KGB was also fashionable though less explicit. He recalled that Washington too could suffer from wealth without taste, but it was able to resolve its problems by engaging interior decorators. "I came home to a shambles," an American once told him. "I thought my wife had hired an interior decorator. Thank Christ we'd only been burglarized."

"Peter, may I introduce you to Teddie," Yelena Akhmerova said.

"Hi, Pete, can I freshen your drink?" said Teddie.

"Teddie lectures at the Institute for International Relations. Neville tells me you used to be in Washington. Teddie knows all about America."

Teddie wore a pale pastel shirt and slacks and a pair of Gucci loafers and Kirov caught the whiff of KGB as tangy as aftershave. A foreign-intelligence analyst from the First Chief Directorate and as suave as they made them.

"Helena is a great kid, don't you think?" Teddie said.

"A great kid," Kirov agreed. Teddie carried on in the same vein, larding his conversation with American slang. You could date an agent's foreign postings from the slang he spoke. Yatsin, the Washington Resident, had confided that the US Residency had given up the old KGB habit of referring to the office in Dzerzhinsky Square as "Moscow Center"—"It was getting to sound like a shop that sold designer espionage." Teddie used words that Kirov found unfamiliar. He had visited a different America.

"Don't mope, old man," Neville Lucas nudged him affectionately. He had found a companion, a younger version of Yelena Akhmerova who had not yet achieved the sophistication of knowing who was important. The girl hung on his arm and interrupted.

"As famous spy, Neville, you know traitors Burgess and Maclean?"

"Don't hang on my arm, there's a dear," Lucas said gently. "Burgess and who? Were they important?"

"You are joking me, Neville!" she laughed.

"Probably." Lucas patted her bottom. "Run along and see if you can find me some bottled beer, Guinness preferably, but anything else will do. Actually I did meet Guy Burgess once," he said to Kirov. "The British press said I was part of that gang, 'the Fourth Man,' but that was all balls. Burgess was a queer and Maclean was an awful snob. Neither of them would talk to me. 'A snivelling little cipher clerk' they called me, which wasn't so far from the truth. I never met Kim Philby. I wrote to him once, but he returned my letter. He'd never heard of me—he thought I was a bloody visiting journalist! But, as I say, I did meet Guy Burgess once—at a party. He did me the honor of throwing up all over my suit. My only English suit. It was a hell of a job to get it cleaned." He thought for a while and added, "Hey ho! Who cares, eh, Peter?"

"I'd better be on my way."

"Actually it's a bloody miracle she'd ever heard of Burgess and Maclean; she must be a history student. Don't go, old man." Lucas put a hand on Kirov's wrist. "Come and meet George." He indicated a settee where a man with slow, patient eyes was watching them.

"Peter, this is George Gvishiani. Peter—George. Can I leave you fellows to get on with it? A word, Peter: George doesn't speak *un mot* of English."

"I—try—little," said the stranger and he gave a meek, appealing smile. He extended a hand to offer a seat. "Please—seated."

Kirov took the seat. The record changed to a slow love song. George Gvishiani, in his brash blue suit with a rose in the lapel, beamed at a couple of girls who were dancing a slow rumba barefoot on the carpet. Neville Lucas sailed past with his girl in one hand and a bottle of Zhigulevskoy in the other.

"I—love—girls," Gvishiani said hesitantly.

"You know Yelena Borisovna?" Kirov said in Russian. His companion turned his eyes away from the girls.

He laughed. "I thought I'd never hear Russian spoken again!" There was no meekness or appeal in that sound; evidently they were side notes reserved for embarrassment, and it occurred to Kirov that, had the conversation continued in English, their deceptive tone would have colored its interpretation. Gvishiani was a more robust character, a small, heavy, dark, intense man, bandit faced and wearing good manners like a Sunday suit. "Here, have a drink!" said Gvishiani and he passed a bottle of dill vodka that he had been keeping secreted by the side of the settee. Kirov took a

48

pull under the other man's scrutiny, wiped the neck of the bottle and returned it. He asked again if his new friend knew their hostess.

"Yes and no. I come to Moscow on business and people lay on a dinner or take me along to a party. One way or another I get to meet everybody." Gvishiani spoke in a knowing way, implying that everything was understood. Kirov had a recollection that Alexei Kosygin's daughter had married a man called Gvishiani. He wondered whether the dead premier's son-in-law and this sleek Georgian were the same, then guessed not: this one was rich but had a homegrown look about him that hit his confidence when a woman like Yelena Akkmerova started spouting English.

"So you're here on business?"

"Sure. Another drink? Sure. I run a few factories in Tbilisi — light industry, consumer goods, you know the sort of stuff. Every couple of months I come here to Moscow to wheedle a bit of cooperation out of suppliers or to kick arses. If I pull it off, then I get my deliveries on time and the workers don't have to 'storm' for the last ten days of the month to make up their quota."

"And if you don't?"

"And if I don't? . . . What the hell, who cares?"

A voice said: "George, you are cheating! English! English! English!"

Gvishiani's face flashed with anger, but he answered: "Apologies, Yelena . . . *Helena* . . . Is difficult."

"No matter. That is not excusing," she replied archly.

"I try more hard." And to Kirov he said: "And you, what do you do?"

"You don't know?"

"Maybe, maybe not. It doesn't matter. Yelena Borisovna invites all sorts: actors, queers, astrologers, *apparatchiks* — even KGB. Who can remember them all? Yelena isn't prudent. She thinks that charm and glamour are a defence to everything. She puts people on show and exploits them. One day she will end up in prison."

"But not you?"

"Me?" Gvishiani answered the question with a simplicity that could have been modesty. "I protect myself by being kind to people. My motto is 'cooperation.' It's the Communist way."

To show that the question did not bear serious consideration, Gvishiani let his attention wander. The two girls were still dancing, eyes closed, bodies swaying, their naked toes hooked into the car-

49

pet. A middle-aged Army general moved between them and, collecting one, slapped his abdomen up against hers and ground away to the music. Yelena Akhmerova stood on the sidelines and watched aloofly.

"Guess who's arrived?" Neville Lucas said, coming from nowhere to stoop and whisper with his beery breath. He smiled innocently. His face was flushed and beaded with sweat. "Here, here, over here!" He motioned to the figure behind him, and with an arm around her waist brought her forward.

"Hello, Lara," said Kirov.

Lara was as he remembered—that is, not the Lara who a little while ago had left him, but the other one who had come to him, filled with a firm but nervous control, every movement a careful placing of her body as if she were dancing, the way she had been when he had taken her from the Bolshoi *corps de ballet*. It hadn't occurred to him before that the separation of men and women, being in part a rejection of the recent past, carried with it the recreation of an earlier past. But maybe it wasn't so surprising that people called up the past's false certainties to pin the fleeing subtleties of the present. Tonight Lara's fair hair was scraped back and pinned to emphasize the elegant bones of her face, and her makeup was heavy and dramatic, though in this place and company appropriate; he wondered if she had reverted to dancing—perhaps just come from the theater? She wore a deep burgundy dress that clung where it should cling and fell where it should fall.

She said: "Hello, Peter, how are you?"

"I'm well."

"I'm glad to hear it."

"And you?"

"I'm well too. Excellently well. Here, darling," she said to her companion, a dark figure standing in the cigarette smoke, and, passing him the boa which was draped over her arm, she asked him to put it away somewhere. In the background a new rumba replaced an old one and the general still gripped his girl. I've seen this film before, Kirov thought. He was aware of the hotness of the room and the effects of that last drink with George Gvishiani. Strange, Lara's facility for picking up the mood and translating it into dance for an audience. Where had he seen the film? Washington—watching late movies in a rented house in Bethesda. Rio de Janeiro as it appears in every B-movie that was ever made. Where is your lover, Lara? Your ardent Latin lover? We have invented a

Moscow café society and rediscovered Rio. Where is your amorous Latin?

Instead, Radek came forward. "Hi, Pete," he said and grinned with satisfaction. He had a new suede jacket draped over his shoulders and a white *foulard* wrapped around his throat.

Kirov must have said something next about not realizing that Lara knew Radek because she became annoyed and said: "Oh, you introduced me to Pasha some time or other, at a party or the theater; or perhaps it was some other occasion when you didn't care enough to remember who was there. Are you going to get me a drink?"

"I'll get you a drink," said Neville Lucas eagerly.

"Would you like to sit down?" Kirov asked.

"No, I prefer to stand." Standing, she could maintain her poise and distance; she could swing her head gracefully, pose it against the lights and nod to the people she knew. Smiling at Yelena Akhmerova, she inquired of him: "Has anyone else moved in with you yet?"

"No."

"Really? Haven't you found anyone dumpy, unattractive and old enough? I thought that women like that were not uncommon."

The cruelty was clumsy and insincere, a thin mask for her own pain. He had never discussed Irina Terekhova with her and she was working only by inference and not information. Irina Terekhova was a small figure seen in a dim, snow-covered street, ugly and ragged with grief, she was the inexplicable change of mood that Lara had discerned in him. The Sokolskoye Incident and the woman with it were a part of the past and now unattainable. Uncle Bog with sympathetic brutality has suggested that, as a defector, it would be legitimate to have her killed. This, however, was said none too seriously, merely to shake Kirov out of his reflections. After all, the KGB didn't do things like that anymore.

"I'm not living with anyone," he said.

Neville Lucas and Radek both turned up bearing drinks for Lara. She smiled with triumph and accepted both, throwing each one back quickly.

"Steady on, girl!" Lucas suggested.

"I have a head for drink," she retorted.

"Oh, absolutely! But leave some for the other customers, eh?"

"Be quiet, Neville!" she turned on him sharply. Then equally suddenly she gave him a long and sensuous kiss on the lips only to say: "There! Better?" She reverted to Kirov, wearing her anxious smile and waiting for—applause? Her lips opened, but Lucas was touching his own and saying: "Good God!" until the repetition faded and he shambled off to get another drink. And at that moment Kirov sensed the cone of silence and a stillness of gesture between himself and Lara. He thought: If I tell her I love her, she'll come back to me. He stirred the emotion aridly. He checked his watch.

"I have to go."

"Must you?"

"Yes."

"Ah." She paused and bit her lip so that for a second Kirov felt a flicker of tenderness toward her. "No one to go home to," she said with sarcasm. "How sad for you!"

"Perhaps."

He left her and pushed a way through the crush of guests, past the general now standing in his socks with his arm draped over his partner's shoulder and his fingers spinning coils in her long hair. He shouldered aside the poet with the Old Believer beard and opened a door. It was the kitchen. Radek was there, helping himself to some *satsivi* courtesy of George Gvishiani who came from that neck of the woods; a cigarette with a column of ash dangled over the food.

"Petya!" he said. He had a sly, drunken grin. "Fuck your mother, what a bunch of creeps! Have a drink!" He slopped some Scotch into a dirty glass and pushed it down the breakfast bar. He ignored Kirov and at the same time addressed him; he babbled something about Grishin and then about Lara. "What sort of bedroom tricks does she do? Hey, don't give me that shitty look, it's an honest question! Where are you going?"

"I was leaving."

"Aw, c'mon, Petya, stay for a drink. If you don't like Scotch, there's a bottle of *Tvishi* here somewhere."

Kirov turned away but Radek was still pursuing the idea of conversation. He said: "The Great Jewish Antibiotics Ring. Why *Jewish?* You still haven't answered that one. Don't go, I'm being serious, why *Jewish?*"

Neville Lucas was on the other side of the door, bumping his way into the kitchen with an empty glass. "Enjoying yourself?" he asked benevolently.

"Why did you invite me here? So I would meet Lara?"

Lucas came over solemn. "As God is my witness, Peter, I didn't know that she would be here." He brightened up. "Come on — forgive me? I'm your friend."

"Sure you are."

He found a bedroom and a mound of winter coats. The room was faintly lit by a table lamp. The coats were heaped about the floor and a half-naked couple were lying peaceably on the bed smoking. The man was thin, his bony chest divided by a line of hair. The woman lay on her back in the ruck of her skirts, her blouse undone and her large breasts hanging splayed and flaccid. The air was spicy with the smell of Afghan hash. The man wore high-top boots, probably a returning soldier.

Kirov took his coat and returned to the press of the party.

"Leaving?" Yelena Akhmerova inquired speculatively.

George Gvishiani asked the same question. "I'm going too. Why don't I give you a lift? We've both had a bit to drink, but I've got a car and a driver."

Kirov accepted the offer. Gvishiani got his own coat and they descended to the street where the Georgian whistled up a black Volga.

"How about a nightcap?" he proposed. "Away from the freak show?"

The car took them to the Intourist, where Gvishiani was familiar with the hotel and known to the barmen. He found a table and drinks, and sat opposite Kirov, the bright blue of his bad expensive suit stamped against the backdrop of the other customers.

"So," he began in a meditative good humor. "What do you think of our Yelena Borisovna and her parties? Not your style, am I right?" Kirov made no reply, which Gvishiani took as agreement, fiddling with the rose in his buttonhole and continuing in the same tone: "An imitation of a Western hostess, I think, though I don't know. I've never been to the West, but I guess you have."

"Have I?"

"The cuff links." Gvishiani flicked a careless finger at them. "Silver and amber — from Sweden?"

"Finland."

"Ah, of course. But still the West — the Promised Land." This observation caused him to muse. "It's pitiful really, when there are so many opportunities here — if you know how to use them."

Failing a reaction, Gvishiani made a few more remarks in the same oblique manner, so that Kirov had a sense of fingers playing delicately over the strings of some instrument, waiting for the resonances of the response.

"Yelena Borisovna thinks that she is being fashionable — what do you think?"

"Fashions change."

"Yes. And we shouldn't be deceived by the surface, by the trinkets, however modern they may appear. I daresay the Tsar's court appeared to be the height of fashion until the moment that the Revolution overtook it." Gvishiani looked up from his drink directly into Kirov's gaze. "And now we have Gorbachev, virtue and abstinence," he said. "Is it a change, do you think? Or are we just shuffling the trinkets?"

"I have no opinion."

"No?" Gvishiani looked for the time from the bar clock. His face was changing from good temper to seriousness. "I've got to go," he said. He moved to stand up, thought of something and, leaning forward, said: "When times are changing, it's useful to have friends and influence. Do you need friends and influence, Pyotr Andreevitch?"

When Gvishiani was gone, Kirov turned to the girls in the bar. Out of an obscure anger he took one home for the night.

5

He sat by the bed waiting for daylight. The floor was strewn with clothes — his — the girl's — and books of poetry: the volume of Walt Whitman given to him by the traitor Oleg Ouspensky; the slim book of verse by Osip Davidov which he had taken from the apartment of Irina Terekhova before her defection. Treachery left poetry behind like calling cards.

The girl stirred in her animal sleep. She had made a nest of the bedclothes and lay face down with her blond hair sprayed over the pillow and the freckles of her pale shoulders as dim spots. He had no recollection of her appearance, no memory of any conversation. She had no history.

He made some coffee and put on a tape to fill the apartment with Mozart, and when he returned to the bedroom she was sitting up with the pillows plumped and the sheets arranged. She had neat breasts with button nipples coiled by small springs of hair, and a flat belly streaked faintly with stretch marks meaning that somewhere there was a child. But he didn't want to think about the child, so he excluded the possibility.

"I'll fix a cab for you," he told her and hoped she would not speak.

"Thanks," she said, looking past him at the furnishings which to her seemed more important. "You live well," she commented.

"I'll go and arrange the cab."

He made her some breakfast which she ate in silence, devouring the kitchen with the food. He left some money on the table, which disappeared while he went to the bathroom. She asked whether she would see him again and he said no. She looked disappointed, so he gave her a maybe, and was touched when she seemed pleased. He held the door of the cab open for her and she thanked him again.

At the office he took care of some paperwork that had nothing to do with the Great Jewish Antibiotics Ring. Now that Viktor Gusev was dead, the antibiotics business could conveniently be left to Bakradze and the boys from Petrovka. Bakradze urged him to do it. The lawyer called and repeated with the same innocence that he thought their relationship had unintentionally soured. He used the word "relationship," which Kirov remembered from his days in Washington where "relationships" — so his American friends told him — were more tangible than diamonds.

Bogdanov turned in late, looking tired and worn. He went to sleep with his head slumped over the rubbish on his desk. Radek stuck his nose through the door looking for a shot of vodka to kill his hangover. He asked: "Why *Jewish?*" — and had a fair shot at dying of laughter. His hangover meant he preferred gossip to work. Kirov was glad when Grishin called him to his office. The interview wasn't planned. Grishin appeared merely to want to chat. Perhaps it was one of those days when something in the air makes work impossible. Grishin rambled about improving the morale of the department by more social contacts after hours, then distractedly inquired about the Great Jewish Antibiotics Ring.

Kirov told him that Viktor Gusev had died.

"The black marketeer? Foul play?"

"Uncle Bog and his team were at the bedside. There's no reason to suspect anything."

"I'm sure that's true," Grishin conceded readily. Then with the same ambiguity that drove wedges into everything he said, he added: "Even so, let's carry on for a while. It can't hurt us, can it?" He smiled, round cheeked and paternal. There was, he implied, nothing more to be said. For a moment Kirov was going to mention the diamonds, but Grishin's equivocation made him hold back and instead he asked: "Why are we pursuing this matter? There are other things to be done."

"You want to be like Radek?" Grishin replied. "You really want me to hand over the remains of the meat racket?"

The answer was astute enough. There was something troubling him about Radek, even if it wasn't that. "I want something more — definite," he said and he remembered something that

Radek had remarked. He added: "I don't believe in the Great Jewish Antibiotics Ring."

"No?"

"No."

"There's no black market in antibiotics?"

"There is — just like there's a black market in hard currency. But there's no conspiracy. People steal antibiotics and they sell them. But that's all there is. There's no organization. The conspiracy is just an invention so that we can handle the problem." This time Kirov felt his own impatience. Grishin was resisting him.

The general weighed up Kirov's words. "Where does Viktor Gusev fit into your scheme of things?" he asked.

"A small-time racketeer. You could drag the Arbat and pull in a dozen Viktor Gusevs every day."

Surprisingly Grishin agreed. "I've often thought that conspiracies are merely a certain way of looking at things. Then again," he said cheerfully, "we're paid for hunting out conspiracies — so perhaps we'd better adopt this one as a working hypothesis? What do you say? Don't look disappointed, Pyotr Andreevitch."

"Do I have authority to take the investigation out of the hands of MVD and the Public Prosecutor's Office?"

"Why don't you come for dinner this weekend at my *dacha?*" Grishin answered. "Bring Larissa Arkadyevna."

Bogdanov had woken up and was sitting behind his desk with a pad in front of him on which he was noting the names of horses. He placed bets for anyone in the department who was interested. "Radek says he's screwing Larissa Arkadyevna. He says he saw you at some party last night."

"I was with Neville Lucas. He set me up to meet Lara. Old age is making him sentimental."

"Neville?" said Bogdanov skeptically. "You've not been falling for his crap about the Good-Old-Days and The-Old-Country-Isn't-What-It-Was? Believe me, whatever Neville was doing, it was with a purpose." He changed the subject. "Fomin called. The results of the autopsy on friend Viktor are in. It's a freak. The antibiotics used to prevent infection after his operation . . ."

"Yes?"

"They killed him." He didn't wait for a reaction. He added quickly and soothingly: "It was contamination of the drugs. Don't get excited about it. Fomin says it's one of those things that can happen. The drugs get manufactured wrong or they're stored wrong or they're just kept too long. Fomin says there's nothing suspicious." He waited for an answer and then prompted one. "Believe me. Bakradze was on the phone as soon as he got the news. You'd think his mother had died. He *really* wanted to talk to Gusev."

Bogdanov really wanted to believe that.

Half an hour later he trudged into Kirov's own office. He inquired: "Have you asked Grishin to give us power to run this investigation or take us off the case? I'm up to my arse in work and don't need this business."

"Grishin wants us to continue."

"What the hell for? Months of work have dragged in a few small dealers and one Viktor Gusev who is well and truly dead. If there are any leads Bakradze is chasing them. If Grishin doesn't trust Bakradze why doesn't he kick the bastard out? What's all this *liaison* stuff? Since when did KGB ever liaise with anybody?"

"Ever since we got morality."

The day fretted to a close in a flurry of sleet. There was a power hitch local to Kirov's floor. The photocopier and the coffee machine went down. The corridors were filled with typists complaining that they couldn't get their work done. Kirov watched them through the window of his office.

"I want a trace on a name," he told Bogdanov.

"OK, fire away. Who?"

"Georgi Vissarionovitch Gvishiani."

Bogdanov recognized the surname. "A relative of Kosygin's son-in-law?"

"I don't know. It's unlikely. Get Tumanov to run the trace and then we'll find out."

Bogdanov checked his watch. "Can it wait until tomorrow? Better still, I'll leave it to the Fire Brigade; it'll give them something more to do than sit around and play cards." Bogdanov had a resentment against the Fire Brigade. They staffed the Center at night against emergencies that never happened, and, when they got bored or malicious, kicked their heels in the empty offices, stole anything that wasn't nailed down and screwed up the filing.

"Whatever you like. It isn't urgent."

Bogdanov noted the name; he called his secretary and had her carry the note to the basket where the Fire Brigade checked for anything pending.

"So who is this Gvishiani?" he asked.

"I met him at a party."

"Last night? The one where Neville Lucas set you up to face Lara? What's our interest?"

"I don't know. Maybe nothing. He's a man who is looking for influence—friends."

"What does he do?"

"He runs an industrial combine in Tbilisi, makes consumer goods."

"Tbilisi—I should have guessed from his name." Bogdanov picked up the phone and called the secretary again. "Anya—the sheet I just gave you: make a note on it to call Tbilisi and do a search of the Georgian records." To Kirov he said: "Not that you can trust those crooks to tell you the truth. What sort of friends is Gvishiani looking for? In the Ministry of Light Industry? In KGB? People choose their friends in strange places. If he's into a racket, it sounds like one that Radek should be investigating. Sunny Tbilisi and all those Georgian girls—just what our Hollywood stars are looking for. Have you talked to Radek?"

"I don't want to talk to Radek."

"Because he's screwing Lara?"

"Not that."

"Why not? Getting paranoid? I wouldn't worry. Radek's getting enough glory without needing to steal ours. It's Grishin who should be watching his back—talking of which, is there any truth in the rumor that he's crossed swords with the Rehabilitation Committee?"

"Where did you hear that?"

"Here—there. But is it true?"

"I don't know."

Bogdanov didn't believe him. Kirov could see the disbelief. I'm tired, he thought. It's nothing more. He looked away to avoid the other man's skepticism. The window faced onto the inner courtyard of the Lubyanka but in this light only his reflection looked back, a faint ghost hanging above the night sky.

"I'm going back to the Butyrka," he said.

"What for?"

"I want to talk to the doctors who were treating Gusev. About the antibiotics."

"What about the antibiotics?"

"Something . . ." Kirov couldn't put a name to the disquiet. He couldn't be sure even that it had anything to do with Viktor Gusev. Perhaps Gusev was only a focus.

"The antibiotics got contaminated and they killed him. It happens. You have the report from Fomin. He tells you it happens."

"Something . . ." Kirov repeated softly. "You don't have to come."

Bogdanov shrugged. "I'll come. Give me time to call my wife and tell her I'll be late home. Then I'll come."

Kirov stepped outside the office. Through the glass in the door he could see Bogdanov with his hand muffled around the telephone mouthpiece. In all these years he had never met Bogdanov's wife. He wondered sometimes if she even knew what Bogdanov did for a living. In a way she was as mysterious as Grishin's prized "spouse and parent," whom he had met only once. But perhaps the mystery lay in being married. Instead of which there were Laras — a succession of Laras. And one Irina Terekhova, the traitor with whom he fell in love.

"We still have the body," the doctor admitted. She was a brisk woman, square and comfortable to look at. "Since he was still technically a prisoner, the autopsy was conducted here."

Off the ward there was a small room. She opened it and turned on the light. There was a collection of mops, detergent and buckets, and Viktor Gusev lying on the floor between a trolley and a pile of chairs. He was covered by a patched sheet.

"Look at him if you want to," the doctor said. "I still have my rounds to do."

"That's OK. Leave us."

Kirov stooped and pulled back the cover from the corpse's face. Gusev was still as remembered. The distance of death had confirmed the irony and aloofness of his expression. The talcum powder that had been used to dress and handle the body fitted with Gusev's smoothness and suavity. The roots of the black hair showed traces of gray. Gusev had used dye, as Kirov had guessed.

Bogdanov let his foot move forward to stir a pale toe that peeped from the bottom of the sheet.

"If we have to go forward with this case, why not leave it to Tumanov? He's a big boy now, he can handle his own jobs and has the sense to know when he's out of his depth. I'm thinking of time—your time, boss. Why waste it on—whatchamacallit—*liaison?*"

"I want to know why Gusev is dead."

"Contaminated antibiotics," Bogdanov answered.

Kirov looked away from the corpse. "That wasn't the question." He examined the walls. It hadn't been possible to reach the full height with a mop; there was a tidemark and a color change, and dried moisture trails dribbled down the wall. Disturbing Viktor Gusev had caused the corpse to seep juices. Kirov knelt and pulled back the cover entirely.

"Jesus Christ!" Bogdanov whispered, and he turned his face away. Kirov continued folding the sheet, then placed it carefully on the floor. He returned his gaze to the body, placing it on the body like fragile porcelain. The breastbone had been broken and the abdomen was slit to the pelvis. After the chosen organs had been removed, the guts had been bundled back into the cavity which was left open.

"I'll stitch him up before we move the body," the doctor said. She was standing in the doorway, leaning against the jamb, her free hand holding a cigarette. She smoked idly and regarded the two KGB men dispassionately. "Finished?" she inquired.

"I've seen enough."

"No injuries? No 'accidental' injuries? That's what you were looking for, wasn't it?" She blew smoke into the room. "Two lots of men watching him, the detective's and your lot. Was he something special, this Gusev, that you couldn't wait to get your hands on him?"

"I don't know."

She laughed. Cheerfully she added, "Don't worry, I'll tidy up." She held the door open and turned the light off behind them.

They stood now in the anteroom to the ward. The patients were huddled over their beds. Those who were on their feet were frozen, staring back through the glass like a still life.

Bogdanov cadged a cigarette from the doctor. She was on the point of disappearing on another errand.

"There's something else I'd like to talk about," Kirov said.

"I'll only be a minute." She smiled with horsy teeth and appraised him sexually with glaucous blue eyes.

Bogdanov kicked the linoleum, examined the burns and stains. "Why haven't you told Bakradze about the girl?" he asked.

"If he knows about Gusev he probably knows about the girl."

"And the diamonds? You still have them? Why haven't you told Bakradze?"

The still life in the ward began a slow movement. One of the prisoner-patients, with large oval eyes slit in the middle the way they paint them on a clown's face, directed a look of recognition at Kirov. It said: *I know you and all the bastards like you that were ever spawned.* The man let his eyes slide slowly up and down then gave a weary fuck-off gesture.

"What do you think Viktor was doing? Buying or selling." Kirov turned away and looked at Bogdanov.

"Search me. But why would he be buying? If he was selling antibiotics for dollars and certificate rubles like we found at his place, why should he spend the cash to buy diamonds? With cash he could do things, pay people for favors, buy things that people want? But what can he do with diamonds worth a lifetime's salary apiece — give them away to get his car fixed? Who needs them? He'd be crazy to convert the proceeds of the drugs game into diamonds."

"So?"

"So . . . I don't know. Maybe there's no connection. Today Viktor is dealing in antibiotics; tomorrow he's dealing in diamonds; and the day after, maybe it's wholesale meat from some of Radek's friends. They're all commodities, and Viktor is a dealer. Somewhere out in the sticks there's a mine where a little bit of the production leaves in the workers' mouths. It filters through the system and finally reaches Viktor, who sells the diamonds for cash. Who knows, maybe the cash we found came from the diamonds and not from the antibiotics."

"Perhaps."

"Sure. And here's a crazy idea: *the Great Jewish Antibiotics Ring doesn't exist!* The whole business is a diamonds racket. We're investigating the wrong thing!" Bogdanov gave a short laugh and coughed over his cigarette. He picked off the ash between his forefinger and thumb and slipped the butt into his pocket. He dumped his enthusiasm. "Who knows? Anyway, why *Jewish?* Is Viktor Jewish? Who's Jewish in this case that we know of?"

"It's just a name."

"But it came from somewhere — from Grishin?"

"Grishin gave it the name," Kirov agreed. He remembered Grishin handing over the papers and saying that they represented all that was known of the Great Jewish Antibiotics Ring. The official title was something else.

The doctor came back. She had a prisoner in tow, a gray runt in prison drabs. She was cuffing him round the ear and abusing him on the subject of cleaning the corridors. Seeing the two men she gave the prisoner a slap and let him scuttle away. She approached Kirov and assumed a pleasant but businesslike expression.

"There was something else? You said there was something else."

"The antibiotics that were given to Gusev, they came from your stocks?"

"Mine?" She found the idea funny. "You think I have antibiotics to waste on vermin like Gusev?"

"They weren't yours?"

She didn't answer but returned his curiosity with amusement.

"Where did they come from?" Kirov pressed her.

"I called Petrovka and spoke to whatshisname."

"Bakradze?"

"The other one."

"Antipov."

"I told him that if he wanted Gusev alive and well, then he'd have to get me some antibiotics."

"You didn't have any."

"Of course I had some," she responded impatiently. "But why should I use my supply? If I gave them to Gusev, then someone else would go without because I have no way of replacing them. I guessed that if Gusev was important, then Petrovka would be able to lay its hands on what was needed." The amusement died in her eyes and for a second Kirov saw desperation. "You know how it is," she said and seemed to shrug off the prison and him along with it.

"I know how it is." His hand reached out toward her shoulder, but he thought better of it and let the hand fall.

"Anytime I can help . . ." she said.

"Of course."

"Anytime."

"Yes." He searched for something to request. It seemed to him that she needed to give him something to excuse her begging for antibiotics. He suspected that her plea to Antipov had been less flippant and had cost more pain than she admitted. And now like other poor people she looked for an act of generosity that was within her means. He asked: "Do you have anything left from the drugs you gave to Gusev?"

"Your surgeon, Fomin, took the remains of the vials with him to do the autopsy."

"You have nothing left?"

She looked disappointed; then as suddenly brightened up. "Wait! I may have the carton they came in."

"Can I have it?"

"I'll try to find it."

"Please."

She left them again to hunt somewhere for the remains.

"Poor bitch," Bogdanov murmured. He prevented any question from Kirov. "I'm just an old softy," he said, and pleated his lips over his snaggle teeth.

That night Kirov called Antipov from his apartment. The detective was at home. He was sullenly cooperative. He coughed his fatal cough and answered the question: "Of course we supplied the antibiotics. We needed Gusev alive and talking. Without him we're back to where we started — chasing the small suppliers and hanging around toilets like a bunch of queers."

"Where did the antibiotics come from?" Kirov asked. But he knew because there was only one answer.

"From Gusev's own supply. Where else?"

6

As promised, Kirov visited Uncle Kolya again. Tatiana Yurievna warned him that the general was feeling better—warned him because the general had rearmed himself with vodka and cigarettes and was feeling feisty but ill-tempered. He had forced her to relent and allow some daylight into the sickroom. It was pale from the thin day, and washed out the colors from the late wildflowers that the housekeeper had placed in a vase by the invalid's bed. Kirov asked: "How are you feeling?"

"Not too bad."

"Good."

"Yes, good."

They went through the polite preambles in the distant and superficially uninterested fashion that characterizes conversations between men when they concern matters of a personal nature. General Prylubin was sitting up in bed and had provided himself with an ashtray that was lost in a mound of stubs and a selection of paperbacks that had failed to hold his interest if the pile on the floor was a guide. Behind his bad temper Kirov detected a note of relief. Death had been deferred and that was cause enough for relief. Both men were aware of this, but neither of them made mention of it. Instead Kirov asked where Uncle Kolya was getting his medication from. There was an ample supply of bottles and tablets.

"I don't ask," the old man answered. "I give the doctor money. How she spends it is her business."

"Doesn't the Service help?"

"The Service would prefer it if I were dead. I'm an anachronism."

"What are you taking?"

"How should I know? Antibiotics."

"Can't you get them legally?"

"Who's to say I'm not doing?" Uncle Kolya raised an eyebrow wryly, but almost immediately let the makings of a smile turn to a frown. "I'm bored," he complained. "I've nothing to do."

"You should read."

"I never learned to read — not books. The Old Woman plays cards, but so badly it isn't worthwhile cheating. Can you come more often?" he asked eagerly; then recognized that he was being unrealistic. Like a child, Kirov thought: his demands had no context other than immediacy. The relationship had inverted. Now Uncle Kolya needed him to satisfy his wants like a parent.

"Why don't you work on your memoirs?" he suggested.

"Don't want to."

"Not for publication — for your own satisfaction."

"Boring."

"Everything?" Kirov humored the old man. "You never did anything interesting? You never met anyone interesting?" Then, suddenly, he asked: "Tell me about my father."

Until then Uncle Kolya's face had been tetchily alive. At the question it fell into a leathery stillness. For a second Kirov wondered whether he had heard. Then: "Why?"

"Isn't it natural? He's my father."

"He's dead. He's in the past. The past is full of dead people — you should stay away from it."

"I've been dreaming about him," Kirov said, and the old man looked shocked, as if Kirov had broken through a security fence that cordoned off the cemetery of dead days.

"Dreams? What do you have to dream about? You hardly knew him. What do you remember?"

"I remember that Beria had my father shot."

I remember that I was born in Minsk in an apartment in Bryanska Street.

No, he didn't remember that. Instead he had walked with his mother, holding her hand, through the ruins of the city and she had pointed to a space and a pile of rubble and said that there he was born, which made him wonder that anyone could be born in such desolation; so that he asked her whether, like Lenin, he had been born in a stable.

He remembered the Hotel Europa. His father's high position allowed him to move there during the crisis of the war into a comfortable suite where food could still be procured from the German military commissariat since the hotel was the base for the politicians. The latter were Byelorussian nationalists. They were holding a congress at the Opera House to work out a basis for their country's independence. They smoked *papirossi* and wore smelly suits, and, like a collection of seedy uncles, dandled the infant on their knees while they talked treason against the Soviet Union. And even now they bequeathed their smells. Children remember smells. Nationalism smelled of unwashed shirts.

"It was Genrik Yagoda who first took notice of your father," Uncle Kolya said reluctantly. He helped himself to a cigarette and offered one to his visitor. A peacemaking gesture, Kirov thought, though he had no idea why this should be so. "This was in 1936. Yagoda was head of NKVD." Cigarette ash fell with a hiss into the vase of flowers. "Later Stalin had Yagoda shot."

"The normal rule with Stalin was that when the head of a department went, then his subordinates went with him. When Yagoda was disgraced, there was a wave of arrests inside NKVD. Two, maybe three thousand Chekists followed him into the execution cellars—no one can be sure about the numbers. Your father was among those arrested," he threw in, using a subdued voice as if the fact were of minimal relevance.

"But he survived," Kirov said.

"He survived," Uncle Kolya agreed, and with a glimmer of cheer added: "How else were you born?" Kirov did not allow himself to be deflected.

"How did he manage it?"

"Chance."

"What sort of chance?"

Uncle Kolya stubbed out the cigarette and dumped it in the vase to float among the flower stems.

"He had the same surname as a dead man."

The dead man was Sergei Mironovitch Kirov.

"The hero of the Leningrad Party. He was killed in 1934 or thereabouts."

"Who killed him?"

"Yagoda. When he was brought to trial in March of 1938, Yagoda was accused of setting up the Kirov murder. In time more or less everyone of importance was accused of the same thing, but in Yagoda's case the accusation was probably true. The point was that Kirov's murder was the excuse for bumping off the leading elements of the Leningrad Party. That was Stalin's object — Yagoda was just an instrument."

Stalin, he said, had attended the lying in state of S. M. Kirov and wept over the bier like a Mafia boss.

"Was my father related to the other Kirov?"

"I don't know."

"Is it possible?"

"Maybe. But you don't understand me. It didn't matter. There were people who could make it possible. Yezhov for example." Yezhov had been Yagoda's successor.

"It's March 1938." They had stopped for a few minutes. The general lit another cigarette and smoked it while studying the burning end. He took a glass of vodka and threw it back in one. He said neither that he wanted to stop nor wanted to continue, and Kirov suspected that both propositions were simultaneously true. Then the old man resumed. "S. M. Kirov is already dead. Your dad is in the Lefortovo prison. Yezhov has plotted with Stalin and done for his old boss Yagoda. He's in charge of NKVD and he conducts the interrogation of your dad personally."

He did not say how he knew this.

"Yezhov was a clever bastard. He understood these things — how they looked — how they could be *made* to look. He made your father an offer. But first he told him a story. He said that it wasn't him — Yezhov — that had ordered your father's arrest. It was Yagoda! That insane monster, not content with the criminal murder of the virtuous S. M. Kirov, was conducting a vendetta against all surviving members of the dead hero's family. In fact, so Yezhov tells it, your father's arrest is positive proof that Yagoda was involved in the murder of S. M. Kirov since why would an innocent man be persecuting the victim's relatives?"

"Offer," Kirov interrupted. "You said 'offer.' "

"In exchange for his life, your father gave evidence against his old friend Genrik Yagoda, who was duly convicted and shot."

The irony in the general's tone was a deliberate cruelty, a penalty for ignoring the warning about the past and its dangers. But now he softened and became Uncle Kolya again. "Don't worry," he said. "It didn't matter whether your father gave evidence or not. Yagoda was a dead man from the moment he became too powerful. That was Stalin's way. He knew that the chief danger to him came from those closest to him. So he had Yagoda killed and afterwards he did for Yezhov and replaced him with Beria. If the Old Man hadn't died first, he would have killed Beria. It's the way things were done."

"Who really ordered my father's arrest — Yagoda or Yezhov?"

"Who cares?"

"Yagoda must already have been in prison when my father was arrested. How could he have given the order?"

"Smart boy. So Yezhov's story didn't make sense, so events were in the wrong order — so what? In this country it's possible to invert time."

7

Bogdanov had been shopping in one of the city's squares where a market had sprung up selling fruit and vegetables. Wagons with number plates from Baku and the South were doing a trade in fresh produce from the tailboards. They were selling tomatoes at thirty kopecks a kilo, aubergines at fifty kopecks, and even watermelons and grapes. But this wasn't a free market: the stuff was being sold at the low state-controlled price. It was part of the system set up by the new Moscow Party organization. The old system had been brought low when KGB and the police had blown the rackets at GUM and the main food shops. In part it was a product of Radek's work in breaking up the meat ring in the Ukraine. In part it was simply inexplicable.

"By the way," Bogdanov continued, "did you know that Scherbatsky's been arrested?" He threw a tomato across. "Here, try, they're not too bad."

Kirov examined the fruit. It was a shade overripe but better than was normally available. He bit into it and closed his eyes to the flavor, imagining — whatever. It was a good day.

"So," he answered, "what's Scherbatsky been arrested for? Not the Chinese watch?"

Bogdanov grinned. "I never did believe that story. No, it was over something else. It seems," he strung himself out full length and grunted as his muscles tensed and relaxed, "that he has a cousin who works for a construction combine. Nice business. Lots of opportunities. The cousin supplies materials *na leva* for any of his friends and acquaintances who want to build a *dacha* — for a price, of course."

"And?"

"So what else is to tell? The cousin approaches Scherbatsky and asks whether he knows anyone who would like a helping hand in the matter of building materials. Scherbatsky talks to his friends and puts them in contact with his cousin. And on the way Scherbatsky acquires a *dacha* of his own, which is not entirely explained by his salary. All of which is just the ordinary way of doing business in this fine country of ours, so that we are left asking: what's so special this time? I'll tell you," he said, and the humor had gone from his voice. "What's so special is that we have a new Moscow Party Secretary who finds the housing program in a shambles through the activities of Scherbatsky and his relatives. This makes the Comrade Party Secretary cross, and also his boss, Lemonade Joe Gorbachev. They wish action. Do I hear you say that Scherbatsky is a member of KGB? 'So what?' says the Comrade Party Secretary, and we all agree—who the hell are KGB anyway? Let's arrest one of those damned Chekists—Scherthingummy will do." Bogdanov paused. He looked at the paper bag that lay open on his desk with the fruit visible. "Fuck their tomatoes," he murmured.

"And Scherbatsky?"

Bogdanov gave a melancholy smile. "Scherbatsky is taking a long holiday in a cold climate. Ten years—if his Chinese watch lasts that long."

Antipov called personally to deliver the remains of Viktor Gusev's supply of antibiotics.

"Have you run any tests on them?" Kirov asked.

"No. We thought you would want them exactly as they were. Untouched."

"Thought we might be suspicious if you opened the package?" said Bogdanov. Antipov gave a go-to-hell grunt. "No need to be coy," Bogdanov comforted him. "Since our little misunderstanding we're all friends; we can talk about these things."

"Are you having any luck in tracing Gusev's contacts?" Kirov asked.

The policeman preferred his question. "It's a slow business. Gusev knew a lot of people, he was that kind of guy. We've had a few suspects in for interrogation, but—you know how it is."

"No rough stuff," Bogdanov fed him the words.

"Some of Gusev's friends are important people."

"Not so accident prone, huh?" Bogdanov took a carton out of

71

the box and spun it in his fingers, reading the label.

"We've made a list of names," Antipov volunteered. "You want the list?"

"Give me the list," said Kirov.

When Antipov was gone, Kirov unpacked the box. The drugs were in vials and bottles, still in their individual cartons. The seals appeared intact. There was an inventory signed by Antipov as investigating officer and the consignment matched with the exception of the items withdrawn and provided to the Butyrka for use on Gusev. Kirov had the carton which had contained the latter; the prison doctor had retrieved it from the rubbish. It too tallied with the inventory and made it complete.

Bogdanov kept up the conversation to avoid talking about Antipov and what-was-the-investigation-supposed-to-be-about in case he didn't like the answers. He pressed Kirov to go to the horse races with him—you need to relax, boss—then gave up and asked: "So where do we go from here?"

Kirov repacked the box. "Put the stuff out for analysis. Have you noticed that the drugs all come from a single source?"

"Some outfit in Bulgaria—Bulpharma—Sofia."

"Run the name through records and see whether it registers. Pull me the file if there is one."

"Do you want me to check with the local *referentura* in case they have something that hasn't found its way back home?"

Kirov paused then answered: "No," without further explanation.

"And the woman, Mazurova? Maybe she knows something. Maybe Viktor was going to Bulgaria?"

The apartment was in one of the Khrushchev blocks in Chertanovo, a relic of another time of change that now stood in the streaming rain. Tumanov, who tried to be laid back with an effort that was almost touching, pointed out his team, two men in a pale-green Zhiguli sheltered under a tree. It was a routine stakeout; the pile of cigarette butts by the driver's door indicated that the car never moved; you could have stuck a militia sign on it. Even the dogs didn't piss on the wheels.

Tumanov tried to be knowledgeable. He talked about the girl in a drawl like a cop in an American gangster movie.

"She comes from Krasnoyarsk. Her parents are dead. Just a *babushka* left and she's pretty far gone; the girl doesn't visit her."

"When did the parents die?" Kirov asked. Tumanov didn't know the answer and took the question as a criticism. "It doesn't matter," Kirov told him.

"I can find out."

"It doesn't matter." Kirov was tired of enthusiasm. He stared through the window, through the rain. Bus queues. A Gastronom shop with a window of tinned fish and dummies of the good things that might or might not be available inside. This year had seen a good harvest: witness the price of tomatoes in the street markets and the piles of apples and cabbages. Meat was available too; and it wasn't the spurious surplus that came when the feed-grain harvest failed and the herds were slaughtered, which meant meat in plenty now and shortages in the months to come. Perhaps things were really getting better.

"She's a smart girl," Tumanov was saying. He used "girl" though she was older than he was. "She has a degree in mechanical engineering." That puzzled him. "What's she doing working as a hostess for Aeroflot? Why isn't she married?"

Kirov speculated on her choices. An engineer in Krasnoyarsk or an employee for Aeroflot with a Moscow resident's permit. How long had she needed to consider the alternatives. Krasnoyarsk was so dull that no one even bothered to tell jokes about it. Instead she could look forward to foreign travel. And marriage? Perhaps Viktor Gusev had offered an alternative. Viktor could proffer more wealth than some worthy fellow engineer in Krasnoyarsk. What were her choices?

They parked behind the other car. Its driver got out and scuttled over to them, his hat pulled down and his coat shedding water. He had asthmatic breath and the general appearance of a Sluzhba goon. Radek had cleared the shelves of anyone with wits. The man tapped the window and Tumanov rolled it down.

"Well?"

"Nothing." The man whistled as he breathed. "No movement. Nothing. She stays in the apartment and does—whatever she does."

"Do we have a listening post?" Kirov asked.

The man looked to Tumanov. "It wasn't authorized."

Tumanov said: "We didn't have the resources. Reproachfully he added: "Radek has commandeered all the best goods, the best troops." He ignored his man, who was indifferent to being second rate, and spoke in a murmur. Another grain to add to his burden of guilt. He probably saw Kirov notching another black mark against his record.

"It doesn't matter," Kirov assured him, knowing that Tumanov would doubt his sincerity. He looked across the bare earth that surrounded the apartment house. The potholes were full of water and rubble. A couple of small cars were roped down under tarpaulins.

"Fourth floor," said Tumanov's man. He handed a piece of paper through the window. A number was written on it.

"I'm going up," Kirov said.

"OK, I'll get my mate."

"I'll do it alone."

"You don't know what's in there."

"The colonel will go up there alone," Tumanov said.

Kirov got out of the car, stretched his legs and looked up and down at the road and the other identical blocks. Behind him a voice whispered urgently: "How was I to know he was a bloody colonel?"

Kirov asked: "Have the militia paid a call yet?"

"No," came the answer, "no, comrade Colonel."

Kirov turned around but the man's face displayed nothing save official respect. Kirov faced the apartment house again and set off across the open ground, avoiding the mud and the puddles.

The elevator was out of action, the stairwell smelled of urine, trash had collected in the corners of the common areas. Kirov knocked at a door covered in peeling paintwork and heard a radio being turned off and the pad of footsteps. Nadia Mazurova opened the door.

Her appearance had altered. Now it was familiar, which was about as altered as you could get. The other changes were superficial: her dress was of brown wool, her blond-streaked hair was pinned back and her ears revealed pearl studs, which he supposed were imitation. She was wearing a cheap though not unpleasant perfume; Kirov noticed it and wondered if she made a habit of wearing perfume under all circumstances as though she spent her life waiting for Viktor Gusev to knock at its door.

She was hesitating and he remembered that he had never given his name. She believed only that he was with the Public Prosecutor's Office.

"Kirov — Pyotr Andreevitch — investigator."

"Please, comrade investigator, come in."

She introduced him to a small square-shaped entrance hall that was hung with damp coats, then into another small room a few meters square which was crowded with furniture: a television set, a folding table, a couch that was made up into a bed and still showed bedclothes peeping from the frayed edges, an old sideboard covered in lace and photographs. A box refrigerator stood on top of the sideboard and purred. An old lady with mumbling lips and a heavy shawl was sitting on the couch and watching the blank screen of the television set. The place smelled of stale tobacco and food.

"You are living here? This is not your apartment."

"For a few days. Please sit down."

Kirov placed himself on a bentwood chair. She took a seat on another, unconsciously measuring out the distance between them and angling her chair so that it did not oppose his. Within the limits of the room she achieved what remoteness she could.

"My friend," she said, "is allowing me to stay here. She lives with her parents. They are all at work."

Five people. Kirov surmised a single bedroom. The couch in the main room would fold into a bed, and on the floor behind the television set was a roll of blankets.

"After Viktor's death I didn't want to be alone," she explained. "At the hostel . . ."

"The girls are not company. They are too . . . merry."

"You're not at work?"

"I had some leave scheduled. Can I offer you some refreshment? A glass of tea? Vodka?" She stood up to action his request and her dress fell loosely, the skirt cut to dip at the waist in emphasis of the shallow drooping curve of her belly as gentle as a raindrop. There was no sexual intent behind the gesture, no invitation in her manner, but Kirov was conscious of her live sexuality. He had felt it before in that first unsatisfactory interview at Gusev's apartment when she described her implausible relationship with Viktor and asked him to accept that she and Viktor were not lovers but something else. "Thinking with your balls," Uncle Bog chided him. Thinking of all the Laras and trying to imagine Viktor Gusev's different way.

"You were looking for me at the hostel," she stated.

"Was I?"

"Your colleagues. Other policemen."

"Probably," he agreed. "Why did you not get in touch with us?"

"It was inevitable that you would find me here. I thought I would wait."

"You were frightened of seeing the police again?"

"Are you really with the Public Prosecutor's Office?"

"I told you so. Why do you ask?"

"I imagined someone—different."

The old lady moved uncomfortably. Nadia Mazurova got up to attend her. She rearranged the old lady in a nest of cushions and shawls, turned on the television but reduced the volume, then went to the kitchen and came back with a bowl of milk and some bread. She dunked the bread in the milk, broke off pieces and fed them to the old woman. Watching her, Kirov detected affection in her actions, affection for the stranger she was ministering to. Her lightness of manner was returning. She wiped the *babushka*'s lips and glanced at Kirov. There was a challenge in her eyes.

"You met Viktor Gusev at a party—isn't that what you told me?"

She replaced the scrap of cotton she was using and wiped her fingers.

"Yes—about three years ago."

"In Moscow?"

"Yes."

"Whose party?"

"Yelena Borisovna Akhmerova. You know her?"

"The film star—yes, I know her. You were moving in elevated circles. The air hostess from Krasnoyarsk meets the famous film star. Strange—yes?" Kirov disliked the teasing note in the last question, but at this stage was curious for any reaction he might draw from her.

"It was the first time I had met her. I was taken to the party by an acquaintance, someone I had met on a plane. Yelena introduced me to Viktor, and from then on Viktor and I were . . ." she searched for a word.

"Friends?"

"Yes—friends."

"Not lovers."

Nadia gave the old lady a quick hug then announced that she would be having some tea, alone if necessary: would Kirov like some? He declined. She left him briefly and he lit a cigarette. From the window he could see across the open ground, the road, the wall, into a factory yard glossy with rain. Tumanov and the

Sluzhba team were sitting in the rear car with the window rolled down.

"How often did you stay with Viktor?" he asked.

Her reply came from the kitchen. That fact itself gave it an oddly domestic note. You could imagine a husband and wife speaking, the way husbands and wives spoke.

"Every month two or three nights, and perhaps a whole weekend once in a while, depending on my duty roster."

"He had other women?"

She had come back into the room.

"No."

"He was celibate?"

She hesitated, then said indifferently: "Sometimes he used prostitutes."

"But he was not a highly sexed man—was he?" Kirov said softly so as to arrest her attention by forcing her to listen. "Otherwise the tension of living with you would have been too much. He looked to you for—other satisfactions. What were they? What drew you together?" He waited for her answer. Her composure appeared complete, but he was aware of a heightened quality in her scent, a small change in her body temperature volatilizing the cheap perfume.

"How do these questions help you in investigating Viktor's business? That's what interests you, isn't it?"

He did not permit the deflection. "Weren't you a part of Viktor's business—part, at least, of his life? He took you to parties, restaurants, theaters, weekends at the *dachas* of his rich friends, perhaps even to their Black Sea villas. Those are the places where Viktor conducted his business. Now," Kirov insisted, "what drew you to him?"

"We were poor," she answered after a moment of bitter consideration.

"Poor—I take it we are talking about spiritual poverty?" Kirov queried with an irony he found distasteful. "There was plenty of the other sort of wealth about."

"We were both poor. And we shared what we had. I possessed what Viktor could give me—and Viktor possessed me."

"Or didn't possess you."

"Oh yes," she smiled wearily. "He possessed me. But as if I were the only one of my kind, far too precious or fragile for a poor boy like Viktor to break. You see, Viktor never really believed that he had me, never really believed that he had anything. That was why

77

he was so greedy: because a poor boy should never have any of these good things and they could always go away." She hung for a second for some receptive sign in his eyes, then added: "Or so I surmised. Viktor could be mysterious. It was never possible to say that one knew him."

Kirov changed the subject. He abandoned irony and insistence. "Did Viktor ever visit Bulgaria?" He threw her some help: "You may as well tell me the truth. I can check."

"No—no, he didn't."

"Or receive visitors from Bulgaria?"

"No."

"Please—think about it."

"None that I can remember."

"He met a lot of people. You met a lot of people. Well?"

"There were no Bulgarians. I should have known."

She should have known, he agreed with her.

He threw away sympathy and tried another version of his character to see what she responded to. He questioned her drily about the details of Viktor's business dealings, the people she met, the places she went to. He demanded details.

But with Viktor there were no details—or from another perspective there were so many details that no picture emerged, no particular detail signified. Nadia Mazurova did not say this but it was the message she conveyed. Viktor in his prime and splendor was a man without limits. His acquaintances bore witness to this in their very variety. Armenians, Azerbaijanis, Byelorussians, Bessarabians, Estonians, Georgians, Kalmuks, Khirghiz, Latvians, Lithuanians—you couldn't believe how big the country was until you knew Viktor, until you sat with him in his large car, rarely the same one twice, outside the railway stations (Kievski, Byelorusski, Savelovski, Rizhski and all the others) waiting for the trains to come in; outside the airports (Sheremetyevo, Vnukovo, et cetera) waiting for the planes to arrive; sat with Viktor's warm arm around you eating spicy tidbits and washing them down with J. & B. Rare while the world arrived to pay court. Viktor entertained royally as befitted his status. Would you like to eat? Try the Aragvi for *shashlyk, satsivi, suluguni* and *tabaka*—the Ararat for *solyanka, bozbash* and *chebureki*. In turn and as the mood and your courtiers suggest, try the Baku, the Belgrade, the Berlin, the Bucharest—the names are enough to conjure with. That was Viktor.

He called this "influence" and maintained that it was a treasure

78

richer than gold, and it must be since it was bought with gold or the nearest thing—though it had to be said that the courtiers bore gifts to defray the charge. In this system of mutual tribute the exact balance of value was difficult to ascertain. One could be certain only that the contents of the visitors' suitcases did not remain the same on the in-coming and return journeys and that on arrival and departure Viktor remained smiling and affable with such charm as had not before been seen in the world.

Names? Ah, that was a different matter. Firstly, there were so many. Secondly they were all false. Moreover, in Viktor's world we are all friends, aren't we, Sasha, Seriozha, Simka, Dimka, Arkasha, Kolya? There was no need for family names in Viktor's extended family even when, as happens in the best of families, a quarrel arose and a knife appeared below the table during dinner at the Ararat and a bottle of *Yubileiny* went onto the floor.

There is however a dark side to this—no, not a dark side—rather Viktor's dealings are seen through a veil. Where there are men, there are naturally women—also provided by Viktor. "My harem," he called them, conscious of his status. They too were a changing throng (except of course for Nadia who had her *special* relationship with Viktor of which the other girls were jealous). Viktor selected them and they did not stay long nor did they know each other. Recruitment was not a problem: Viktor's kindness and consideration were legendary and he never *misused* you (said the other girls, and Nadia Mazurova agreed, though not in those words). The entertainment of the harem was first class, but during the business dealings the girls sat idly by, dying of ennui and peered through their veil of isolation. Sasha, Seriozha, Simka, Dimka, Arkasha and Kolya joked and had a jolly time; they patted each other on the back and compared bellies (You should lose weight, Sasha, be as slim as Viktor). The girls retired in boredom to the restaurant toilets and there exchanged their real names and promised to keep in touch.

Or so Nadia Mazurova told it. And she added a few facts that stuck in her mind—like the time at the Aragvi restaurant when Viktor burst into tears.

"Over what?" Kirov asked.

"Something—something had upset him."

"Who was there?"

"I don't remember," Nadia Mazurova answered hastily. "Sergei and some of the others—I forget."

"Viktor cried about *business?* That doesn't seem likely."

"No."

"Then about people. A girl?"

"Maybe."

"You?"

"No. It's not important. You wanted to know what Viktor was like. He was emotional. He cared about people."

And Kirov let the matter drop there. He was convinced that, whatever mystery might surround Viktor Gusev's personal life, he remained at bottom only an unimportant racketeer, whose story was clear except for some odd discrepancies which would resolve themselves in due course. And for that reason the rest of her story could be dismissed as irrelevant, but for one fact. Nadia Mazurova had reminded him that the only mystery of abiding interest was the relationship between men and women.

8

I am gifted with a personality.
Alas you see only my mannerisms.
Is it a wonder that, with such thin stuff,
You hold me in contempt?

Kirov found the poem in the volume by Davidov left to him by
Irina Terekhova. The book had become a nomad object that wandered around his apartment, now by his bedside, now browsed in
the bathroom; an unexpected reminder as inconvenient as a guilty
conscience. Osip Davidov was a bad poet, but like other bad writers could strike the occasional chime from some facile truth and
set it ringing for a while. To prove Davidov's point, Tomsky turned
up at Kirov's apartment.

Tomsky worked the American desk in the First Chief Directorate. He serviced Yatsin and the Washington Residency — occasional bagman, occasional translator of Yatsin's official-speak into
intelligible Russian, occasional pimp if allowed to join the KGB
entourage on a diplomatic visit. He was a mustache grower, never
entirely with or without one. His apartment was in the same block.

"Are you going to ask me in — invite me for a drink?"

"Come on in." Kirov let Tomsky through the door and fixed
a couple of drinks. While he waited, Tomsky picked among
the books, looked at and discarded Davidov's poetry and then
carelessly took a seat. He was so relaxed that he could have
fallen apart with tension. Kirov handed him a drink. He noted
the gold identity bracelet and the Porsche key ring: Tomsky

collected Western junk and wore his latest mustache like a souvenir.

"Is this business or pleasure?" Kirov asked.

Tomsky smiled, threw back his drink and said: "Personal — I'm doing a friend a favor."

"A friend?"

"Scherbatsky."

The only Scherbatsky Kirov knew was the subject of the Chinese-watch story, another of Vanya Yatsin's odd-job men.

"I'm glad he's thinking of me."

Tomsky treated this as a joke.

"How's he doing?" Kirov remembered that Scherbatsky had been arrested. Something to do with the Moscow City housing fraud.

"He's OK. Unhappy, but OK. He's under house arrest. His apartment has been sealed and he's living with his parents in Kavrov."

"And his wife?"

"You knew he was married?"

"I heard he bought her a watch."

Tomsky laughed again. "That's Scherbatsky for you!"

There was only so much laughing you could do; Tomsky began to fidget and then handed over a slip of paper with an address written on it. "Scherbatsky's place. He'd like to see you."

"And why would I want to see him?"

Tomsky shrugged. "A favor? Call it a favor — don't you collect favors? I thought everybody did. Friends do each other favors — it's called Communism."

"People keep telling me that."

"Suit yourself. I've done what I promised." Tomsky bridled.

Kirov stopped him. "What does he want to talk about?"

"Do you really want to know?"

Kirov found what the other man reminded him of — bad films, people acted them all the time when they were looking for a role.

"Not particularly."

That got Tomsky laughing again.

"He wants to talk about serious business, he tells me. Serious — you understand serious?"

Kirov didn't know which looked more exhausted, the horses or the crowd. Since the races were fixed, form hardly counted

82

and a good tip was better than an eye for horse flesh. Uncle Bog had neither and so consistently lost money.

They met by arrangement outside the hippodrome entrance by the heroic statuary of rearing stallions and well-muscled men. Bogdanov had smartened himself up and looked more sleazy than the touts. Normally morose, he was grateful that Kirov had taken up his suggestion to go to the races. Kirov never speculated on where Bogdanov got his pleasures, and here was Uncle Bog, pleased.

They went inside. Bogdanov placed a couple of bets and they stood on the two-tiered stand to watch the horses lose his ten rubles, which was all the tote allowed. Kirov told him about the visit from Tomsky.

"He's a friend?"

"No."

"And Scherbatsky? I thought you didn't know Scherbatsky?"

"I don't."

Bogdanov shook his head and took a pull on a bottle of vodka he had bought from some character on the stairwell. "It tastes like diesel fuel," he said after his third choice fell in the final stretch. "How about a beer at the Bega?"

"OK."

The racecourse restaurant was a decent enough place. They got in the beers and went to stare out of the windows. Bogdanov had forgotten about the horses. He had the fretful look he wore when things were happening that he didn't understand.

"Did you see the girl?" he asked. "Did she have anything new to say?"

"Gusev was never in Bulgaria. He had no Bulgarian friends."

"Uh huh? And how was he getting his supplies from Bulgaria?"

"She doesn't know."

"The hell she doesn't."

Kirov tasted his beer. It was warm and flat.

"Antipov and his men visited the hostel where she lives."

Bogdanov let his eyebrows flicker. "He hasn't mentioned it. In fact he hasn't mentioned the girl at all; you'd think he'd never heard of her existence. Now why is that? What does he think she knows?" He looked down onto the track. "I had a tip on that one, the horse in the white socks. A winner? No? By the way, the result of the check on Georgi Gvishiani is in. Moscow say that he's a crook, into some racket involving furniture and consumer goods.

Tbilisi say that he's a son of the soil, a great Communist, as honest as the day is long." He glanced at Kirov. "The guess about Radek was a good one. Twelve months ago his team took a look into Gvishiani's business."

"What did they find?"

"Nothing. The investigation was dropped. Shortage of re-sources—Radek wanted every man he could get in order to break the Kiev meat ring. Meat shortages have a higher profile than stolen furniture, so the business of Gvishiani could wait. And why not? I could find you a dozen Georgi Gvishianis, the whole country is rotten with them. Catch one and another one springs up. Even Lemonade Joe Gorbachev can't put a stop to them."

Kirov nodded without replying. Gvishiani wasn't important, just a stray thought wandering across a confused landscape of facts: Viktor Gusev, the contaminated drugs that killed him, the unexplained cache of diamonds, the woman. Why hadn't he pressed Nadia Mazurova harder? Why hold back?

Bogdanov meanwhile was asking more questions about Gvishiani: did Kirov want more information on the Georgian; did he want some Sluzhba talent to follow Gvishiani about—"a couple of guys who can read and write." More to the point: what did Georgi Gvishiani have to do with anything?

"Nothing—just a thought. Forget about him."

"Uh huh." Bogdanov had turned and was leaning with his back to the window, watching a bunch of hook-nosed Armenians sur-rounded by paper parcels representing souvenirs of Moscow and drinking their winnings. He made a comment about the number of niggers you see around town these days and, casually turning around, asked: "Have you ever bumped up against a Director's Case?"

Kirov unwound from his thoughts. He glanced at the other man who was burying his head in a beer as though the question had never been asked. "Twice—perhaps three times. Is that what you've found?"

"I don't know what I've found," Bogdanov answered bluntly. "I hoped you might know."

Kirov knew about Director's Cases, or all that could be known. Some subjects were too sensitive to be handled anywhere but at the top. If an investigation threw up a reference to a Director's Case, it stopped there. Perhaps someone continued with it, perhaps not, you never discovered.

"What have you got?"

Bogdanov told him.

"I ran a search against the Bulgarian outfit, the drug manufacturers. It drew nothing apart from gossip and dirty stories — the usual stuff."

"And?"

Bogdanov eased up. "Another beer? Do you know Krapotkin — Sergei Pavlovitch? He's a systems man, he wrote some of the data-collection programs."

"Go on."

"Well, he taught me a trick. I've used it a couple of times, there's nothing fancy to it; sometimes it works and sometimes not. Have you ever handled a case when you suddenly find yourself stepping on somebody's else's toes? You arrest a guy and it turns out he's someone's informer; you run a surveillance operation and you find that the place is already wired but no one told you. It's all a matter of paperwork, the files aren't up to date, or the data isn't logged or cross-referenced."

"It happens."

"Yeah," Bogdanov found amusement in some recollection. "I'll get the beers," he said. He shuffled off to the bar and pushed the Armenians aside. He returned with the drinks and continued: "Where was I? Falling over people? Sure! That was Krapotkin's problem. It happens all the time. The systems, he says, are there but people don't use them — Krapotkin gets religious about this because he designs the systems. In fact, he says, the only part which is guaranteed to work is the finance bit, which is because nobody can spend money without accounting for it. And this part of the system works every which way as an audit check. *That* is Krapotkin's point.

"Let's say you have a subject which you think should be on file, but isn't. Provided it's a key word logged on the finance data base, if you punch it in, the computer will spill out all the costs and charges logged against it and give you the case number. What does it matter if you aren't interested in the accounts? Now that you have the case number you can call up the main file. It's a useful cross-check. A gimmick."

"You used it this time?"

"I was curious. I tried to find Bulpharma on the main files and drew nothing but rubbish. So I decided to see if anyone had been spending money in that direction. They had."

"How much?"

"Three quarters of a million rubles."

There was a hush in the restaurant. By the bar two of the Armenians were shoving each other. The crowd was silent and tense in expectation of a fight.

"Let's talk about this outside." Kirov dumped his beer untouched and collected his hat. "You had enough of racing?"

"I only ever lose."

They left the stadium in a drift of early leavers and walked in the direction of Begovaya metro station, ignoring the touts and the currency changers who mistook Kirov for a Westerner. Bogdanov maintained a morose silence until they were clear, then began again.

"The stuff I uncovered had a finance code against it. I asked Krapotkin about it. 'It's on open budget,' he says, and I ask: What's 'open budget'? 'Open budget,' so Krapotkin tells it, means that the expenditure is recorded, but there is no sum set against it for control purposes. Three quarters of a million rubles spent on Bulpharma? 'Peanuts!' says Krapotkin. 'Make it a million — ten million! There's no limit on what can be spent!' " Bogdanov halted. "What I didn't need Krapotkin to tell me is that the only time the sky's the limit is on a Director's Case."

"I'll talk to Grishin."

"When?"

"Tomorrow."

"It's a weekend."

"He's invited me to his *dacha*."

"I don't think it'll help."

"Why not?"

They stopped again to let the crowd pass. Bogdanov moved to the shelter of a wall and lit a cigarette, spitting loose strands of tobacco onto the pavement. He watched the people and the bright autumn sky and chewed over the end of his cigarette.

"It wasn't one of ours. It was a GRU operation — I know: what the hell were military intelligence doing investigating a pharmaceutical plant in Bulgaria? But that's the way it was — Krapotkin is certain — all the costs were charged to the Aquarium. And it gets worse. I've come across Director's Cases before — ours, theirs, it makes no difference. You can't get anything out of them, *but* they carry a main-file record so that new data can be logged into them. This one doesn't."

"Are you sure?"

"Positive. According to the main file it doesn't exist. You take my point? GRU had a team in Bulgaria for four months and spent three quarters of a million rubles — and apart from a few entries on the accounts, *the whole operation doesn't exist*. Boss, I'm starting to get bad feelings."

Bogdanov had run out of words. He leaned back against the wall, thin and strung out like a torn poster. Kirov suggested they move on. He proposed they find somewhere and have another drink. Forget about the GRU investigation, everybody spied on everybody; it probably had nothing to do with the present business.

"Maybe — maybe," Bogdanov agreed without much conviction. "But there could be a way to find out."

"How?"

"The finance file has a name attached to it. It's a long shot, it could simply be a clerk who collects the expense claims. But there has to be a chance that it's the acting case officer."

"Who is he?"

"Heltai. That's it, no first name, no rank. Just Heltai. To me he doesn't sound like a Russian. You look as though you've heard of him?"

Kirov shook his head. He didn't know any Heltai. The name was just a breath that shivered the surface of forgotten memories, so light that it could not be grasped.

"Pyotr Andreevitch! I'm glad you could come."

"It was kind of you to invite me, Rodion Mikhailovitch."

General Grishin wiped his hands on his rough cord trousers and extended one in friendly fashion. Kirov's arrival had caught him chopping wood at the shed by the side of his brick-built *dacha*. Kirov had watched him from the road before announcing his presence. Grishin, a small figure in a blue check shirt and red suspenders, sweated away at the woodpile with a look of peaceful effort, pausing only now and then to take a swig from a bottle and study the sky, which was stained with yellow-gray clouds and swirling with crows from the woods behind the house.

"Do you think we'll have snow?" Grishin said doubtfully, and then, with simple pleasure: "It really is good of you to come. My wife — my mother — they see so few . . . I'm glad you came."

"I look forward —"

"Yes. Well, let's go in. Do you think it will snow?"

Kirov examined the clouds. Heavy with snow like a pregnant woman; the crows cawing in distress over the still treetops.

"I think so."

They walked along the path to the house.

"You've been here before?" Grishin asked.

"Once," Kirov reminded him. They had walked in the woods where Grishin took potshots at the crows who ravaged his winter vegetables, and in a quiet clearing they discussed obliquely the people who had to be killed or terrified to solve their particular problem. Afterwards they sat around the family table and ate peasant food lovingly prepared by Grishin's wife.

There was a story about Grishin's wife: that she was a country woman whose manners unfitted her for the *beau monde* of the KGB chieftains, even that she was religious, which would have been in bad taste. It explained why she was never seen around the general's Moscow apartment, nor shopping in the city, and why Grishin never took his holidays at the KGB villas in the principal resorts but went, no one knew where, off into the bush. The woman was a near idiot, it was said.

"Pyotr Andreevitch Kirov — my spouse and my parent."

The two women bobbed in acknowledgment. The wife was pale and distant and dressed in a homemade woolen frock and apron. The mother was round-cheeked like her son, in shapeless clothes trimmed with bits of lace so that she looked gift wrapped like the presents Kirov remembered from the past: Uncle Kolya in his thin romantic period, standing on the apartment landing and bearing gifts.

"Shall we eat?" Grishin said, coming directly to the ostensible point of the invitation. Kirov glanced at the table. It was set for two. "Men's talk," said his host. The women were gathering themselves to retire to another room. Grishin hopped to the door and opened it for them, then returned to his guest. He sat down, evidently uncomfortable with his own shyness, unable to explain it. The woman is a near idiot, Kirov recalled — and Grishin is in love with her, which explains everything.

They drank iced vodka with the *zakuski.* The general's wife had prepared a simple borscht and *shash!yk,* and Grishin ate it with what appeared to Kirov to be contrived gusto. The two men sat in silence, occasionally exchanging smiles. Grishin eased the collar of his shirt and the belt of his trousers. He avoided Kirov's curiosity and studied instead the furnishings of the world he had created outside the confines of Moscow, a little territory of overstuffed chairs, ornaments in tarnished frames, a cast-iron stove that burned sweet logs.

"We live in changing times," he suggested, repeating the litany that rang these days through the corridors of Dzerzhinsky Square.

"So I hear."

"Oh, we do, we do. Food? More food or another drink?"

"Thanks."

"Food? Drink?"

"Another drink."

Grishin poured more vodka. Kirov picked up the glass but left the liquor untouched.

"We must change with the times in order to survive. We must become—what? Butterflies? Frogs? It's difficult to be sure." Grishin's philosophizing meant that he was drunk. "I knew your father," he went on. His eyes searched out a response. Cunning drunk. "And your uncle, General Nikolai Konstantinovitch Prylubin. Ah, I forget: he wasn't your uncle, was he? Just a family friend."

"You knew Uncle Kolya?"

"I worked for him—just as he worked for your father, and your father in turn served Beria, and before him Yagoda and Yezhov. Yes. But in those days I was unimportant, a mere captain."

Kirov took a sip of the vodka and asked if he might smoke. Grishin busied himself for a moment feeding logs to the stove though the room was overheated. In the next room the old woman was berating her daughter-in-law for something. The idiot!

"Because of your father, I always took an interest in your career. I recommended you for the Washington posting. I suggested you handle the Ouspensky Case. You may recall my telling you that I was responsible for cleaning out the Paris station after he defected. I knew Oleg Ouspensky's character and that if anyone could bring him back it was you. And I was right. An old-style Chekist would have frightened Ouspensky, made him back away. We could have killed him, of course, but even then times were changing and we wanted him alive. We needed a new kind of man to get him—a *changed* man."

But after the Ouspensky Case there had been no place for changed men. They had pulled Kirov out of Washington and put him through months of dangerous debriefing to see what particles of himself he had left over there. That was ten years ago, since when America too had changed, and anything left behind was in a place that no longer existed. Grishin was well aware that the Ouspensky Case, while an operational success, was a personal blow. Only Kirov's sidekick, Vanya Yatsin, who lacked the imagination to see the humanity of a traitor like Oleg Ouspensky, had risen after the event to become Washington Resident. Grishin looked at his guest sorrowfully and helped himself to another drink.

"Yes," he murmured. "That's how it was."

"I didn't realize you knew my father."

"Nikolai Konstantinovitch didn't tell you?"

"Uncle Kolya has told me very little."

"Probably for the best. Your father lived through difficult times. We all did." Grishin stared remotely into his glass. "And even those days, which one might have thought had gone beyond all change, become reevaluated. It seems that even the past won't lie down unless we drive a stake through its heart." Kirov was reminded that Grishin was spending time with the Rehabilitation Committee, which contributed to *perestroika* by resurrecting the names of the dead and the undead and offered them to the Politburo for reconsideration of their past crimes, actual or alleged. Of late the Committee had been sitting more frequently and there were rumors that the proceedings had at times become heated. "The Great Jewish Antibiotics Ring . . ."

"Yes?"

"It represents the way things are going. We must liaise with and support the other agencies in maintaining the law — unless, of course, we have evidence to prove that those agencies are corrupt. In the past we were inclined to be — arrogant? Though I'm sure we meant well. It represents a change of style. Radek seems to understand it. Radek," he mused, "who would have thought it? And you?"

"I've tried to cooperate."

"Yes, yes, I suppose so. I had thought," Grishin said abstractedly, "that your background and training would have fitted you for the times. And instead — instead I get a feeling that you are holding back as if you have no faith in what is happening. Radek on the other hand . . . Radek will go far. Shall we go for a walk?"

They put on their topcoats. Grishin loaned Kirov a pair of boots and disappeared into the other room to inform his wife. Kirov waited on the doorstep, watching a car disappear in the direction of Zhukovka. Grishin emerged, unsteady on his feet, held Kirov's arm, and together they took a path into the silence of the woods.

They walked awhile. Grishin stooped occasionally to pluck a mushroom from the bole of a tree or among the fallen pine needles. He threw the odd stone at the treetops as part of his perpetual feud against the crows, and the disturbed birds rattled and flapped out of sight among the branches.

"Viktor Gusev is dead," Kirov began. "He died of contaminated antibiotics—his own."

"Ironic," Grishin replied. He proposed that they take a seat on a tree stump in one of the clearings.

"The antibiotics were produced by a factory in Bulgaria."

"Really?"

"The factory was the subject of an investigation in 1984. It was run by GRU as a Director's Case and the data-logging procedures were violated in order to suppress any main-file record." Kirov waited but Grishin's expression revealed nothing. He picked up a stick and stirred the leaf litter. "You knew about the investigation?"

"Stories."

"What stories?"

"Andropov died in 1984. He was too young to die, people were curious. Work it out for yourself." Grishin picked up a milk cap that was buried among the leaves; he spun the grub-wormed fungus in his fingers and discarded it.

"Are you implying that Andropov was murdered?"

"I'm not implying anything. There would have been an investigation however it was that Andropov died. I'm simply trying to tell you the way that some people *thought*. That can be as important as the truth. It was no secret that Chernenko was opposed to Andropov. So, when he came into the succession, he ordered an investigation into Andropov's death since he didn't want anyone blaming him for the convenient event—in particular, given that Andropov had been head of KGB, he didn't want to give KGB an excuse for a witch-hunt. Do you understand? It didn't matter whether Andropov had been murdered, but everyone had to act as if he had been."

Kirov halted.

"Rodion Mikhailovitch, I need to visit Bulgaria. Everything suggests that the antibiotics have their source there."

"Make a formal request."

91

"I can't do that. I don't want to notify the local *referentura*."

"Why not?" Grishin glanced from the damp mulch at his feet to Kirov, and Kirov had again the sense that he was being asked to read Grishin's intentions. The moment passed, Grishin stood up and started brushing the dirt from his pants. "Let's go back," he suggested. He made no further reference to Kirov's request and Kirov could only guess that he had understood its significance. GRU had run an investigation in Bulgaria for a period of four months; and during the whole of that time KGB's local *referentura* had not picked up the activity and notified Moscow. On any view that was curious.

They walked a while longer by a foresters' path. Grishin was intimately familiar with the wood and they took a different route for their return. In the clearings snow was falling, lazy snow that would not last. The general remained in his strange mood; even his grunts and sighs as he maneuvered by the ruts and fallen branches were like snippets of code. Kirov was left to speculate on the reason for Grishin's invitation. To talk about my father—Yuri Andropov—the Great Jewish Antibiotics Ring? It occurred to him that in some way he was considered dangerous by Grishin, but any attempt to explore that idea made no sense.

"Why *Jewish?*" he asked to break the oppression of silence. Grishin stopped abruptly and gave him a fleeting look of cold suspicion. Then he was smiling again.

"It's just a name."

"I didn't invent it. You gave it to me."

Grishin acknowledged the fact with a nod.

"The case has a history," Kirov suggested. "Something before my involvement."

"A history. It has nothing to do with the present."

"Tell me."

They exchanged cigarettes. Grishin removed his cap and beat the snow off it. He took Kirov's arm and moved him to the shelter of the trees. He found a place to perch himself heavily on a log, and invited Kirov to take a seat next to him. For a moment he sat in cautious silence and Kirov felt the other's small, intense eyes picking at him like fingers. Then Grishin began.

"Have you heard of Academician I. A. Yakovlevitch?"

Kirov had: Yakovlevitch was a defector—no, not a defector: a *refusenik* Jew. He had been a surgeon or some such thing.

Grishin drew on his cigarette and cast his eyes loosely about the trees. "It comes back to foreign policy," he said. "Jews in the Soviet Union—they don't fit. I don't know whether it's a matter of racism or something else; but they don't fit. That's just a fact."

Kirov nodded. Grishin took this for agreement and he went on: "The Israelis want them out of here, the Americans want them out of here, and, God knows, we'd be glad to see the backs of them. But"—he paused—"there's the matter of our own pride and prestige—and what would we do with all the others, the non-Jews, who want to leave? The whole business is a nuisance, a distraction."

"I can see that."

"Can you?" Grishin's thoughtfulness still seemed misplaced. Kirov still had the feeling that he was missing some clue to the other man's mixed approach of affection and caution, and wondered what had changed. Grishin continued his explanation: "Andropov decided to make a gesture—not to release any Jews, you understand. He decided to pillory a few in order to make the others shut up. The idea was to arrest one or two, bring them to trial in a glare of publicity, and frighten the rest."

"And Yakovlevitch was picked for this?"

"Yes. He was to be the lead conspirator in the plot. He was ideal—the plot was ideal. Yakovlevitch could be made to fit into a popular scenario: the anti-corruption drive, the antibiotics shortage, the Jewish problem. Yakovlevitch was a Jew and a doctor. Tie him and a few associates to the illegal trade in antibiotics and there you had a dramatic solution to everything! The Great Jewish Antibiotics Ring!"

"But it didn't happen," Kirov pointed out.

"No, it didn't happen."

"Why not?"

"Oh, there were changes."

"Such as?"

"Andropov died, and Chernenko wasn't interested in picking up an old KGB plot; you could never tell where it had been—or, more to the point, where it was intended to go. Chernenko ordered the investigation closed and kicked Yakovlevitch out of the country. Only the name survived."

"And was there any truth in it?" Kirov asked.

"Why do you ask that now?" Grishin answered sharply.

"Curiosity."

"Well, there wasn't any truth in it, not a shred and nobody cared,

because that's the way that business was done. Remember that."
He stood up abruptly and said they should press on back to the
house. Kirov followed him. On the way he asked if Grishin had
ever come across a GRU case officer named Heltai. Grishin said he
didn't know him and asked where Kirov had come across the
name.

9

In those days adults called him Petya. He was a boy on holiday with Uncle Kolya in Riga on the Baltic coast. They were at their hotel whiling away a dreary day moodily sipping lime tea in a sheltered spot on the terrace while behind them in the dining room, viewed dimly through a french window, the waiters played cards.

The stranger was a fat man. He came from the direction of the sea, barefooted with a pair of two-tone shoes hanging by their laces around his neck. His face was hidden by the broad rim of his straw hat, the jacket from a gray double breasted suit flopped open over a striped pullover, and a pair of trousers from another suit were rolled at the bottom to display his white feet. His strange glamour was readily apparent.

He approached them, taking the steps two at a time, sheltering his hat under a newspaper, his other hand carefully holding a box tied with string. He placed the box on their table, shook the newspaper out onto the paving slabs, then took a seat.

"Hope you don't mind if I sit with you?" he addressed Uncle Kolya, and, offering a hand, he announced himself: "Heltai — Ferenc Heltai." Then he looked away back to the sea where the cold rain blew from the rolling mass of cloud.

On removing his hat he showed a round pallid face. His red hair was cut to a stubble, and, like many red-haired men, he appeared to have neither eyebrows nor eyelashes, which with the round blandness of his features gave his face an open fascination. He caught the boy staring at him, but, thinking he was interested in the contents of his box, asked: "What do you think it is, then?"

"I don't know," Petya answered.

"Guess."

"I can't."

"Go on, make a guess," he repeated, but when the boy couldn't he lost interest and the boy was left to look at the enigmatic box while the stranger engaged Uncle Kolya in conversation, occasionally casting an eye at the waiters who casually returned his glance and continued their card game.

Petya did not know how old this newcomer was; he was himself of an age when the age of other people was a mystery to him. Thinking of him later, he supposed the stranger was in his late twenties, made older in appearance by his weight. He spoke Russian with a Hungarian accent and in an odd dialect of his own making which seemed to consist of stilted official phraseology mixed with the coarsest of abuse, of which he was apparently unconscious since he delivered oaths with perfect coolness. He had the habit of laughing at the end of each remark as if it must necessarily be funny.

Because Petya had become embarrassed by staring at him, he tried to follow the conversation without looking in the other's direction. So his view drifted over the roadway where raindrops were bouncing from the cobblestones, and he saw two girls also coming, like the stranger, from the direction of the sea. Their printed cotton dresses were soaked and they giggled with discomfort. They too came up the steps onto the hotel terrace where they took the table next to the two men and the boy, and the elder of the pair began to shout for a waiter and finally went over to the french window and rattled on the glass. The waiter came and took their order, and Ferenc Heltai also ordered a beer. That action and the direction they had come from gave Petya the idea that he and the girls were in some way linked. He was a stranger and they were other strangers who fitted inside him like a doll. Take the girls apart and they would reveal more strangers.

Uncle Kolya dealt with the other man cautiously. The Hungarian was more open—indeed he seemed anxious to talk. He was attracted to the older man; his manner and his authority inspired confidence, and the colonel (as he then was) eased him along with small prompts and murmurs of sympathy. Petya could not understand what they were talking about, but as the conversation developed he realized that Uncle Kolya was subtly interrogating the other man, drawing out his story; and he admired then and often later the skill and power his uncle displayed. He wanted to acquire that ability, that power to take a stranger and reveal his secrets and strangeness.

The girls meantime were making themselves comfortable. The elder one had taken off her headscarf and was shaking her hair and wringing the moisture out of the scarf. Her companion was sitting back in her chair and seemed to be looking longingly out toward the sea. This was what attracted Petya's attention to her; he wanted to understand what was out there, somewhere beyond her sight. Occasionally her hand passed over her dress, smoothing out the lines and picking out the damp folds. The pattern on the dress was of primroses. The wet material clung to her. She wore no brassiére, but her breasts were covered by a cloth tied halter fashion about her neck so that they fell in a natural line. The boy was, of course, intensely interested, but he endeavored to cover his interest. He leaned forward on the table, resting his chin on his hand with his eyes peering above the splayed fingers and the fingers stroking the down on his lip and chin.

Having stirred the waiters into action, Uncle Kolya kept their new companion supplied with beer. Heltai, mistaking this interest for friendliness, continued to be forthcoming, but, probably in recognition that the boy's attitude was less complicated, less dangerous than that of Uncle Kolya, he drew Petya into the conversation.

"It's a cake," he said. "In the box—a cake, a Ruslan and Ludmila cake." By way of explanation why he was carrying the cake about in the rain, he went on: "I bought it in Leningrad. A specialty. Hard to come by. I daren't leave it in my room or the hotel staff would steal it, so I have to take it everywhere. Last night I went to the cinema. The night before I went dancing. Both times I took the cake." He swore and laughed. "Did you guess it was a cake?"

Petya shook his head.

"Ah—" The red-haired man smiled at him. "Then you'll never grow up to be a good policeman."

There was a message for the colonel in this last remark since Heltai began to talk of police matters, but he continued to treat the boy as entitled to listen. It was his first introduction to the secret life, and although the details were lost on him he understood immediately its fascination. The stranger spoke of people Petya didn't know. He mentioned in particular a man called Laszlo Rajk, an enemy of the people who came to a suitably nasty end.

But was he an enemy of the people? Heltai wondered. In 1950 —
yes. In 1956 — no: because Imre Nagy and the gang of Fascists who
had taken over the country had rehabilitated Laszlo Rajk.

Heltai was amused by this paradox. He continued to talk about
AVH and a building at 60 Andrassy Street in Budapest where he
and his colleagues in AVH had wrestled like theologians with the
soul of Laszlo Rajk. His mood was alternately swept by laughter
and sadness as he puzzled over this old problem, and he ended by
staring at the beer bottles he had accumulated on the table and
fiddled with the string tying the box which held the Ruslan and
Ludmila cake.

And the girls, they drank glasses of tisane and continued to unfold their skirts, trying to get each panel to dry. The prettier of the
two caught Petya's shy glances, and, pausing over her drying exercise, studied him coolly. In the street a black limousine with curtains at the windows pulled up. The rain had stopped and steam
rose from the bonnet.

"I must be going," their companion said, and he placed some
money on the table. He shook hands with the colonel and the boy
formally and collected his box. A driver in an MVD uniform came
up the terrace steps and approached — not Heltai but the girls.
They laughed, picked up their bags and followed the driver down
to the limousine. Their Hungarian acquaintance watched them
and then with a brief goodbye left. Petya last saw him walking
barefooted along the hotel terrace, still guarding his precious cake.
The girls had reached the car, and the younger one looked back
and blew a kiss in Petya's direction.

"What does that man do?" he asked Uncle Kolya.

The colonel pulled coins from a small purse he kept in his
pocket. Then he suggested they leave.

"But what does he do?" the boy pressed him.

"He tortures people," said Uncle Kolya.

10

Ivan Pavlovitch Scherbatsky was living at his parents' apartment in Kavrov, which was a miserable place unless you liked factories. On the strength of Tomsky's invitation, Kirov decided he would pay Scherbatsky a call. There was a lull in the Gusev case: the only development that promised a lead was the discovery that the labels on Viktor Gusev's stock of antibiotics, both those retrieved from the rubbish at Butyrka and the consignment handed over by MVD, showed a break in the series of package codes. One interpretation was that Viktor had sold part of his stock before the police raid. Kirov asked Bogdanov to check the Moscow regional hospitals for any deaths similar to that of Viktor Gusev. In the meantime there was Scherbatsky.

He spoke to Tomsky again, but the Washington bagman, having paid off whatever debt he owed Scherbatsky, didn't want to take any more risks — after all Scherbatsky was under arrest. All he had to give was a new version of the Chinese watch story.

According to Tomsky, a year or maybe two years before, because of his American experience Scherbatsky had been asked to carry a bag of tricks from San Francisco to Taiwan and pass it over to the Illegal Resident, an old man name of Harry Korn or Kornilov, depending on accounts. It was a joke among the KGB foreign sections that Taiwan was a black hole: nothing went in or came out except once a year a report and a request for money. This was because there was no diplomatic cover for a large station and because no European could get anywhere with the Chinese. It was a shoestring operation and Harry Korn was pathetically glad if anyone stopped to say hello to him and there was no holding him back when Scherbatsky dropped by in person. Harry wined him and dined him and took him on a tour of Taipei's renowned barbers' shops where Scherbatsky had his hair well and truly clipped. And at the end of it all Harry gave his friend a watch which he picked up at a street market in Wanhua but swore was the genuine article. This was the famous Chinese Rolex.

Tomsky didn't guarantee that a word of this was true.

Scherbatsky's parents occupied an old-style apartment in a pre-Revolution villa on the outskirts of the town. It was a handsome place with a ragged garden set behind a broken wall and it might have been turned to something better, but around its original isolated position the planners had built a couple of iron foundries, and across the potholed surface of Raspletin Street stood an electrical repair shop with a yard full of old *Biryusa* refrigerators and *Raketa* vacuum cleaners, which they were cannibalizing for parts. In the garden a man was working among the stumps of hewn-down birches, clearing brambles and elder saplings to dig a patch of winter vegetables. Kirov approached him and asked for the Scherbatsky apartment.

"Who wants to know?"

"A friend."

"Is that so?" The gardener let his spade fall and wiped the clay from his hands on the seat of his pants. He was a tall man with striking fair hair and blue eyes that gave his face, fitted with the regular features and rattrap mouth, the empty look of a doll. "You'll be Kirov," he said matter of factly. "I'm Scherbatsky. Were you stopped on your way here?"

"No. Are you watched?"

"On and off. I'm here on my promise to behave myself. The local boys are lazy sods, but if the GAI post back at the junction noted the Moscow plates on your car they'll probably send someone to look you over. Tell them whatever you like; the morons will believe you. Let's go inside and have a drink."

Scherbatsky left his tools to lie among the turned earth and picked his way by a path of shattered paving stones to the house. A swarm of children poured out of the door and scattered across the garden.

"This is an old-fashioned place," Scherbatsky said. Part of the large dim hallway had been curtained off, and behind the curtain someone was cooking. "We share the kitchen with two other families, the bathroom too. I guess I should have found my parents a better apartment, but," he shrugged, "on the road to success, who thinks about the past? In any case they like it here. The children. Me, I don't like children."

"Is your wife with you?"

"My wife," Scherbatsky repeated flatly. "No. I told her to get a divorce. In these cases it's safer to get a divorce. It's the least I can do for the bitch."

He opened a door off the first-floor landing. It took them into what had once been a large room, since clumsily divided so that the central light hung from a point near the wall and had been rigged with flex and tape to give some light from the middle of the room over the mass of furniture.

"Take a seat," Scherbatsky invited. He hunted for a bottle, found one and poured a couple of measures. "Make yourself at home—sorry about the mess. Know what it's like—too many people, falling over . . ." he turned around with a grin of sociability plastered over his face. It fell as his eyes registered Kirov's cool patience. "Look, take a bloody seat, will you? *Sorry—*" he caught himself, "sorry—nerves." He sat down on an overstuffed chair and gestured toward another one that stood crammed between an ancient radio and the wall. His lips glided over the rim of his glass and left its contents untasted. He put the glass down and regarded it guiltily. "It's easy to drink yourself stupid. Stuck here. Anything like this ever happen to you?"

"Once," Kirov answered, remembering the lonely months after his return from Washington bringing the returning defector Oleg Ouspensky. Limbo time. Unreal days spent nursing Ouspensky in his fool's paradise of freedom for the benefit of Western media before they buried him under the icy ground as happened in those days when they did things differently. "Once," he said, but didn't elaborate. He said it coldly, meaning he was fresh out of sympathy for anyone in the same boat. He had decided to make Scherbatsky work for his sympathy: it was the interrogator's treasure, to be expended sparingly.

"I suppose," Scherbatsky began at last, "that you want to know why I've asked you here." He wasn't bothered about a reply. "I know about Viktor Gusev."

Kirov had expected many things, but not that. Scherbatsky

worked for the American desk and had no business with the Gusev case, shouldn't even know the name Viktor Gusev. Then the connection came to him.

"Through your cousin."

It was Scherbatsky's turn for surprise. "How did you know that?"

"Your cousin worked for a construction combine. Gusev worked for the city authorities. He handled budgets for construction work on the water system. It fits that they would meet."

"OK," Scherbatsky grunted circumspectly. "Well, that's what I have to offer — information on Gusev. Interested?"

"Perhaps. In return for what?"

"For help, what else? Will you have another drink?" Without waiting he got up to pour one and talked as he poured. "Who would have thought that with my record I'd be facing corruption charges out of the construction racket? It's incredible!"

"Is it? It depends on whether or not you're guilty."

"Don't be bloody stupid, of course I'm guilty! What's that got to do with anything? Here," Scherbatsky handed over the glass.

"You knew it was illegal."

"Sure it's illegal! That's not the point. Nobody ever told me it was *wrong!*" He finished his drink. He had brought the bottle over and now poured himself another one but let it lie.

"What do you think of my prison?" He waved an arm to take in the crowded mass of dull wood and upholstery.

"There are worse."

"That's what they tell me. 'We're being good to you, Ivan Pavlovitch' — that's the story — in return for my cooperation."

"Who are 'they'?"

"Komarev from Special Investigations and Petruk from your lot — he's the case officer but I don't know who he works for."

"Radek."

"Shit!" Scherbatsky murmured and took a sip from his glass. "Radek is a star. He'll want to make a big production out of this business. I was hoping . . ."

"What?"

"That Petruk might be working for you. I've heard that you're a reasonable man. Is there any chance . . . ?"

"No."

"Ah — well, so much for hope."

Kirov let him drift for a few seconds in hopelessness. "What cooperation do they want?"

"They don't tell me."

"Isn't it obvious?"

"Nothing is obvious. Even confession isn't *obvious.*" He spat the word out. "Crime and confession aren't related—you know that. Confessions don't close the door on a crime, they open new doors onto other things. What am I supposed to confess to? What do they want the confession for? They don't tell me. I'm supposed to guess."

"What's your guess?"

Scherbatsky didn't answer. Instead he asked miserably: "Are you frightened of pain?"

"Yes."

"Me too. I'm frightened that they'll take me inside—understand? I don't think I could take it if they really gave me the business."

"That's not Radek's style."

"Isn't it? That's not what I've heard."

"Not these days. There's been a change. You're here, aren't you?"

"For how long?"

Scherbatsky got up and took a few paces about the room, halting by the window. "Our friends have arrived." Kirov joined him and saw the black Volga sedan parked in the street and a man quizzing the children. Not GIA, the highway police used yellow patrol cars. A call from the traffic post back at the junction to the local MVD? A wind had got up and the branches of the wild elders swayed. The cracked bark was hung with liverish swags of Jew's ear fungus (why Jewish?). Scherbatsky stared at the view indifferently and continued to talk.

"What do you know about my case?"

"Your cousin was in a racket doing illegal construction work. You found customers for him."

"It sounds simple when you put it like that. But have you ever thought who those customers might be? The names?"

"It's not my case."

"Oh, for God's sake, don't be such a prig!" Scherbatsky snapped. Then: "Sorry. Temper temper, must watch our tempers. Forget what I said. Not priggish, eh? Cautious, yes?" He took another sip of vodka, toasted the world outside the window, and turned away so that his face was now in shadow and his hair a halo against the light. "Does Radek really want the names?"

"Why shouldn't he?" Kirov answered neutrally and found Scherbatsky watching him with a sly regard as if he had uttered some deep wisdom. It was a response to the interrogator's air of power as if Kirov's every banality had become as subtle as the word of God. Having striven to create this effect, Kirov was depressed by it. He wished that Scherbatsky would be finished — but in an interrogation even the interrogator had a price to pay. Scherbatsky said: "Does Radek want the names I know? Or does he want some other names? You understand *'other names'?"*

Kirov understood. One of Grishin's stories came back to him. Academician I. A. Yakovlevitch had figured as an "other name" in one version of the Great Jewish Antibiotics Ring, dropped into the plot because at a certain time and place his name was convenient. Had the surgeon appreciated his danger, or had he passed in ignorance through the whole episode? Scherbatsky couldn't leave the idea alone.

"It can't be me they want. They can't put me on trial. A KGB major involved in corruption? It would be unthinkable. It has to be someone else that they're after."

He chose to ignore the fact that these days you could put KGB majors on trial.

"Maybe they'll retire you," Kirov offered as consolation, and he saw the other man brighten up. But he couldn't avoid the thought that like the Great Jewish Antibiotics Ring this conspiracy floated free of any form, a name without content, a conspiracy waiting for conspirators to join it. His curiosity was mixed with his boredom. The Moscow construction fraud tingled with hidden meaning — yet Scherbatsky, dull and greedy and as predictable as the pages of a cheap book, lay as a thing without interest. Kirov asked: "What do you have to offer me?"

"The location of Gusev's *dacha.* Interested, huh? You didn't know there was one, did you?"

Scherbatsky's smugness was irritating but Kirov ignored it. Losers often gloated over their petty successes, and Scherbatsky was a loser: he bought Chinese watches and thought he had a smart deal.

"There had to be one somewhere."

"Somewhere — Where's 'somewhere'? There's no way anyone

could know about Viktor's place unless he'd been there."

"Why's that?"

"Because Viktor was a clever sod. Too clever by half. Yes," Scherbatsky repeated thoughtfully, "too clever by half. He took the *dacha* in the name of one of his subordinates—all the paperwork, everything. The poor devil probably doesn't even know."

"But you do."

Scherbatsky laughed. His voice descended to a low chuckle, then, catching the hysterical undertone, he sniffed and took another drink. "You're not drinking?" he asked. Kirov raised his glass as a token. Scherbatsky ran his fingers through his hair and stared into his own glass as if he could hide in it.

"I can't bear pain," he murmured. "I can't face Radek tearing my brain out."

"It isn't like that."

"I'll give them any names they like—true—false—I don't give a damn. Get Radek to understand that. Find out what he wants, who he's moving against."

"I'll do what I can," Kirov promised.

"Do that." Scherbatsky paused as if some urgent idea had come to him, but it was a repetition of an earlier theme. "Why don't you take this case over? *Believe* me, it's in your interests."

"Why is that?"

Scherbatsky shook his head. "Forget it. I can't say . . . I mean . . . oh, stuff it, I'm pissed." Then, with a show of warmth, he reached into his pocket, found something and forced the object into Kirov's hand. "Here, take this—we're friends, aren't we?" Kirov uncurled his fingers and looked into his open palm. It held a watch—a Rolex. The story about Scherbatsky's Chinese watch was wrong in one particular. It was made for a man.

"Nice, huh?" Scherbatsky said. "Keep it. It's not a good timekeeper, but that can be fixed. The gold is real gold plate."

Kirov put the watch down. He examined the other man's face and saw fear, guile, relief at having accomplished an unpleasant task. It was possible to read anything one chose—even friendship. The best interrogator in the world could never really know. If you polished at the surface long enough, you would see only your own reflection. He looked away at the watch which glinted dully in the sunlight among the tobacco haze and the dust motes. The wind rattled the windows. Scherbatsky nibbled distractedly

105

at a broken nail. A bottle clinked against a glass.

Something dangerous had happened but Kirov couldn't say what.

As Kirov walked through the garden, brushing aside the dry canes of the dead weeds, one of the men in the black Volga sedan got out, pointed a camera in his direction and ran off a roll of film.

11

Tatiana Yurievna complained that Kirov shouldn't talk to his uncle about the past. It got him excited and then he smoked and drank to calm himself down. Why all this talk about the past? It had nothing to do with the present where things were done differently.

"How is he today?"

"He's all right!" Uncle Kolya shouted from the depths of the house.

"Sick," said Tatiana Yurievna, who was not going to let a mere man's opinion prevail. But grudgingly she allowed Kirov to cross the threshold into the interior with its smell of pine and old people. He noted strange objects, pinned to the wall, posed over doors or on pieces of furniture: pieces of wood and straw, cloth, paint — he hadn't time to examine them. With ill grace the housekeeper was letting him into Nikolai Konstantinovitch's bedroom. He had an idea that she was displaying charms and icons. It would not have surprised him if she was attending church, praying for the old Chekist who was lying in his bed and complaining.

"Go away, Old Woman," Uncle Kolya told her. She looked at him crossly, and in the name of tidiness roughed up the bedclothes to annoy him until the general lost his temper and made her leave. Then he turned on Kirov, allowed his cheek to be kissed, and said: "What are you here for? More talk about the past? More bad dreams?"

"Some nights."

The general wasn't prepared to display any sympathy. "They must be making delicate consciences these days."

"You may be right," Kirov agreed rather than fight the point.

And maybe it was true, though he doubted it. He suspected that the horrors of the past were committed by men who were no less moral but merely saw things differently, though sometimes so differently that their visions of bliss could appear monstrous. His father for example. He asked: "Why didn't the Germans shoot my father?"

Minsk has fallen.
The road disappeared into the woods beyond Romashkovo with its graveyard on the hill by the disused church and the station. From it led a lane of yellow hardcore with birch trees on both sides standing deep in leaf litter dotted with the red caps of fly agaric. Behind the odors of mist and dampness the ripening stinkhorns contributed their smell of rotting meat.

As they drove along Bogdanov kept up a conversation about Uncle Kolya. How was the old man? Any better? The idea was to sound concerned like a real friend should be, but Bogdanov's lugubrious voice made him sound bereaved so that you would think Uncle Kolya was dead.

"You did see him today, didn't you?"

"I saw him — he was well."

"Good, good. What did you have to talk about?"

"Nothing. Keep your eyes on the road."

They had talked about Minsk.

In the great German advance during the summer of 1941 the city of Minsk fell. That was how Uncle Kolya told it. The old man abstracted himself, gazed at the ceiling and recited the words as if reading them off a tombstone. The city of Minsk fell and he himself escaped the fall because he was on a train heading east with a cargo of political prisoners whom NKVD felt it impolitic to shoot out of hand: even in wartime the interrogations had to go on. "In a way they saved my life," Nikolai Konstantinovitch said thoughtfully. "Not that it saved theirs."

When the Reds were forced out of Minsk by the Fascists — he resumed, using the expression "Reds" as if they were a different sort of Russian — Andrei Nikolaievitch Kirov, the father, stayed behind. "He was still needed for political work. He couldn't get a permit to move."

The Germans shot every Red they could lay their hands on: commissars and NKVD men naturally, but also ordinary Party mem-

108

bers. It wasn't so difficult to find out who they were — after all everything was meticulously recorded — and in any case there were people who were only too willing to tell on their neighbors. The occupiers were easily able to set up a puppet nationalist government for Byelorussia, and Minsk was its capital.

"What happened to my father?" Kirov asked.

"What do you expect? He was betrayed and arrested. The German SD held him." And that, Uncle Kolya said, should have been the end of Colonel A. N. Kirov just as surely as when he was locked within the walls of the Lefortovo.

"Why do you mention that? In 1941 it wasn't the same thing."

"Wasn't it?" Uncle Kolya replied with a hint of the affectionate contempt the old can have for the young. "In both cases wasn't your father still a policeman, a professional, a valuable asset for anyone who needed that sort of thing? And the Germans did need him. They knew they hadn't got all the Reds. They had a mass of collaborators, but who was to know which ones were genuine and which ones were planted by the Soviets?"

"But the Germans were enemies."

"So what? In 1940 they were friends, in 1941 they were enemies, who could tell what would happen in 1942?" The tone sharpened. The old man broke off. He called Tatiana Yurievna and asked for a bedpan. "And take this one away, it stinks!" He returned his attention to Kirov and said curtly: "Your father was a professional. All other loyalties weren't worth shit. Either you understand that or you don't."

"Go on," Kirov prompted him softly, and he learned how the SD recruited Colonel A. N. Kirov. He was valuable. He knew who the Reds were. He would make them talk. The Germans moved him and his wife and child from their apartment in Bryanska Street to the Europa Hotel where he could keep a safe eye on the politicians and their futile congresses. He was safe.

"Until the Reds returned," said Uncle Kolya.

Tatiana Yurievna brought the bedpan. She and Kirov levered the old man and positioned him so that he could use it. He sighed and a stream of urine rattled into the steel dish. The housekeeper removed it and settled him in the bedclothes again. He stared bleakly at Kirov and said: "Don't worry about my dignity. I'm still alive and kicking, still surviving, huh?" And he went on.

The Reds returned and the NKVD squads cut a swath through the ranks of the collaborators, the lukewarm and the stragglers who failed to flee in the baggage of the retreating Germans. New drafts of humanity for the camps and the execution cellars.

"Was my father arrested?"

"Of course," Uncle Kolya answered. "But not for long."

"Why not?"

Kirov did not expect the answer.

"Because your father was a hero."

Uncle Kolya explained. Far from being implicated in the murder of thousands of loyal Communists, Colonel A. N. Kirov — contrary to appearances and the careful records kept by the Germans — had secretly assisted the partisan forces, placing their cadres in the heart of the Fascist occupation government and masking their acts of sabotage.

"Who rehabilitated him?" Kirov asked.

"Lavrenti Beria."

And Beria, said Uncle Kolya, would never tell a lie.

"Do you want to hear about my researches into hospital deaths?" asked Bogdanov for the second time.

"Tell me."

"One case, maybe, at the Botkin Hospital. A girl aged thirteen. Burst appendix. Peritonitis. Maybe complicated by the antibiotics used — no one will say. Frightened of responsibility. It's the way it goes."

"Who supplied them?"

"Would you believe the father? The hospital said, 'Thank you very much,' and didn't ask any questions, and who can blame them."

"What's the father's name?"

"Kliment Vasilyevitch Ostrowsky — Party member, respectable but no big shot."

"Has he any connection with Viktor Gusev?"

"Nothing in the regular way of business. But . . ."

"What?"

"He works in the jewelry trade."

The lane ran out in a wide patch of beaten ground shaded by trees and studded with shallow pools of frost-hazed water. Footpaths ran off on either side into the hollow cover of the wood.

"Viktor liked his seclusion," Bogdanov commented as he got out of the car and beat his arms against his chest to fight off the chill here in the shadows. "Are you sure that Scherbatsky was giving

110

you a straight story about this *dacha?"* Kirov paced the length of the clearing and examined the paths. The first ran through a maze of brambles and thickets toward a wooden shack a hundred meters off into the trees. The second had been cleared to the width of a truck and the ruts infilled. It headed for a good-sized cottage with a shingled roof and a collection of sheds and outhouses. He checked the sketch map that Scherbatsky had drawn and took that direction.

The house was of good construction: gleaming paintwork and at least a half-dozen rooms. A patch of grass lay in front, faded from its struggle with the trees, and in the middle was a barbecue pit deep in white ash that still smelled sour and woody in the close air. There was even a tennis court; the net hung limply and the surface was covered in a drift of leaves.

They examined the outhouses, pushing open the unlatched doors. The first was an old earth privy dating from some earlier building; it was out of use and stacked with tools. The second held a supply of vegetables, earthed up, straw covered or hanging in bunches from the roof; a smell of onions, apples and mushrooms and a trace of creosote. The third contained a generator; power cables ran off to the house and an oil tank stood outside resting on a brick foundation. Next to it was a well with an electric pump. Bogdanov proposed they check the house.

The windows had been fitted with winter panes. They were clean and unbroken and reflected the gray sky and the thin silver fingers of the birches. The door had a mortise lock, which yielded easily to Bogdanov's keys. Inside the place showed signs of a break in.

The two men stood in the doorway. The immediate view was of upturned furniture and displaced ornaments and carried the air of violation that comes when images of stability are disturbed, so that for a moment they hesitated until Bogdanov said: "He took care of his comforts," and suggested that they get down to business. Then he walked into the room, in turn banging the doors that ran from it, and the disorder became an aspect of normality. "There's nobody here," he reported and slipped his gun back into his belt.

Kirov looked the room over. Pine walls, carved beams, concealed lighting, too many mirrors. A feeling of method in the chaos. He saw that nothing had been broken.

Bogdanov made the same point, picking up a porcelain vase and replacing it. He pushed a finger into the debris inside an ashtray and opened a cigarette box. "Whoever it was took his time. The smokes are gone." He opened a cabinet and rummaged among the liquor. "No full bottles."

Kirov directed his attention at a pile of books and magazines. The books were mostly classics, new editions in bright bindings; Viktor hadn't possessed them long. The periodicals were also about books, back numbers of *Literaturnaya Gazeta* and *Molodiya Gvardiya,* and a flick through them showed marginal notes written in a fine hand. It was necessary to suppose that Viktor Gusev had spent his weekends here reading through the quiet evenings, perhaps in the company of Nadia Mazurova. As an image it was more inexplicable than the diamonds spilled from Gusev's guts.

"What do you think they were looking for?" Bogdanov turned over a chair and exposed the burlap covering of the underside. It had been neatly slashed with a razor. He turned over another and found the same. The scatter cushions had received similar treatment. Kirov picked one up; the stuffing had been searched but largely replaced, only a few traces lying about the floor. The question came of itself: why such care when the fact of the break in and search was undisguised? A woman's tidiness? Or an attempt after violation to restore the inviolate, which was essentially a male illusion? There was an absence of malice, and its effect was disturbing.

Between them they slowly covered this first room, marking what had been disturbed and what not. Some things, like books, had been moved to uncover what lay behind them but otherwise left intact. Others, the soft furnishings in particular, had been thoroughly taken apart. The selection suggested an object of a certain size, small enough to be hidden but not such that it might have been cut, folded or pasted to the inside of a book. Not a document. Nor the diamonds, which could have been secreted anywhere and would have required the demolition of the whole place.

They moved to the next room which proved to be the bathroom. It appeared intact, but here too the delicacy of the search left its fine traces. Kirov remembered Gusev's taste for body oils and lotions, but found only a few dregs in the assembled bottles.

"What do you think?" Bogdanov asked. "Found what they were looking for or just helping themselves to souvenirs?" He eyed the bidet. "Fancy piece of plumbing—what's it for? Joke—joke—I'll check the next room."

Adjacent to the bathroom was a bedroom. The furnishings continued to betray Gusev's uncertain sense of style. A dressing table in the heavy Tsarist manner. Some mildly pornographic lithographs. Bed sheets of oyster-colored silk (was it possible to buy such things?). By the bedside an open book lay on the floor— *The Brothers Karamazov*. Kirov saw Viktor Gusev struggling with his unexpected wealth and the culture which his new acquaintances had brought to him, and striving to change himself into something else, probably unsure what that something else might be. This however was supposition. The facts were a mere collection of objects bought by a black marketeer and open to any number of constructions. Kirov discounted his analysis and focused on the careful attentions which the searchers had given to the room. He found the electronic bug in the table light.

Bogdanov returned from the kitchen with a spoon and some bottled red currants. "The power's off. The stuff in the freezer has gone bad." He levered the lid off the bottle and asked casually: "What do anchovies taste like?"

"Salty."

"Are they good?"

"Not on their own. Did you find anything?"

Bogdanov dipped into his pocket and produced a small object which he threw onto the nearest table. Kirov held out the bug he had found in the bedroom. The other man nodded.

"Adequate but not the latest equipment. Viktor must have installed these himself—suspicious bugger. I wonder where he got them from? Where is his recording machine, have you found it?"

"No."

Bogdanov wiped the berry juice from his lips. It left a scarlet stain like a bruise across his cheek. He glanced about the room then tested another door. It was locked. He tried it with his keys and, when that failed, kicked at it until the doorjamb splintered. "After you," he said.

The new room was small, windowless and in darkness save for a glimmer on one wall which revealed a narrow table and a bentwood chair. The table held a film camera fixed to a rostrum and a tape recorder. On the floor in the far corner were a projector and a tripod-mounted screen rolled up and stowed in a vertical position. The faint sheen of daylight came through a sheet of one-way glass set into the wall flanking the bedroom. "Fuck your mother," Bogdanov murmured. "It looks like Viktor was in the film business."

113

They searched the room and found nothing else except a box-shaped case that might have held films or tapes but didn't. A check of the camera magazine and the tape deck showed that both were empty, and the dismantled light fitting revealed no more bugs. They returned to the main room and in silence smoked a cigarette.

Bogdanov stirred himself first. "Any theories as to what's going on? I'll fix a drink while you think that one out." He got up and busied himself among the remains of bottles in the cocktail cabinet, leaving Kirov to think his thoughts and flip through a couple of issues of *Literaturnaya Gazeta*. He studied Gusev's notes, which were brief but frequent: *I don't understand — why this conclusion when the opposite could be true? — bullshit! — I don't understand!!* The latest numbers were without notes and appeared unread as if Viktor Gusev had given up his struggle to comprehend.

"Well?" Bogdanov handed over a glass of Ararat brandy. He took a sip of his own, crossed the room and tried the light switch against the fading day. "Well? What is it all about?"

"I know why GRU investigated the Bulgarian factory," Kirov answered.

Bogdanov expressed no surprise, just a weary: "Go on, tell me."

"Someone thought that Yuri Andropov was murdered."

"Wonderful! This, I take it, explains why an antibiotics racketeer has a gut full of diamonds and a secret *dacha* complete with camera for taking dirty pictures. I can't wait to hear it." He halted there then added in a regretful murmur: "Fuck them! Who cares what they do to each other? Just don't tell me the details. It's not our problem, boss. Just something we bumped into in the dark. All we have is a little case of racketeering — nothing to make us stars, but enough to give us a glow of satisfaction in the evening. There's no connection with the other thing."

"Maybe." Kirov realized that wasn't enough for an answer.

They finished their drinks. Bogdanov volunteered another. He asked: "Did Grishin give you this story?"

"He told me there was a rumor." No, not a rumor. Grishin had implied a more substantial basis, urged the point upon him and then withdrawn it. Like bait. Solve that one if you can. "He had something else to say. He told me how the Great Jewish Antibiotics Ring got its name."

"Why *Jewish*? He gave you the answer to that one?" Bogdanov's laughter suggested that this was the joke of the century. A belly laugh with ornaments of tears and coughing, another time and

114

place you might have believed it. Instead it reverberated around the empty building and as abruptly died.

"Do you remember Yakovlevitch," Kirov continued, "the surgeon who was allowed to leave for Israel?"

"No—but if you say so."

"Yakovlevitch and some other Jewish doctors were going to be implicated in the antibiotics black market."

"Grishin told you that? Is there any truth in it?"

"The story is true, but the plot was a fiction. Andropov set it up as a warning to the *refuseniks*. After his death Chernenko dropped the idea."

"And the connection? Are you telling me there's a connection?" Bogdanov pressed him, but now more circumspectly.

"There's no connection," Kirov answered. "It's just a story."

Andropov's death, Yakovlevitch's departure and the death of Viktor Gusev. Stories.

The rest of the search turned up nothing but further hints of Viktor Gusev's ambiguous character and signs of the carefulness of the first searchers. The two men locked up the house and stepped out into the rain, which had blown in from the west and spattered from a dark sky onto the debris beneath the trees. Bogdanov pulled down his hat and took long ungainly strides across the soft ground, talking the while above the rainfall.

"So who was here and did they find what they were looking for?" He paused and added: "The diamonds—do you still have them?"

"Yes."

"Have you filed a report on them or told Grishin?"

"No."

"Why not, for God's sake?"

"Because there are people who want to know what happened to them. And as long as they keep looking for them we have a chance to find out who they are and the significance of the diamonds."

Bogdanov stared up at the sky and made a comment about the weather. His glance fell down and wandered among the trees before returning to Kirov. "Get rid of them," he said. "Turn them in. If they're discovered and you haven't reported them . . . You know what I mean. Don't give Radek a case against you."

"Radek has nothing to do with this."

Bogdanov shook his head. "Radek wants your scalp. He may be a shit, but he isn't a fool. Get rid of the diamonds."

When they reached the clearing where the car was parked, Kirov remembered the shack that lay along the other path and suggested they inspect it. They took the narrow path, weaving between the brambles and the dripping boughs until the cottage came into view, a paraffin lamp driving the twilight from the window. They halted there and heard a crack of a twig breaking somewhere in the trees, but that was all it was and nothing happened, just the cottage built of rough-cut logs, earthed up at the base of the walls, with a corrugated iron roof that was patched with tar paper. The rain drummed on the roof and ran off into puddles. A woodpile was stacked next to the shack and next to that was a privy and then a chicken run occupied by sodden hens. A loose pig paused from rooting in the birch mast and gave them a cold glittering stare.

They knocked on the door and it opened on shaky hinges. An old man stood in the doorway. He wore a shawl and a rabbit-skin hat with the flaps down and was smoking a pipe of pungent *makhorka* tobacco.

"Who are you?" he asked.

"Friends, grandad," said Bogdanov. "Let's just call us friends." He stuck his foot in the door.

The old man examined them indifferently. "All right, 'friend,' you'd better come in." He stood back and let them enter a single room dimly visible in the smoky light of an oil lamp. A fug of tobacco and woodsmoke from an iron stove in the middle of the room made the air as thick and tangible as if it were nailed to the walls, and beneath this covering the place was densely furnished with an old man's junk, of which a large part was a number of elaborately carved musical instruments and a collection of photographs in silver frames. The bed was a straw palliasse and a pile of newspapers. The rain made a rhythmic drumming on the roof.

"Walking in the country, were you, comrades?" The old man eyed their shoes slyly. "A right pair of farm boys, I think."

"How did you guess, grandad?" Bogdanov picked his way through the maze of the old man's litter and peered through the window in the direction they had come from. "What do you say, boss, is there someone out there or not? No? Any opinion, grandad?" Kirov had moved some papers from a stool and taken a seat. The cottager took a place opposite him, leaned forward and leered like an old sinner. "Good view," Bogdanov commented. "I say 'good view,' grandad, you hear me? Yes?" The old man spared him a brief glance of amused malevolence.

Like the querulous old man in a Chekhov play, Kirov thought, wondering whether that gave him an angle of approach to the other man. He asked: "Do you live here alone, grandfather?"

"Whose business is it?"

"My business," Kirov answered lightly enough.

"I don't care for your business."

Kirov looked away unoffended. On a table, next to a fragment of a broken balalaika that the old man had been mending, stood a Dresden figure of a shepherd. He sought for its female companion.

"Gone," said his host, reading his thoughts. "Broken. Care for these things, do you?"

"Shouldn't I?"

The old man replied peevishly: "You're a Chekist, aren't you? Don't bother denying it—I can smell them." He reached from his seat to a box of kindling, took a stick, flipped open the stove and lit the wooden spill. He applied it to his pipe, drawing in his hollow cheeks with the effort. "You're a Chekist all right, even if you are a funny looking one."

"You know all about them, do you?" Kirov inquired mildly.

"Sure I do." The voice was sharp but with a note of pride. "I've been worked over by the best—by *real* Chekists. Five years in Kolyma. Who ever survived five years in Kolyma? Me, that's who! Semyon Kuzmich Dubanov!" He snorted again and descended mumbling into silence.

From the window Bogdanov signaled that Dubanov was crazy. Kirov thought not: Dubanov was simply playing out the role of old man in the way that people without imagination played out the roles assigned to them. He was struck only by Dubanov's pride, which, from the other side, had been shared by Chestyakov himself, former terror of the KGB lecture halls, now dead and a real Chekist if ever there was one. The two old men would have found things to talk about, even a common sympathy. After all, in their separate ways they had both survived.

"It's there again," Bogdanov said.

The rain had stopped. The drumming had ceased, to be succeeded by the gurgle of water running off the roof and the pat-pat of drops falling from the eaves onto the earth. A rustle of trees.

"What?"

"Someone—something—out there."

"A fox," said Dubanov. "After my chickens."

Kirov looked to Bogdanov who shook his head. Outside, the pig gave a squeal and came trotting past the window.

"Why have you come here?" the old man asked with a nervous interest.

A little way off a car engine sounded during a lull in the wind. Bogdanov held a hand to the window glass, masking out reflections, and peered into the gathering darkness.

"Who was it broke into the *dacha?*" Kirov asked. He had one half of his attention alert for more sounds from outside. Tense. What is it this Dubanov knows? I'll miss it if I can't concentrate. "You saw, didn't you. Here with nothing to do but look out of the window—you saw, didn't you?"

Dubanov spat a gobbet of phlegm onto the stove and watched it sizzle. Kirov wore a mask of patience. Bogdanov watched for movement in the darkness. Finally the old man said scornfully: "Is this the way they ask questions nowadays? All nice and friendly and lovey-dovey? Aren't there any serious minded people anymore?"

"Sure there are," Bogdanov answered abruptly, and with a long stride he reached the Dresden figure, raised it above his head and dashed it to the floor. He stared at the shards of porcelain, then at the old man. "There, does that suit you? Serious enough?" He approached Dubanov and grabbed the scarf that the old man wore around his throat. "Now answer the nice man's questions," he muttered, "or I'll tear your head off and whistle down the hole." He released his grip and let the other man fall back. Dubanov collected himself but displayed no fear, only a bitter satisfaction.

"They were your lot," he said. "More damned Chekists!"

They left the cottage. Night had fallen and the rain dripped a curfew of spatters from the trees. The bird cherries bordering the space around Dubanov's shack, stirred by a breeze, made passes against the dark backdrop, and the pig scratched at the door like a family pet to the noisy sulking of the hens.

"So who were these 'Chekists'?" Bogdanov asked. The old man had got to him and he was feeling peevish on his own account. "Our lot?"

"KGB, MVD, who knows?" Kirov answered. But it was a good question. According to Scherbatsky the existence and location of Viktor Gusev's *dacha* were a secret.

"Trees — I hate trees," Bogdanov said morosely. Around them the trees stored their silence, the soughing of boughs, the creak of wood, the splat and patter of water, the silence of incidental noise. Stars and a hazy moon broke through the wind-shredded cloud. An owl gave a hunting shriek.

They made their way back toward the path. Bogdanov, with a city dweller's delicacy, tiptoed among the sodden leaves to avoid muddying his shoes — tip tap — *oh, shit!* — tip tap along the path between the brambles and the dead branches covered in moss.

Crack.

They froze. A cold sleet drifted from the east in a sudden shower that crackled off the dead leaves. *Crack.* Not the sleet though it drove against their coats and their faces burned under the sharp cold.

"Some bastard is out there," Bogdanov whispered. "I heard a car earlier, did you hear a car?" He stepped away into the trees and disappeared. Kirov walked on.

Step — step — feet placed uncertainly on the glistening surface of leaf mold. A bad place to stand and fight especially when he carried no gun. More sleet fell in a sharp dash and then as suddenly stopped. A bird clattered in the treetops. Kirov slipped into the shadow of the birches, where the tangle of brambles plucked at his clothes.

He saw the man.

The figure wore a leather coat and a slouch hat, and carried a camera slung by its strap. His hands held a pair of night glasses which for the moment he wasn't using. He stood in full view twenty meters away along the path, caught by the moon through a new break in the cloud. A professional — a Chekist, as Dubanov would put it — but careless with the arrogance of the mediocre.

Movement. Bogdanov breaking out of the trees to the stranger's rear. The man turned. Kirov let out a yell and ran at him. The stranger hesitated, glanced both ways, and swung out with the binoculars, catching Bogdanov on the head. Bogdanov slipped on the wet leaves and took a tumble into the undergrowth. Then Kirov was onto his target.

The momentum of the charge carried them both into the blind darkness of the trees, scrabbling among the roots and the leaf fall, trying to keep a footing on the treacherous surface. The stranger's leather coat was slippery with moisture; he struggled and struck out blindly, but each man was invisible to the other. A few meters away Bogdanov was swearing and crashing through the trees in pursuit of the unseen.

Flash. A set of headlights came on. The stranger, seeing Kirov, tried a clumsy head butt. It had enough force to drive him back, but then Bogdanov was onto the stranger. Already more men were appearing, four of them from the direction of the waiting car.

"Jesus Christ!" Bogdanov felled his first victim with the grip of his revolver. He turned and fired a shot into the trees. He set himself square on toward the newcomers and found himself staring at four guns. "Shit, boss," he murmured. "What do we do now?"

They faced each other. Two groups. Without turning aside, Bogdanov kicked his first, fallen assailant when he showed signs of movement. Kirov stepped forward.

"Where's your chief?"

From the left of the line one man moved. Kirov studied the others and sensed reluctance.

"Your orders don't include killing me," he said.

The other man considered the point then answered: "Back off. Give us that idiot back and we'll call it quits."

"What security do I have?"

"Like you said: my orders don't include killing you. Not for the time being. Now back off."

"He's bluffing," said Bogdanov.

"My orders say nothing about you," the newcomer answered. "As far as I'm concerned, you can be dead meat."

"He's bluffing," Bogdanov repeated.

"Let their man go."

"Boss?"

"He's a know-nothing, not worth keeping."

Bogdanov moved back from the groaning form. Two of the others came forward and seized their companion by the heels. They dragged him backwards, then a third man took hold of the shoulders. They heaved the body upright and retreated through the trees.

Bogdanov watched them, then put a hand to his head where he had been hit. "I feel terrible," he said almost cheerfully. He stepped groggily aside and was sick into the moonlight.

12

When Kirov was ten years old his mother took him to a circus. It wasn't in Moscow but in Sverdlovsk where his grandparents lived. He stayed there for several months. It was some time after the arrest and disappearance of his father, and although his presumed murderer, Beria, had by then fallen, there was still some tension because of the ambiguity of the elder Kirov's history. In fact, for a while, Uncle Kolya himself vanished only to emerge months later, pale, thin and taciturn.

He went to the circus with his mother, his grandmother, Nadezhda Viktorevna, and one of her ancient friends, a crone with steel teeth and a mustache like Uncle Stalin. The party sat in the dense, perspiring crowd, watching the sawdust ring, and passed a bottle of soda water and a piece of dry sausage, which went from hand to hand like contraband. They sat complaining of their neighbors and the people in front whose heads were too large, and they saw what they could of the acts.

Now, years later, the memory returned a second time as he drove to Kavrov, to the house in Raspletin Street where Scherbatsky, owner of the famous Chinese watch, was holed up with his parents. Scherbatsky, the only person who knew that he would be paying a visit to Viktor Gusev's *dacha*.

That day at the circus two clowns came into the ring. They wore the Italian costume of glittering silver jackets and breeches, white stockings and black pumps, and their faces were made up as white as chalk. They carried a box the size of a man, its sides hinged and the whole thing collapsed together like a flat board for carrying purposes.

So, with much fooling and gestures to the crowd and little courtesies to each other, the two clowns proceeded to unfold and erect the box. The band played and the drums and cymbals punctuated the high points. In essence the thing seemed simple—to put up the box. But as they opened it up, first one clown and then the other would find himself inside the box then outside as a flip or fold of one side of the contraption changed its shape. That, of course, was the joke. Although the two clowns were supposed to be constructing the box together, each was in fact trying to trap the other inside it.

"What is it called?" Kirov asked his mother.

She turned and asked his grandmother who duly asked her friend and the answer was passed down the same line.

"It's a Chinese Box," said his mother.

"Thank you," Kirov answered and he returned his eyes to the two clowns, this time with understanding. For he knew that such was the nature of the Chinese Box that it was impossible to say who was inside the box and who outside.

The horde of children still played in the unkempt garden of the house at Raspletin Street. The repair shop over the road still moved its stock of cannibalized spare parts. There was no answer at the Scherbatsky apartment and the neighbors played hard at being out. Kirov went down to the basement and rooted out the old man who acted as *dvornik* for the building.

The old man claimed to know nothing except that four men in two cars had turned up the previous day and the Scherbatskys, parents and son, had left with the callers. The old people had appeared nervous, but the younger Scherbatsky, who in the *dvornik*'s long memory had always been a cocky kid, had made no fuss at all. On the contrary, he seemed pleased. Pleased or relieved? asked Kirov, but the distinction was lost on the old man. What was he carrying? Nothing. Nothing? A bag. Be precise—a grip, a document case, a shopping bag? A small suitcase. And the parents? Nothing—well, maybe the old lady carried her knitting. So one small suitcase between the three? That was it, for sure.

Kirov took the old man's keys and opened the apartment. The single room had an undisturbed appearance, tidier than Kirov remembered it. Holiday tidy was the thought that came to him, in the way that his grandmother had left her own apartment neat and clothed in a mysterious millpond stillness whenever she left it for any length of time, locking the door of the shrine behind her with a grunt and a bob of obeisance to the household gods. And Scherbatsky's mother had done the same, or so he supposed, running his finger over the furniture to check the absence of dust, searching the corners for a trace of dirty crockery or unwashed laundry, all absent. The family had been prepared to meet their visitors, taking with them only one suitcase and leaving behind the bulk of their clothes, Scherbatsky's as well as his parents'. What was the deal? A couple of nights away—or as long as it takes, but with all comforts found? Had Scherbatsky expected his visitors when he asked Kirov to help him? Kirov searched more thoroughly, finding the drawer where Scherbatsky kept his shirts and underwear, shoving his hands into the pockets of the other man's suits and turning them out. He checked the cupboards, the tins, the ornaments; found the family nest egg of ruble banknotes, greasy and tied with twine, and the box with the campaign medals won by Scherbatsky's father. He checked the bed and the mattress, the couch made up for the son, the needlework basket and the box refrigerator that sat under the radio. They all spoke of tidiness and preparation, and said that the family expected to return and had therefore taken nothing in the way of excess: one suitcase and some knitting to amuse the mother. The only unaccounted-for item, which was the more strange for its uselessness and triviality, was a Chinese watch that didn't work.

Back at the office Bogdanov tried to grab his attention on the subject of Ostrowsky. "You remember Ostrowsky—jeweler—daughter died at the Botkin hospital? I've got him staked out. Tumanov is running a Sluzhba team, but I can't keep them forever. If I don't take them home to their mothers I'll have to marry them."

Kirov promised to get around to the game plan for playing Ostrowsky.

"No joy with Scherbatsky?" Bogdanov hazarded a guess. "He wouldn't tell you who was playing games at Viktor's place?"

"Scherbatsky's been taken in. The apartment was empty."

"Taken in as in 'arrested,' or something else?"

"I don't know. He had visitors—maybe MVD, maybe Radek's man, Petruk."

"I know how you feel: with all this liaison stuff it's difficult to be sure who's running the show. I'll make some inquiries. If Scherbatsky is in detention, he should soon show up."

Tomsky was surprised to receive his call and tried to get Kirov off the line. The American desk was in a panic trying to produce a briefing that would explain the latest unpredictable vagary of American foreign policy. "I've got everybody on my back. What do you want?"

"Where's Scherbatsky?"

"How should I know? Is that why you called me?"

"You were in contact with him — and now he's cleared out of his parents' apartment."

"So? Try his own apartment or his wife's parents. Why don't you talk to Radek, his section is handling the case, isn't it? Or don't you boys speak to each other anymore?"

An hour later Tomsky called back. This time he was more cooperative. He apologized for not giving a serious answer before. "But, honest to God, I didn't know where Scherbatsky was. And this place, it's a madhouse. Every time we think we know what the Americans want, they change their minds. How Gorbachev thinks he can negotiate arms control with them, Christ knows."

"What news do you have?"

Tomsky was offended to be cut short in his complaint. "Oh, sure, Scherbatsky. He just telephoned."

"When?"

"Like I said, just now — five, perhaps ten minutes ago, right out of the blue. He told me to say thanks for your visit and everything is OK."

"Where is he?"

"I don't know, he wouldn't tell me and the call didn't last long enough to place a trace. What's wrong, you don't sound happy? You sound as though you don't believe me?"

"I believe you."

"You should. Ivan Pavlovitch says that it was you who gave him the idea."

"What idea?"

"All that talk about things changing, about legality." Something was amusing Tomsky. "Do you watch television?"

"Which program?"

"*Twelfth Story,* this week's edition."

Kirov sometimes watched current affairs programs. *Twelfth Story* was one of the better ones because it took live questions over the telephone. Tomsky meanwhile was explaining his point.

"Boris Kravtsov was in the studio. That's right, our very own Minister of Justice. He was talking about the new revision of the penal code. He said a lot about securing the rights of the defendant under Article Fifty-eight of the Constitution. You understand? After you talked to him Scherbatsky watched television and saw this program. And it came to him that, strictly speaking, he wasn't actually under arrest, or, if he was, the arrest was technically illegal."

"So?"

"So," Tomsky gave an abrupt laugh, "Scherbatsky's gone and hired himself a lawyer!"

They waited in the New Arbat, watching the shoppers struggle in the fading light. Moscow, even before the true onset of winter, was a city of short brilliant days and long melancholy twilights made duller by the electric lighting and wan interiors of the shops. Tumanov, who had already had several hours of keeping surveillance, was bored and drummed his fingers on the nearest wall, yawned and whistled a tune until Bogdanov told him to shut up. To Kirov he said: "Is that true, Kravtsov was really on his hind legs and saying that sort of stuff?"

"I didn't see the program, but the speech was reported in the papers."

Bogdanov appeared distressed as if discovering a neighbor's immorality. "He ought to know better than that," he commented, and making a vague connection he asked: "You don't suppose for a second that Scherbatsky really has got himself a lawyer, do you?"

Tumanov threw a glance over his shoulder, and thinking it a smart remark said: "Since when do lawyers turn up by the carload and take whole families away?"

Bogdanov told him to shut up, but added for Kirov's benefit: "Still, he's right. I can think of people who do provide that sort of service—but they don't include lawyers."

Kirov could also think of people who provided that sort of service. But usually not in broad daylight. And how to explain the *dvornik's* observation that Scherbatsky left with a smile on his face? It represented a subtle variation on the old themes of arrest that Kirov could not as yet understand. For now he answered the question.

"I don't believe in the lawyer. But something happened to change Scherbatsky's attitude. Perhaps Radek offered him a fair trial."

"And Scherbatsky believed him? Pigs might fly!"

"Our man's here," Tumanov interrupted. He pointed to a figure holding a briefcase in one hand and a shopping bag in the other and bumping into the other pedestrians. "He's pissed again. He was pissed at lunchtime — you should have seen him staggering along Gorky Street, I thought the militia would grab him for sure, knocking all the respectable citizens sideways and then into the Ocean fish shop to buy something." The man turned off the street and into the Agat jewelers' store.

Bogdanov was weary with waiting. He saw Ostrowsky and was tired with the thought. He asked: "Did you recognize him from the photograph?"

Kirov shook his head.

"Me neither. I sometimes wonder why we bother — with the photographs I mean, fat lot of good that they do us. Still it's Ostrowsky all right, Kliment Vasilyevitch, and as respectable as my mother-in-law. I can't see him dealing with Viktor Gusev. Viktor's too shiny, too flash: all those tarts, Ostrowsky would shit himself with fear."

"He was dealing with Gusev." Kirov felt for the diamonds in his pocket. Somehow they had to be explained. Bogdanov remained unimpressed.

"If he was, he's got nothing to show for it, no car, no *dacha*, no holidays you'd care to go on and he lives in a crummy apartment with his one-and-only-ever-loving wife. In my book those mark him as an honest man; and so says his file — read it, it's all in there. Ask yourself: if he was in business with Viktor, what was he doing with the money?"

People came and went. A woman in a sable coat glided to the entrance to the shop, accompanied by a young soldier who carried her parcels. She flounced and let the full skirts of the coat swing, obviously enjoying it for its sheer sensual pleasure. For a moment she reminded Kirov of Nadia Mazurova, but it was a fleeting resemblance. Nadia Mazurova was limited by her relationship with her provider, Viktor Gusev; and Viktor, struggling with his gimcrack ideas of style could never achieve that level of suavity.

"He's gone to hell since his daughter died," Bogdanov continued on the subject of Ostrowsky. "His wife blames him. An only child and no hope of anymore. Poor sod," he added, having no children of his own. "He goes home at night and has to face her. She chews his ear and naturally he's too polite to smack her in the face. And what's he supposed to tell her? That it's all Viktor's fault and

126

everyone is very sorry? So he takes it for a couple of hours, then finds himself a liquor shop, buys some vodka, and sits outside getting quietly drunk — we have that from the local drying out station. Two reports. The militia have had to drag him off the street. They feel sorry for him, so you won't find the entries on his file. And at the shop his staff are covering for him. They like him." He turned to Kirov and said unexpressively: "He's a decent guy. Do you really want to give him the business?"

Kirov watched the street and the woman going into the Agat store bearing her burden of other people's dreams.

"What do you suggest?"

Bogdanov recognized a professional question. Without enthusiasm he exercised his imagination.

"Me and Tumanov go in and soften him up. Death. Stress. Piece of cake. You turn up as the Guardian Angel. Love and Understanding. Ostrowsky spills the story and nobody notices the bruises. Guaranteed." Bogdanov checked his watch. "Ten minutes and he leaves. Bloody easy. It's a shame to do it." He waited. "Well?"

Kirov returned Bogdanov's gaze blankly, seeing for a moment only the jeweler.

"The money was for his daughter's future."

"Shit! Why didn't I think of that?"

"It doesn't matter," Kirov answered. With the death of his daughter it had ceased to matter to Ostrowsky too. Perhaps now he would buy a *dacha*, take a decent holiday; even buy his wife a fur coat in exchange for the daughter they had lost. It was equally possible that in a fit of maudlin drunkenness Ostrowsky would burn the money. If the jeweler had really given up hope, was there anything to offer in exchange for his knowledge? Was there any threat that wouldn't be welcome to him as a chance to pay off his debt of guilt? Kirov felt that Ostrowsky was more problematic than Bogdanov suggested.

They waited. Not ten minutes but forty went by. Bogdanov had an old policeman's mindless stamina and dozed out his boredom while Tumanov fidgeted impatiently. The beautiful woman in the sable coat came out of the Agat store, still handing out smiles like tips to anyone who noticed her. And Kirov did notice her, and wondered what Viktor Gusev would have given to possess her. A half of his kingdom. Fairy-tale stuff. Ostrowsky emerged from the shop at five thirty and headed in the direction of the Arbatskaya metro station.

"What now?" Bogdanov asked. "Where do you want him arrested? Say the word anywhere between here and his place. It makes no difference. He doesn't stop or talk to anyone. He doesn't have any rendezvous. There's nothing to be gained by following him — am I right?" he said to Tumanov. "So take your pick."

"I want to speak to him alone." Kirov had decided that the jeweler was too fragile for any other method. "It's OK, I know what I'm doing. I'll call you later."

Ostrowsky was in no hurry. He walked unsteadily and paused regularly to look into shop windows. Once he stopped a passerby and asked for a light and looked as if he wanted to engage the man in conversation but the stranger shook him off. Finally he reached the metro station where he put down his parcels and fumbled for the five kopeck fare.

Arbatskaya links through to the Lenin Library station. Ostrowsky transferred and took the first train heading northeast on the line to Preobrazhensky Square. Kirov got into the same carriage and stood beside him in the press of passengers, in the silence of the crowd, which was broken only by the announcements of the stations. Ostrowsky stood in a nodding torpor. For the first time Kirov could see him clearly: mid-brown hair straggling from under his fur hat, lobeless ears that were red and veined with cold, drunken somnolent eyes. The other man turned his head and gazed vacantly along the carriage length. A small round nose and slack mouth, shaving nicks and a mole on the left cheekbone.

At Kirovskaya they transferred stations again and changed trains for the Kaluzhsko-Rizhskaya line. Ostrowsky began to show anxiety. He searched in his shopping bag and produced some powdered eggs then a parcel wrapped in paper. He unwrapped one end of the parcel under the curiosity of his fellow passengers and sighed as the head of a pike peeked out and looked at him with its dead glazed eyes. This appeared to satisfy him and he repacked the bag. He pulled himself together and stood more upright. Kirov watched and interpreted. Ostrowsky had checked his purchases in order to limit or avoid a quarrel with his wife. But the quarrel would not be about fish, or perhaps it would: the jeweler and this wife would argue about the pike and the powdered egg, and the subject of their daughter would be fought out in the bitter silences. The announcer meanwhile called Rizhskaya.

They left the train and emerged onto Prospekt Mira. Ostrowsky maintained his rigid attempt at sobriety, staring fixedly ahead and colliding with whoever got in his way. A militiaman scanned him idly but took no action. Close to Rizhskaya the rail lines heading north cluster, and somewhere in the angles Ostrowsky lived in one of the apartment houses in a dim and melancholy street, empty but for a man carefully removing the wiper blades from his car before leaving it for the night, and a black Volga with a whip aerial and two occupants contriving to look suspicious. Kirov did not follow as Ostrowsky entered the nearest apartment house. Instead he approached the car and the two men inside, a driver and the heavy help—"A pair of stars from Sluzhba remedial class," according to Bogdanov, and all that he could get after Radek had cleared the place of talent for his larger, more colorful operations.

Kirov tapped the window of the vehicle on the driver's side. It opened and a wrapped up figure leered out.

"Bugger off," the man said calmly. Kirov showed his badge and watched the driver freeze and stammer his apologies to the Comrade Colonel. Kirov told him abruptly to be quiet then asked what time Ostrowsky usually came out.

"A few minutes either side of seven o'clock, comrade Colonel. There's a liquor shop a couple of blocks away. He goes there. Then he gets pissed." He chanced a smile at his companion. Kirov knew its meaning.

"Where's your bottle?" he demanded.

"Bottle? I don't know what you mean, comrade Colonel. It isn't allowed. Not on duty."

"I'm not here to enforce the regulations, I just want the bottle. Hand it over."

The passenger reached to the space by his feet and came up with a half liter of Streletskaya. He leaned across the driver and handed it through the window.

"I was taking it home for tonight," the driver said feebly.

"Sure you were." Kirov slipped the bottle into his pocket.

He checked his watch. Six thirty. He walked back to the metro station, found a call box and telephoned Bogdanov at home.

"Any messages?"

Bogdanov said that Bakradze had sent round the MVD file on

129

Nadia Mazurova. His story was that the Public Prosecutor's Office hadn't known about Gusev's girlfriend until yesterday. On top of that there had been a backlog of inquiries on the MVD main computer; call Ogaryov Street yourself and they'd confirm it; the whole system down and everyone trying to remember what it was they used to do before the place was computerized and who the hell had the keys to the archive copies. It had taken all day to pull the girl's record. "And only then because of my influence," said the lawyer smoothly. So far Antipov and his Anti-Corruption Squad first team hadn't been able to interview her, but Bakradze was releasing the papers in the interest of friendly relations.

"I'm going to marry that guy, he's so considerate."

"Anything else?" Kirov asked.

"Yes," Bogdanov answered. "There's a note on your desk. Grishin has agreed to the Bulgarian trip."

Ostrowsky emerged from his apartment at seven fifteen. He was wearing the same hat and coat as before, but this time his gait was steady and his face held a flushed determination. Kirov recognized the evidence of the quarrel with his wife and for a second he considered this wife who would be destroyed because he proposed to destroy her husband, but who in herself had been so insignificant in his calculations that nothing remained in his memory of her record and he could not bring to mind her name. He suppressed the thought of her and drove her into the shadows of moral blindness in the company of all the Laras and the other casualties of his life. Ostrowsky meanwhile walked vigorously down the street, intent on suppressing his wife by other means.

They walked, fifty meters between them, their footsteps breaking the rime as it formed on the frosting puddles, through the dull streets pale and patchily lit, past a dim bread shop, past carefully tended Zhigulis swathed in covers like babies. In the otherwise empty roadway an Army car cruised out of the darkness and the driver, freelancing as a taxi, offered Kirov a lift. When he refused, the driver took it for a negotiating ploy and offered a lower price. Kirov rejected it. Throughout the exchange his eyes were kept focused on Ostrowsky until the soldier, bored by bargaining, finally noticed and asked: "What's this, then? Is he your boyfriend? Are you going to use my car or not?"

"No." Kirov walked away.

"Faggot," said the soldier. "Bloody queer!" he shouted. He stuck his head out of the window. "Faggot! Brown nose! Faggot!"

And Ostrowsky noticed nothing.

He reached the liquor shop, its window glimmering a dull blue. It was empty of customers, which in the ordinary way would mean that it was empty of stock, but Ostrowsky still went in. The assistant, without waiting, dipped below the counter and produced a bottle in a newspaper wrapper. Ostrowsky paid no money but took the package and left the shop. The assistant closed the door and began to shut up behind him, leaving Kirov to wonder what the deal was. Jewelry for vodka? Not likely: you couldn't easily divide jewelry into the small portions that form the currency of everyday life. Not that it mattered. He couldn't chase Ostrowsky into the crannies of his existence: how he paid for his washing machine to be fixed; how he came by those theater tickets that people were killing to get. Diamonds and drugs and Scherbatsky with his Chinese watch. It was enough mystery. Ostrowsky was walking toward him, staring intently at his own feet.

Kirov stepped forward. He blundered heavily into Ostrowsky's right-hand side. The bottle went flying from the other man's grasp and shattered on the pavement. Ostrowsky froze, then mutely turned his head and examined the shards of glass and the pool of spilt liquor.

"I'm sorry — my fault," Kirov volunteered, and his eyes examined the other man and saw only his absence.

"My only bottle," Ostrowsky answered listlessly.

"I know what you mean. Hard to get." These days sympathy about the liquor shortage was the entrée to casual conversation with strangers, so much so that rumor had it the CIA Moscow Station had abandoned its dreary history of passwords to do with cigarettes and matches. "Damned Lemonade Joe!" Kirov added with a probably unnecessary touch of realism.

"Lemonade Joe," Ostrowsky agreed reflexively.

"A drink?" Kirov's voice had arrested the other man's eyes and he was now looking at him with disconcerting nakedness. As Bogdanov had said, it was easy: the jeweler was in such a state of moral shock that he had no business being on his feet. "I've got a bottle," Kirov added.

"Have you?"

"Let's share it."

"Why?"

"I broke yours. Remember? It's only fair."

131

"What's fair? Life?"

"No, not life," Kirov conceded. God, spare me the philosophy. Ostrowsky looked as if he would make a point of it. And the words would be the same as they always were because suffering was too common for novelty and people were too ordinary for eloquence. Don't tell me about suffering or the sympathy I feel for you now will turn into boredom. "Let's have that drink. It'll keep out the cold." Kirov looked along the street. "Do you know anywhere we could go? Where do you usually go?"

"I know a place."

"Pyotr Andreevitch."

". . . Pyotr Andreevitch. A good place." With this statement Ostrowsky set off unsteadily and after a few meters took a corner to the right. Kirov followed.

They reached a complex of apartment houses with walkways and underpasses striped with cold shadows black on gray; spaces that rustled with urban nighttime.

"In here?" Kirov asked as they stood at the mouth of a dark subway. Ostrowsky shrugged his shoulders: why not? Kirov examined the path which stretched to an invisible end from which came the sound of breaking glass as evocative of place as a native chant, suggesting, as the dark corners of the city sometimes did, another Moscow, forbidding and ill-defined in its shifting cloak of snow.

"It's kids," said Ostrowsky. "It's the kids that break the glass." He said this indifferently so that you could be persuaded that he had immunity in the way that idiot saints and drunks sometimes had even though the street gangs that operated in some areas of town rolled drunks like Ostrowsky for a few rubles and the hell of it. "Just kids," Ostrowsky repeated and sat down, resting his back against the concrete wall. Kirov sat next to him and passed the bottle across, and they remained like this for maybe five minutes, guru and acolyte as it seemed to Kirov, remembering a time in Washington when one of Yatsin's legmen took an embarrassing interest in Hinduism and wanted to shave his head and wear orange — was it possible that times like that existed? The bottle went from hand to hand, Ostrowsky drinking and Kirov brushing his lips against the bottle neck while his eyes studied the water stains trailing down the concrete along the paths made by the wooden shuttering, and then the jeweler started to sing in a tearful light tenor.

"I've spoken to Viktor Gusev," Kirov said as the echoes of the song died away in the underpass. Ostrowsky, listening to his own echoes as if to a departing train, nodded and then said: "What's that, Pyotr Andreevitch?"

"Viktor—I've spoken to him."

"Ah," crooned Ostrowsky soulfully. "Bastard."

"Bastard," Kirov agreed. He tried to read the other man's anger, but Ostrowsky was somewhere on the other side of anger, stranded in a flat emotional landscape. "He shouldn't have done it—sold you those drugs for your daughter."

"No, he shouldn't have."

"Or sold his stolen diamonds to you. Trouble, that's what comes from buying from Viktor."

"I didn't buy diamonds from him."

"Oh?"

"No. Have another drink."

"You first."

"Drink, dammit!" cried Ostrowsky. Then: "He was a bastard, Petya! He killed my little girl!" He slumped forward, his head buried in his hands. Kirov put an arm around him. Ostrowsky turned his face and Kirov nursed it against his coat—*there, there*—until he could steady the other man and sit him upright to see the tears coursing down his cheeks either side of the button nose. And even then it seemed to him that Ostrowsky's grief was a dull, worn-out thing.

"I have news for you," Kirov said comfortingly. "Viktor is dead."

They began again. In this second phase Ostrowsky was calm and coherent. Kirov had remarked this form of transition before and had no explanation except that it was in some way related to emotional exhaustion. Sometimes it worried him to be able to watch and predict these phenomena of behavior and yet to have no understanding.

"Viktor had a source of stolen diamonds. He was selling them to you."

Ostrowsky shook his head.

"What then? How did it work?"

"I was selling them to Viktor. He was doing the buying."

"I don't believe you."

Ostrowsky shrugged indifferently. "It's true, all the same."

"Why?" Kirov was thinking back to the time when he and Bogdanov had tried to answer the same question. Why should Gusev have exchanged usable cash in certificate rubles and hard currency for a commodity as inflexible as diamonds? How could he spend or dispose of diamonds? Viktor might well smile his secret smile.

"Maybe they were for his girlfriend," Ostrowsky answered, leaving Kirov to work that one out, and without prompting he began to explain how the business had been transacted. They had a rendezvous point in the Park of Economic Achievement. Viktor would have lunch over the road at the Kosmos with his cronies and his flashy girlfriend Nadia something-or-other, and then come to the Metallurgy Pavilion where they made the exchange. How did he pay? From thick wads of small-denomination bills, the sweepings of the illegal trade in tourist currency, on the last occasion a suitcase full.

"Why didn't you eat with him?"

Ostrowsky smiled and stared dreamily at the darkness. In retrospect he regretted not taking up Viktor's invitations; after all you only live once and what is life without a bit of high living, even with some risk attached? But then the prudent jeweler in the romantic soul of Ostrowsky had reminded him that the purpose of this activity was not for himself. Ostrowsky had refused. He didn't want to get too close to Viktor and the high-rolling Georgian Mafia he was tied into. Once was enough. He had accepted once? Yes, once.

"Why?"

"Because . . ." Because like other prudent men he had committed adultery once, got drunk and insulted his boss once, stolen something moderately valuable once so that he could tell himself that life was not an entire barren expanse.

"Where did this happen?"

"The Aragvi."

"Who was with Viktor?"

"I don't remember."

"Why not?"

"I was drunk." Viktor failed to turn up on time for their appointment. Ostrowsky hung around in the park moving from pavilion to pavilion in a state of terror, thinking that the Fraud Squad had got Viktor and it was only a matter of time before they got him. So he trailed through halls of exhibits, losing imaginary tails, and with a burst of imagination he decided that in darkness he could wipe out his fears and his pursuers, and accordingly he left

134

the park by the main entrance to Prospekt Mira and bought a ticket to the cinema near the space obelisk. And there he shivered in the darkness and watched the film *Iron Harvest*. Afterwards he felt an access of courage and returned to the park. Viktor was there, full of drink, good cheer and apologies; arm around his good friend Ostrowsky; pressure of other business; never let a friend down; make it up to you. The jeweler consented to a drink, and a few drinks later he wound up at the Aragvi with no clear recollection of what followed.

"Who was with you?"

"I don't remember."

"The girl?"

Yes, the girl — Nadia Whatsherface. Ostrowsky recalled her now. Maybe another couple of girls as well, Viktor was passing them round like cigarettes.

"Including this Nadia?"

"No, not her. She was special."

"Special?"

"Special! Special! I don't know what makes that kind of woman special."

"And the men?"

"I don't know."

"Names?"

"I can't remember. It wouldn't help. Viktor used to give people different names."

"Georgians?"

"Georgians — Armenians — who knows?"

"Which?" Kirov insisted.

"Georgians!" Ostrowsky answered sharply. "Two of them, one of them a gangster and the other one an *apparatchik*."

"You could tell?"

"The clothes. One of them waved his arms all the time. He wore expensive jewelry — gold bracelets like Americans wear. The other man was quiet."

"Could you recognize them again?"

Ostrowsky didn't answer. His eyes began to swim as if to remind him he was drunk. Kirov proffered the bottle.

"Who the hell are you?" the other man asked limply.

"A friend. Have that drink."

From the shadows at the end of the underpass came a clatter of boots and a shout of voices. Ostrowsky drank deeply and subsided into silence. Kirov got to his feet, his legs aching from squatting. The focus on the pains of his own body made his companion disappear, as though Ostrowsky were drinking himself to physical as well as mental oblivion. Somewhere in the darkness a fight was going on: he could hear the dull smack of fists and boots, the sharp grunts and exhalations of breath. It occurred to him briefly that that was what Ostrowsky was looking for in his nightly excursions. Someone to beat the guilt out of him.

At the end of the passage he found the two Sluzhba men beating up a youth. A second lad lay doubled up on the ground holding his abdomen. As Kirov approached the two policemen left off kicking and looked blankly in his direction through eyes misted by violence. Kirov pointed down the passage and told them that Ostrowsky was there; they should clean him up and take him home.

"Be polite to his wife. They've just lost their daughter."

Kirov reminded himself that in due course he would have to file a report on Ostrowsky's involvement with the diamond smuggling ring. The penalty was theoretically death but the jeweler was likely to be more lucky.

The Andropov Version

Gorki's death took place in the crudest possible circumstances. A box of evidently poisoned sweetmeats had been given him and he and two male nurses to whom he offered some all died quickly. An immediate autopsy showed that they had indeed been poisoned. The doctors kept silence.

Robert Conquest
The Great Terror

13

The Aeroflot flight terminated in Sofia, a small airport with the shabby provincial charm of a village bar in a southern clime, where the airline desks stand as dingy as fairground booths and people mill in the hall clutching cardboard suitcases and packages tied with string, and the air is aromatic with Balkan tobacco.

Kirov took a yellow Mercedes cab to the Hotel Vitosha, where he checked in under the cover of Hans-Jürgen Becker, a West German businessman selling industrial air compressors to the foreign trade organization Isotimpex. The Vitosha was a high-class hotel built by the Japanese in the seventies and starting to show its age. It sported a swimming pool, a bowling alley of erratic reliability, and a collection of African students who sat in the foyer bar drinking Astika beer, as a relief from cooking in their hostel rooms and worrying how to explain their Bulgarian wives to the folks back home.

Jack Melchior, who had traveled a great deal on business before the matter of bigamy limited his area of operations, schooled Kirov in the ways of Westerners in his supposed line of business. "Have a shower and go to the American bar. All these hotels are the same, but once you're in the bar it doesn't matter where you are." As evidence Jack had described the restaurant at the Holiday Inn in Abu Dhabi. "The bloody place wouldn't stay still! It was French on Monday, Chinese on Tuesday and Indonesian on Wednesday. The day I left, they were preparing for the Oktober Bierfest, complete with oompah band!" Jack had been under stress in Abu Dhabi. "Bad case of Businessman's Blight. I thought I was irresistible to women and could drink the world dry." The changing restaurant unsettled him. He took to visiting the Sheraton to eat in the Mexican restaurant and drink in the English pub. "I went up-country and stayed in the Al-Daffrah Ramada," he mused. "There was a band out from England, doing gigs at spots all around the Gulf—a jazz band—used to be famous in the sixties." He paused and thought about the sixties. Why are we talking about this now, Jack, here in the Mezhdunarodnaya with snow on the window ledges and a KGB listening post in the next room? "Do you know what tune they played, Peter?" "No, Jack, I don't know what tune they played." " 'Moscow Nights,' Peter! 'Moscow—bloody—Nights'!"

Kirov showered and changed and had a cocktail in the American bar on the top floor of the Vitosha. Outside it was nighttime and the mountains brooded on the horizon among the stars. Yellow tramcars rattled down the hill toward the city. Kirov drank slowly and watched the whores parade around the bar and listened to the man at the white piano fumble over an old Sinatra song. Then he went downstairs to the Lozenets restaurant and ate a light meal of *shopska* salad and fish. The interior of the restaurant was empty of customers. A group of Japanese sat at a table on the terrace around a bottle of whisky, and the waiters in their red folk costume lounged in a corner and told jokes. From the gallery two musicians descended bearing an accordion and a violin and went to the corner. And there they struck up their music and serenaded the waiters with a love song. Kirov watched the Japanese talking, silent on the other side of the glass, and listened to the music from across the empty tables. Watching, listening, observing the distant world. As Melchior had hinted, travel offered poignant pleasures. To sit in a deserted restaurant, and there to dine on loneliness.

The night before Kirov left, Bogdanov brought a bottle of vodka to Kirov's apartment. They had a few drinks and then Bogdanov asked: "What's the penalty for getting caught? Grishin isn't exactly going to stand behind you, is he? *Unofficial,* I think that's the word he used to describe his sanction for this trip."

"I don't know the penalty for trespassing on the local Resident's territory. A complaint to Moscow? A reprimand? Nothing much."

"Nothing much." Bogdanov agreed too readily. It left a knot in Kirov's stomach that he could still feel when he rose at six, dressed from his unpacked suitcase and selected the day's identity from those which Bogdanov had prepared for him.

He took a tram to Lenin Square and hired a car without a driver at the Balkan Sheraton, then drove out of the city, picking up the Botevgrad Chausee and the highway to Varna. It took him on a straight road through hills that lay rich and sunny under the southern autumn, and for an hour he passed only a few carts crossing the highway and the occasional truck, while beyond the farms and their sandy fields the sharp slopes rose covered in juniper and laurel.

At Botevgrad he turned off the highway by the link to the town, a road of posts and cables and low apartment houses with sagging balconies. A man on a donkey cart gave him directions for the Bulpharma plant, and he skirted the main part of town until he found it. He presented himself at the gate.

The plant buildings were new and stood away from the road, fenced off on the far side of a sandy lot. The gate was guarded by a conscript. To one side stood a ramshackle booth where an untidy young woman took note of the callers and phoned through to the protocol office. A collection of workers outside the gate bought grapes from the back of a truck and paid no attention to the dark-suited official calling himself Hristov who was demanding to see the cadre's officer.

After five minutes a man appeared from the main building to receive the visitor. He was a small person, swarthy as a Turk, with a habit of looking at his feet while talking. He introduced himself as Senior Plant Engineer Nikolaiev and explained that the plant director and his deputy had not yet arrived and that he, Nikolaiev, had no instructions to expect any visitor, let alone one from the Party's Central Cadre's Office. Could he help? Could he make Comrade Hristov comfortable in the protocol office? Offer any refreshment? If he noticed the accent, he made no comment. He opened the gate and bobbed excuses like a man accused of a crime.

At the protocol office Kirov showed his credentials and signed the register. With a display of common sense Nikolaiev invited his visitor to wait while he confirmed the credentials with Sofia. He disappeared and returned five minutes later with the news that the Central Cadre's Office would not be open to receive inquiries before 9:30, apologized again and asked if Comrade Hristov would mind waiting for a while in one of the conference rooms. The plant director would arrive at nine; he would introduce Comrade Hristov as soon as confirmation came from Sofia. With a mild show of impatience Kirov consented to the delay.

He was left alone in a conference room to study the furnishings and the view from the window over the drive to the main gate. As soon as Nikolaiev had slipped through the door, Kirov tested it to make sure it wasn't locked. He ignored the fact that his hand was shaking.

A man who exercises authority has the right to exercise authority. That was one of Chestyakov's maxims, taught to all the students sometime in their second term. Human psychology cannot resist a plausible show of authority: doors open; security systems fail. "If you convince them of your authority you can walk bollock-naked into a nunnery," said the old man. "Just don't get caught when the Mother Superior arrives."

The main gate remained closed and the workers passed in and out through a side gate, bringing their purchases from the vegetable truck. Kirov watched them and steadied his nerves with a cigarette, and after a moment returned to the door and stepped out into the corridor. "Don't smoke!" said a voice.

The speaker was a small busy woman in a white coat and carrying a clipboard. Kirov examined his cigarette but made no attempt to extinguish it.

"I'm looking for the cadre's office," he told her.

"End of this corridor and turn right. And please don't smoke," she added more cautiously. This time Kirov obliged her.

Beyond the conference rooms one wall of the corridor was glass and overlooked a production area. It was white tiled and occupied by a series of stainless steel vessels, a control panel and various pipe runs. A few workers in aseptic white glided silently about the space. The atmosphere was remote, inaccessible. The idea that contamination of Viktor Gusev's antibiotics had originated here began to lose credibility. But if not that, then what? How did Bulpharma and the GRU investigation figure in the scheme of the Great Jewish Antibiotics Ring?

He found the door of the cadre's office. The room was heavily furnished with files and occupied by a typist and a female clerk. The latter looked at him without interest and resumed her interrupted conversation with the typist.

"The director wants information on personnel," he told her.

"Help yourself."

"Where do I look? He wants to review staff movements for 1984 and disciplinary actions for the same period."

"Over there—second shelf. The files are in date order." The woman scrutinized him now but without any sign of suspicion. "I love the suit," she said, and the secretary giggled. Kirov threw her a smile and a kiss, helped himself to the files and found a space to work. Ten minutes later he was finished. It was five past nine. He returned to the conference room where Nikolaiev was waiting.

"Where have you been?" the engineer asked. He was nervous and prickly.

"To the toilet. Has the plant director arrived yet?"

"He's in his office. There's someone with him. He'll see you at nine thirty."

"Fine. In the meantime I need to go back to my car." Kirov let the other man see his easier side. "I left the lights on." Nikolaiev nodded and relaxed.

They returned by the maze of corridors to the protocol office.

"Do I sign out?" Kirov asked. Without waiting for a reply he picked up the register and scanned it for any names following his own. There was one in neat italic handwriting: W. Craig.

"There's no need," Nikolaiev said hastily and took the book out of Kirov's hands.

Behind the receptionist's desk a door was open to an inner office and through the open door an American voice said: "Have you checked this guy Hristov out?"

Back in Sofia Kirov returned the hire car. It was time to reinforce his identity as Hans-Jürgen Becker. From the Sheraton lobby he made a call to Isotimpex and, giving no name, asked for the buyer, Mr. Dukov. He was informed that Mr. Dukov was at lunch. In the square he picked up a cab and had it take him to the Isotimpex office in Chapaev Street. At the protocol office he presented his credentials and requested to see Mr. Dukov, citing a previously arranged appointment. When he was informed that the buyer was at lunch, he brandished a telex and complained that he was used to being better treated. He left them with a brochure on West German air compressors and promised to return the next day.

From Chapaev Street he took a cab across town to the West German embassy in Anri Barbjus Street. He paid off the driver and hung around on the pavement long enough to be recognized, then went inside and read a copy of *Die Zeit* for a quarter of an hour before reemerging with the signs of a successful visit written upon his face. He returned to the city center, had lunch at the Budapest and found a public telephone across the street in a yellow shell tacked to the wall of the film institute.

He called the Vitosha and asked in English to speak to their American guest, Mr. Craig. So sorry, no guest of that name was registered. Kirov phoned the Balkan Sheraton. A woman receptionist answered. Mr. Craig *was* a guest. A man's voice broke into the call: Mr. Craig was not presently in his room; would the caller please state his business and leave a number at which he might be contacted? Kirov promised to phone again. He replaced the receiver, walked the short distance to Lenin Square and took a tramcar to the Vitosha.

He had no serious concern about being followed, but his skin prickled under the eyes of all the people who were not following him. Old Chestyakov used to call it "spy's itch." Depending on how often it occurred it could be sound instinct or bad nerves. He watched his fellow passengers for the one who was deliberately not watching him; he stared out of the window at the apartment houses ranged like dominoes up the hill, and thought that someone out there was also feeling uncomfortable as the day's anomalies dropped into his work tray: the nonexistent Hristov, the unrecorded appointment with Mr. Dukov, the telephone caller at the Vitosha and the Sheraton who did not leave his name. Was it one person who was aware of these discrepancies or three? Indeed did they exist as discrepancies yet? The name of Hristov might still be a puzzle only at Botevgrad and not so far notified to Sofia. Mr. Dukov might even now be applying himself to his afternoon's work without checking the messages that came in during lunch. The abortive calls to Craig might be ignored or simply logged on an operator's notepad until the security police made their next call for passport collection. Dependent on these variables and a dozen other chances was the time that it would take for someone to make the connection and draw the conclusion that led to Kirov. Dependent on *chance*. Kirov got off the tram at the crest of the hill and walked across the road to the hotel. And still nobody was following him.

Kirov entered the lobby of the Vitosha in a press of other guests. He went to the desk and while the clerk was occupied with another guest glanced at his mailbox. It was empty. He examined the boxes of the guests in rooms 503 and 609 who had checked in at the same time on the previous day. One of them was also empty; the other contained a telex and a passport. From the desk he went to the telex room, identified himself as the guest in 609 and asked at what time his telex had come in. The girl was pert and obliging and told him that the telex was an overnight transmission. He thanked her, left the telex room and went to the coffee bar in the lobby where he bought a cup, smoked a cigarette and worked out the inferences, though they were clear enough: last night's passports had been returned before breakfast; the guest in 503 had collected his; the guest in 609 had not bothered to check his mail all day. The police had retained Kirov's passport. Conclusion? Nothing certain. Inefficiency was as plausible an explanation as suspicion.

The lobby was crowded. Half a dozen African students were sitting at one of the tables with a couple of beers between them. Kirov put on his jovial face and asked if he might join them. He gave them his act as the bored businessman looking for company and bought a round of drinks. Four of the men were West Africans led by a big Nigerian called Bernard, who was studying economics and losing his taste for socialism. The other two were South Africans with withered faces and quick narrow eyes; they had a look of faith about them and an interest in unspecified subjects that kept them in Bulgaria. Bernard was indulgent: they had even less money than he had and prospects even thinner than his own with his uncle's wholesale millet business in Lagos. He confided that the South Africans earned pocket money by spying on the others, then confessed generously that he didn't care, he would be leaving the country in April and the Bulgarians were welcome to it. He drank his beer and looked carelessly about in case another had arrived.

"You looking for a woman?" he inquired. Another party of students had arrived, his compatriot and the two South Africans left with them.

"No."

"Well, you're looking for something — aren't you?" He gave a knowing smile and leaned back in his chair to spread his fat, glossy bulk.

"You can do me a small favor if that's your business."

"Maybe. How much?"

"Five dollars. Here it is." Kirov produced the note from his wallet.

"To do what?"

"Go to the reception desk and ask for Herr Hans-Jürgen Becker. If anyone asks what you want, tell them you found some business

145

papers in the elevator and are returning them." From his bag Kirov extracted a brochure on air compressors; he gave it to the other man with his firm's card and the money.

Bernard considered them. "Is this going to earn me a night in the cells?"

"I shouldn't think so."

"Ten dollars."

"No."

Bernard was still looking at the five-dollar bill. His tongue passed across his lips, then he shrugged and said brightly: "OK." He got to his feet and his big body lumbered toward the reception desk. Kirov moved from the coffee bar across the lobby to the cigarette kiosk where he bought a pack of Phoenix. At the desk Bernard introduced himself to the clerk. Kirov watched the dumb show. The girl disappeared into the back office and returned with a man. Bernard and the supervisor engaged in conversation for a minute or so, then the latter raised his hand and beckoned to two others who were loitering in the lobby. They approached the desk and placed themselves on either side of the Nigerian. After another minute's conversation, the two men from the lobby took Bernard gently under the arms and escorted him offstage. He maintained an affable smile throughout.

Kirov left by the main doors and stepped out into the autumn sunlight. He crossed the highway leading to the city and joined the shirtsleeved crowd waiting by the tram stop. When the number 2 tram arrived he caught it and traveled to Velcova Zavera Square where the tram stopped before its picturesque meander downhill through Svobodata Park. He set out on foot using the cover of the tree-lined avenues to lose any tails.

What had happened? He hadn't expected as quick a reaction from the local security police. Who were they looking for: Pyotr Andreevitch Kirov, Comrade Hristov or Hans-Jürgen Becker? His guess was that they wanted to talk to Becker; ask him to explain certain discrepancies in his papers and conduct. At this stage they could be little more than curious; otherwise the surveillance at the hotel would have been thorough and men would have been drafted in, instead of which they had relied on the hotel's own people. OK, so Kirov told himself, no general alarm and nothing too bad: he still had some time.

He left the park by Nezabravka Street near the sports hall and crossed to the Moscow Park Hotel, which didn't as a rule cater for Westerners and where no one would look first for a German salesman.

146

There he checked in as Engineer Anton Alexandrov on business from Varna.

Kirov showered and slept and it was seven thirty when he woke. Night had fallen. His room lay under the pitter-patter stillness that sounds as if someone else is there but is just the breathing of the building. He shaved, packed his small bag, turned on the radio and left the hotel without depositing his key. He walked the three blocks to the main Lenin highway and picked up a bus into the city.

The bus dropped him in Russki Boulevard by the National Assembly near a café where the customers were still sitting outside in the mild evening air. Kirov ordered a coffee, found a telephone and called the Balkan Sheraton, asking for Mr. Craig. The call was switched to the room and an American voice answered: "Craig here."

"Wrong connection," Kirov replied and replaced the handset.

He left the café and walked to Lenin Square through streets empty of traffic except the fleet of black Mercedes parked outside the Party headquarters. In Moscow the first chills of winter were snapping the air, but here the balmy nights of summer had extended late into the season and the men in shirtsleeves and the women in their light print dresses had an easy way with them so that you could forget how things stood, and the idea of being followed by one of the pretty women whose perfume he could smell as they passed along the pavement had its sinister charm.

The Sheraton chain had refurbished the old Balkan hotel. It had designer *belle époque* deco and the Americans had changed the management style so that the staff were now as neat and assiduous as Mormon missionaries. Kirov checked with the desk and saw that Craig was still holding his key, which meant he had not left the hotel. He wrote a brief note, left it with the receptionist and an instruction to page the room, and went to the bar where he ordered a Zagorka beer. He sat on a stool facing the door and waited for the police to arrive. Instead, a man came into the bar with a woman on each arm and an expression of curiosity and amusement on his face.

"I wasn't expecting you, Mr. . . . ." Craig spoke in well-modulated Russian, although Kirov's note had been in English. The American was pleased with the effect of surprise he produced. "Can I buy you a drink? Ah, I see you've got one. Have you eaten

147

yet? We were going to eat here," he smiled at the women, "and you're welcome to join us."

"I haven't eaten."

"Be my guest. Bring your beer. I have a table for three arranged, but I'm sure that another place can be set."

"Thank you."

"No trouble." The American raised a hand and conjured up the waiter who had trailed him to the bar. He spoke to the man in Bulgarian and asked for his table in the restaurant to be laid for four. The waiter nodded deferentially and left to carry out his commission.

"You get good service here," Kirov remarked.

"I get good service everywhere," Craig answered evenly and treated the other man to a studious look with no hostility behind it as if he had no use for hostility and paid people to hate on his behalf. Kirov put his age at forty, a big man with a handsome monumental head and thick hair cut as neat as a toupée and starting to go gray; then he revised the estimate upward by ten years. Americans of that class and style carried their years well, their features fined down and firm on exercise, a good diet and an attention to image; unlike their Soviet counterparts, who withered on stress, cigarettes and drink or grew fat and sly on success. Craig dressed to match in an open cotton shirt, an expensive woolen sweater and checkered trousers with a touch of golf-pro chic. "Are you going to bring that beer . . . ?"

"Peter."

". . . Peter. Call me Bill. My friends call me Bill."

"Bill."

"OK. Good of you to join us." Craig slipped his arms around the waists of his two girlfriends and quit the bar, leaving Kirov to follow.

"So you want to talk English or Russian?" Craig asked as they sat at their table, now set for four. "Take your pick, the girls don't speak either, except Minka who can talk dirty in Russian."

"Where did you learn to speak Russian?"

"My grandparents came from the old country a million years ago."

"Your family is Jewish?"

"Part Jewish, part Irish, part nigger—in America who knows?"

"You have a good accent."

"Sure," Craig answered indifferently and ordered the wine. "I

148

take it you've no preference? The local Cabernet Sauvignon is OK." He told the waiter to bring some *shopska* salad and some mineral water. "Do you mind if I do the ordering? I know what's available and what these guys can cook. Where are you staying?"

"Another hotel."

"The Moscow Park? High-class Russians normally stay there unless they're bunking in one of the embassy apartments."

"You meet many Russians?"

"A few. I'm a sexy guy, the KGB can't get enough of me."

"You've had dealings with KGB?"

Craig treated this as a joke. His face broke into a smile of immaculate white teeth. "They don't exactly advertise but you get to recognize the house style. Now I'd say that you were KGB."

Kirov didn't reply.

"KGB, MVD, GRU, I've got no prejudices."

"You've met GRU too?"

"Maybe."

"In 1984, for example, in the spring. What were they looking for?"

"You tell me. Guilty people? Isn't that what you characters are always looking for? Find the guilty people and afterwards you can find out what they're guilty of. You're talking to the wrong man, Peter. I'm just a businessman." Craig snapped his fingers and ordered more drinks. The two women giggled. The waiter came with the salads and took the American's order for the main dish. Having finished with the waiter, Craig ignored his guest and attended to his girlfriends, taking from his pockets a couple of trinkets, which he gave to them in exchange for a kiss.

"How long have you been dealing in Bulgaria?"

Craig stopped stroking his partner's hand. "Ten years, more or less. My company provided the technology for the Bulpharma plant."

"Your company?"

"The Lee Foundation. I'm surprised you don't know them. Didn't you do your homework before visiting us?"

"I prefer to get direct answers."

"Are you sure you're not KGB?" Craig observed tolerantly, and the women giggled at the joke though Kirov believed the American that neither woman could understand them. But Craig spoke a fluent body language of easy gestures, smiles, hugs and caresses, even if most of it was lies or at best equivocal, and his companions could pick up the joke from the raising of an eyebrow. Kirov merely noted this characteristic and that the other man was trading on his sexual presence, in recognition of the fact that sex and power were interchangeable currencies and easily confused. He had never before had a man so clearly flirt with him — if flirt was the right word since the American's attentions were directed at the women and it was intended only that Kirov should be seduced by the display of power. He found it neither attractive nor repellent: the poverty of human eloquence meant that every emotion, intimacy or intensity was expressed, at least in part, sexually. And, however masked, this was as true between men as between men and women.

"Would you like one of the girls?" Craig asked.

"What do you do for the Lee Foundation?"

"I'm the European Vice President."

"Does that mean you visit the USSR?"

"I sell to the Soviet Union but I don't need to go there. Your guys know pretty well what they want."

"You've never been to the Soviet Union?"

"Didn't I say that?"

The main course arrived. Craig had ordered *shashlyk* for everyone and red wine to go with it. The manager and the head waiter came around and in English with American accents inquired with untypical piety how the meal was going. Craig thanked them and slew them with a smile so that Kirov wondered if charisma was neat white teeth, a good orthodontist and the right dentifrice.

"Be my guest," Craig proposed. "Take one of the girls. I've got a spare. No charge. I know you can't be gay, since the KGB wouldn't have sent a faggot alone on a foreign mission. What do you say? You think they're working for me? I should be so lucky! The Bulgarian Ministry of the Interior pays them and our every loving embrace is on tape, isn't it, my doves? I can't speak for social diseases, but security-wise, Peter, they're as safe as they come." He tweaked the breast of the blonde. She glanced quickly at all the people who were not looking and then her face smiled a smile while her eyes looked dully at Kirov. Craig announced: "I've got to take a leak."

"I'll join you."

"Well, what do you know?"

They adjourned to the toilet and urinated from adjacent stalls. Craig pissed like a horse with a vigorous animal grunt and talked the while. "What's wrong with you? Frightened of leaving me alone? Thought I'd go to the police?"

"Why should that worry me?"

Craig fastened his fly and took in the fancy appointments of the room. "What are you really up to?" he asked. "Who the hell are you? Is this an off-the-record visit so that I can't even go to the john without you following me?"

"That worries you?"

Craig turned. He smiled. "No, it doesn't worry me." He had finished at the washbasin, grunted again and patted his hair at the mirror. "I think you're the one who's worried. I get the feeling that this visit of yours is strictly below-the-line."

"You know about these things?"

"Go screw yourself." Craig charmed his own image with a smile and checked his teeth for stray food. When he turned it was as if he didn't expect Kirov to be there. "Look, I'll buy you a last drink and then you're finished. I pay my dues and for that I get people to throw out the riffraff. No offense, it's been nice talking to you, but I'm tired."

They returned to the restaurant. "Peter's leaving," Craig told the two women. He was ill-tempered now and called for the bill without taking coffee. Kirov bade him goodnight and left the hotel for the square and the mild evening.

He walked a while, feeling the contradictions of the febrile night which clothed the sky in purple and the streets with easy passersby who were busily not spying on each other. He thought of Moscow, where you couldn't believe in Craig and his seraglio, nor Viktor Gusev and his, which was perhaps why the Great Jewish Antibiotics Ring remained an enigma since its main actor was an implausible creation, out of time and place; maybe Viktor had created himself out of the books he struggled to read. Kirov passed a mosque. It was shuttered and in shadow. A few men with black hair and black mustaches sat in the shadows watched by the police and watching in turn with empty eyes the warm quiet night walk past them in its shirtsleeves.

There was one part of his plan that he hadn't explained to Grishin or even to Bogdanov. It was necessary that he be arrested. It was the surest way of finding out who was interested in his case and in the plant at Botevgrad. Logic said that the risks weren't serious, but now in this strange place where the warm breeze stroked his face like balm he felt that he had escaped something. A pedes-

151

trian stopped him and asked for a light for his cigarette. He had wandered back to the Sheraton, which was brashly bathed in floodlights and whispered *America* across the square to him and anyone else who wanted to hear. He toyed with the idea of returning to the Moscow Park where the Bulgarian police were impatiently waiting in his bedroom following the call which Craig must by now have made. But even if he wasn't afraid of arrest, a few more tired and unprofitable hours of release still appeared desirable. "Traveler's melancholia," said Jack Melchior, who knew. "Have a drink." So Kirov did. He returned to the Vitosha and braved the sloppy surveillance of the lobby security staff who knew by now that he was at the Moscow Park. He descended past the envious Africans, the diligent Japanese and the lavatory lady (ten *stotinki* in her saucer) to the nightclub.

In the nightclub the floor show was halfway through. A chorus line, in spurious peasant dress that trailed braids and ribbon over a boned and body-hugging costume, posed and kicked to the accompaniment of a florid male singer who was delivering a bland number in Spanish. Kirov took a seat and ordered a drink while he watched the bored crowd and thought of the traitor, Neville Lucas. "Why is it, Peter, that there's so much to do in life and so little to do on Sundays?" Lucas was an expert on foreign travelers. "Lonely — lonely. Never — listen to your uncle Neville — *never* get drunk in a crowd. You'll hate them or feel compassion for them. Or worse still, you'll talk to them. I used to talk to strangers. I used to be the weird bloke who sat next to people on trains and spoke in a loud voice. That was before I came to Russia and got respectable." Lucas smiled innocently. You could know a spy for a lifetime, and in his will he would bequeath you another person as his legacy. What did Neville mean about Sundays? Am I drunk?

Kirov finished his drink and ordered another. He watched the foreign businessmen in their twos and threes, the Party stars with their smart middle-aged wives, who walked belly-out like the prow of a ship as they crossed the floor, and, in the corners, the policemen and the gangsters with their girlfriends, whom they kept as close to themselves as their sins.

How long? How long? Kirov checked his watch and cast an eye over a table near the floor where two girls sat together. The cabaret had finished. He got to his feet and asked one of the girls to dance. She was blonde and lively, plump, cynical, badly dressed and made-up and wholly attractive. Her name was Louise, French-style, she said. They danced a while, laughed a lot and she suggested that he take her home with her friend Jacqueline and her companion, an inebriate Dutchman. Kirov agreed.

They left the hotel by the lobby. By now the security guards were twitchy. Kirov halted and gave his partner a kiss and laughing together they caught a taxi outside the door and the girl gave directions.

"You're nervous," she said with mechanical coyness.

"No." He looked from the windows of the car into the black and starry night. She cuddled into him, eyes closed and alert. He felt her against him, soft as a baby asleep and yet tensely awake. The car pulled up after a mile or so outside an apartment block. The girl got out, invited Kirov to join her and then gave directions for her friend and the drunken Dutchman. Kirov waited on the step and breathed in the air. He was abroad, on a warm night, with a fat whore. He was oddly happy and wondered if this were freedom.

At four in the morning he was arrested.

The police broke down the door, dragged the girl naked from bed and hit her around the face a couple of times for form's sake then politely asked Kirov to get dressed while telling the girl to quiet the baby who was screaming in her cot. The girl huddled in a corner among the washing and the unironed clothes, sobbing. Kirov lifted her to her feet, comforted her, head against his shoulder with her tears burning his face, and gave her some money and a final kiss on the cheek. Then he went with his captors, clip-clip, their shoes echoing on the bare silent stairs past silent doors with ears glued behind them and out into the street where a car waited by the pavement.

They drove without speaking. The streets were empty, the sky pale with a bright moon and the skyline a soft silhouette of trees. Sofia was a city of trees and pleasant parks; in other days and other times you could fall in love with it. And now they were in Nezabravka near the junction with the main highway and faced by the long bone-white shape of the Soviet embassy behind its fence and floodlit garden, where they were expected at the gate and admitted almost without interruption.

They bundled him out of the car and through a side door and frogmarched him down the corridors and through the checkpoints with the same firm gentleness, no rough stuff, just a strong firm grip as long as he cooperated. A couple of heads poked out of

153

doors and watched him with neutral curiosity, cipher clerks relieving their boredom on the uneventful night shift. His captors ushered him into a security elevator with a coded call button and they were whisked a couple of floors to a carpeted lobby with a guard manning the night desk and a woman with a sleepy look and a stenographer's pad who regarded him with hostility. They knocked at a door before introducing him to a room. His two companions pushed him through the opening and closed the door behind him. A light shone in his face.

"Turn the light off," he said. That first moment was all that was given him to establish his dominance over his captors. The light came from an anglepoise placed on a desk in the center of the room and directed at the door. "Let's not play games. Can I smoke?" Kirov patted his jacket for cigarettes. A pack of Belomors was thrown toward him and a hand with a lighter extended from the circle of light. With a click the lamp was switched off and a gentler glow filled the room from the strips concealed in the cornices.

"Who are you?" a voice inquired flatly.

Two figures became visible. The speaker was sitting behind the desk. He wore a short-sleeved shirt open at the collar; his face was unshaven, he had half-moon spectacles and thin hair scraped straight back and oiled. It was an uninteresting face, large-pored and slack with tiredness. The speaker eased the spectacles off his nose and spun them in the stubby fingers of his left hand.

"Who are you?" he asked again.

"Kirov — Pyotr Andreevitch — Colonel in the Second Chief Directorate of the Committee of State Security of the Soviet Union."

"Fuck your mother," the man murmured, and glanced over his shoulder at a second figure who was lounging in a chair against the farther wall. A soldier in an unbuttoned uniform with colonel's tabs.

"Who am I speaking to?" Kirov asked.

"Gavrilov."

"The Resident?"

Gavrilov glanced over his shoulder again and then nodded. "I run this show. Now what the hell are you doing on my patch?"

"I'll sit down."

"Sit down, smoke, take your shoes off — who am I to object? A real live colonel from Moscow!"

"You can check my credentials."

"Damn right I can!"

"Contact General Rodion Mikhailovitch Grishin. He'll vouch for me and tell you he authorized my visit."

"Authorized your visit? Well, that's all right then, isn't it? You can walk into here and wander all over the goddamned place without letting anyone on the ground know. I suppose it didn't occur to you to let me know that you were coming or tell me what you wanted in case I could help you out?"

Kirov didn't answer. Gavrilov's anger only confirmed that nothing was going to happen to him. Gavrilov spoke in a low voice to his colleague and returned to the questioning.

"What were you doing in Botevgrad nosing around the Bulpharma plant?"

"I'm investigating the source of antibiotics being sold on the Moscow black market."

"And that's all?"

"That's all."

"Why did you ask to see the cadre's office?" the soldier intervened smoothly.

"I was checking for familiar names."

"Find any?" asked Gavrilov.

"No."

The colonel asked: "Why did you go looking for the American at his hotel?"

"Curiosity," Kirov answered blankly. The colonel received the answer in the same fashion. The GRU station chief? The other man gave no introduction. Gavrilov meanwhile was on the internal phone, asking his secretary to contact Moscow Center to verify Kirov's details and get a photograph and fingerprint match.

When he had finished the colonel took the handset from him and ordered mineral water and coffee. "Do you want a sandwich?" he inquired casually and without waiting put the order to the secretary, then took up an earlier point. "Why did you not notify the *referentura* that you were coming here?"

"I didn't need any local assistance."

"Why did you use false identities—two, or maybe you have some more?"

"I'm conducting an investigation. I took security precautions. You seem nervous about the Bulpharma plant?"

"It produces medical supplies for the Army."

"Ah."

"Yes."

Gavrilov turned to his colleague. Kirov again read anger and un-certainty. Gavrilov wanted him off his hands. What was he into? The black market? The GRU investigation? What was that about? Two more conspirators to add to the Great Jewish Antibiotics Ring? Kirov felt a wave of tiredness hit him. Travel and tension. A sense of an explanation that was retreating from him toward the tip of understanding like an object pursued in a dream. Should he be frightened?

They gave him sandwiches and a chair in which to doze away the remaining hours of the night while the lines between Sofia and Moscow buzzed with urgent inquiries. In the morning they put him on a plane. First they roughed him up mildly. They guessed he was in no position to complain.

14

They escorted him to the airplane and let him go. There were two of them, in wedding suits, smiles like passport photographs and cement in their eyes. Kirov was bundled with their civilities onto the plane and assured that their thoughts would go with him. He could still feel them as the dark landscape unfolded and he hummed the tune to "Moscow Nights," remembering that the tune did not apply to his Moscow but to another remote city, a distorted mirror image. "Don't you feel it?" Neville Lucas once asked in an unguarded moment. "Have you never felt it?" To which the answer was, Yes—but not here.

Once before there had been a sinister world. It was Washington during the time when he was bringing home the traitor Oleg Ouspensky. Washington where the CIA would buy the drinks, call you by your first name and show pictures of their kids. The world of the ambiguous "Have a nice day," where friendliness and insincerity clasped each other so that conversation became unintelligible.

"Yes, Neville, I've been to places where it's possible to be frightened."

He drove to Dzerzhinsky Square and called in at the office. It was nighttime and the Fire Brigade were manning the duty office, playing chess and sorting cables to the music of the decoder. They turned toward him with their dead-fish stares. "Don't go up. The place is full of mice."

The power to the elevator was cut and a guard blocked the stairs. "You can't go in."

"Why not?"

"Don't make me laugh."

He caught sight of Kruchkov from Special Investigations crossing the floor with a telex in one hand and a bread roll in the other.

"Semyon Mironovitch! What's going on?"

Kruchkov turned his nearsighted eyes, registered blankness, then recognized Kirov and fitted his face with a smile. "Hi, what are you doing here? It's OK," he said to the guard. "He can come in. What are you doing here?" he repeated.

"I've been away on a trip. I wanted to check my mail."

"Good trip—bad trip?"

"Bulgaria."

"Hmm—so-so. Good weather but not much chance of making anything on expenses."

"You've been there?"

"No."

"Oh—I thought you had. I heard that Special Investigations had a team in Sofia after Andropov died."

Kruchkov froze in the act of offering a cigarette. "Where did you get that one from?" he asked.

"I heard it was you or GRU."

"It was GRU." Kruchkov paused and his face cracked with a grin. "Fuck your mother! Good try, but not good enough! How the hell did you hear about that business?"

"Just a rumor."

"Well, leave it at a rumor. And finish the cigarette downstairs. I can't let you in any farther."

"You haven't told me what you're doing."

"Haven't I? Well, don't worry about it. It's just a routine security audit. In and out overnight so that we don't interrupt the flow of work."

"I don't remember it happening before."

"No? Well, we don't advertise. But believe me, it's just routine. Would I be talking to you like this if it weren't? Look, I've got to go. Apologies again for screwing up whatever you wanted to do. If it can wait until morning you'll never know we've been here. Give my love to Lara—ah, I'm forgetting, Lara isn't living with you any more, is she?"

"How did you know?"

Kruchkov looked at Kirov with a sympathy that didn't hide a sense of superiority. I know something that you don't know, it said, and Kirov had encountered it often enough to recognize that it usually masked cheap secrets that weren't worth the having. But you could always be wrong. "Someone must have told me," Kruchkov was saying when Kirov interrupted him.

"What is Ferenc Heltai like?" he asked.

"Heltai?" Kruchkov answered in a long lingering way that had a dozen question marks from beginning to end. "Never heard of him."

Bogdanov moaned that the Fire Brigade must have been in during the night. Someone had messed up the papers he kept strewn on his desk. "And not for the first time. Grishin has complained. Every night lately it's the same. Have they been through your stuff?"

"My papers are filed."

Bogdanov picked up a bunch of telexes and leafed through them. "They've tried to put them back in order but it isn't the way I left them."

"It wasn't the Fire Brigade. At least, not last night. Special Investigations were in here."

Bogdanov froze barely perceptibly, then casually put the papers back and asked: "I wonder what those spying bastards wanted?" He turned to the subject of Kirov's Bulgarian trip. "So tell me what happened. What did GRU turn up during their investigation?" The questions flicked off his tongue like dandruff off the shoulders of his shiny suit, so easily that you wouldn't know the answers were important. He wants to know and doesn't want to know. He can't handle the truth. Kirov felt a surge of annoyance and put it down to tiredness.

"GRU gave the plant a clean bill of health. If there was any contamination of products from the Bulpharma plant, it didn't arise at the production end. And I don't believe that the plant is directly involved in the black-market trade. GRU scared them and they're still scared. They wouldn't dare to divert production illegally."

"So the Bulgarian lead is a dead end?"

"I don't know."

"Why not?"

Because the Bulgarians hunted him down? That wasn't an explanation, it was an inevitability from the moment he had visited the plant. Perhaps the opposite. They had taken their time before picking him up. Except that it was standard procedure when handling

159

an unknown quantity and, if they had identified him as a Soviet citizen, the Bulgarians weren't going to wade in without checking first with the local *referentura*.

"The Resident sits with the GRU station head."

"So?"

"They take decisions together."

"Is that a serious comment? Are you telling me that GRU are running the *referentura?*"

"It would explain why the Resident failed to report that a GRU team was investigating the plant."

"But why? Why would the Resident side with GRU? We've been kicking their arses for so many years it's become a habit. You know how it works, you were in Washington."

Kirov was in Washington where the GRU team were as clean and wholesome as poor relatives and the station head didn't say boo without the approval of the KGB Resident. All in pursuance of the unwritten rule that said that the military was subordinate to the political even if the Americans didn't have any political secrets you couldn't read about in the newspapers. Remizov, who had been Resident at that time, wouldn't even allow his army opposite number into his office.

But now things had changed, and in a changing world anything was possible.

He returned to his office and called registry to tap the computer for any record kept by 8th Department relating to the American, Craig. He also called the MVD Central Files Section in Ogaryov Street and put through the same request. Then he turned to his mail.

To: Colonel P. A Kirov
    12th Department
    Second Chief Directorate
    Committee of State Security

REFERENCE: STAFF MOVEMENTS — SPECIAL HOSPITAL KUNT-SEVO

With regard to your inquiry concerning staff movements at the above institution for the period 9 February 1984 to 9 August 1984 covering personnel above the

grade of Assistant Pharmacist, our records indicate the
following:
Academician I. A. Yakovlevitch
suspended from duty 13 February 1984
dismissed 27 April 1984 with loss of benefits
emigrated from USSR 2 May 1984
deprived of citizenship 2 May 1984
present whereabouts not known.

Chief Pharmacist G. D. Orlov
resigned 5 May 1984 with preservation of benefit
reposted 7 May 1984 to No. 2 Pharmacy, Tula
present whereabouts No. 1 Pharmacy, Cherepovets

(Signed) Yu. A. Belinkov
Directorate of Personnel (Special Section)
Main Hospital Administration
Moscow Region, RSFSR

"Did you know that Yakovlevitch had been on the team at the
Kremlin clinic?" Bogdanov asked.

"No."

"Was he treating Andropov?"

"Work it out—he was suspended after Andropov's death." Kirov
put the paper down. The words continued to jump out of the page.
Code—everything in code. There to be understood if only he possessed the key. He didn't want to contemplate the alternative—that
the Great Jewish Antibiotics Ring was without shape or form, a
conspiracy looking for conspirators.

Bogdanov asked what "whereabouts unknown" meant.

"Yakovlevitch is in America."

"Then why 'whereabouts unknown'?"

"The hospital administration lost interest in him when he lost his
pension rights. They don't care where he is. Send a cable to the
Washington Residency—for Yatsin's eyes only—ask him for
Yakovlevitch's address."

"Isn't that going to stir the shit?" Bogdanov said flintily. "And
what for? Where's the connection with our business? Boss, this investigation is going all over the place."

"Send the cable."

* * *

In the quiet of lunch hour Kirov wrote down the possible theories.

First Theory:
The Great Jewish Antibiotics Ring is a simple black-market operation. Viktor Gusev was a Moscow racketeer with access to drugs from Bulgaria. He died from an accidental dose of contaminated antibiotics.
Evidence: Gusev's flat and dacha *show that he was living beyond his official income. Wholesale quantities of antibiotics were found at his apartment. The labels indicate that they came from Bulgaria. MVD had a tip-off that Gusev was the head of the racket.*
Problems: Why was Gusev buying diamonds from the jeweler Ostrowsky? Why did Gusev and Ostrowsky's daughter both die of contaminated antibiotics when a check at the plant indicates no production problems? Who broke into Gusev's dacha *and what were they looking for?*

Second Theory:
The Great Jewish Antibiotics Ring was a plot by the KGB at Andropov's instigation to implicate Academician Israel Abramovitch Yakovlevitch and his Jewish colleagues in the illegal trade in antibiotics. The object of the plot was to provide a basis for harassing refusniks *and an easy explanation of the medicines shortage.*
Evidence: Grishin organized the case against Yakovlevitch.
Problems: Why did Chernenko terminate the investigation after Andropov's death? If the plot was so straightforward, why didn't Chernenko adopt it? How does this version square with a GRU investigation of the pharmaceuticals factory, if the whole scheme was a fabrication?

Third Theory . . .
Kirov halted there. He wasn't certain that there was a third theory. He remembered only that Grishin had given an explanation for GRU's interest in the pharmaceuticals plant. Someone thought that Andropov had been murdered. Drugs supplied by the plant had been used. That someone had presumably been Chernenko. He had been responsible for the funeral arrangements for the dead man and so must have seen the autopsy. The problem with this version of events was that the most logical person to have organized Andropov's murder was Chernenko himself, who had lost the lead-

162

ership race on Brezhnev's death and had every reason to fear Andropov's moves against the old Brezhnev gang. In which case, having contrived the medical murder of Andropov, he was unlikely to have advertised the fact by ordering an investigation.

Kirov stared at his notes and the words seemed to drift. Three versions of events, each straying into the others and the only common thread the Bulpharma plant, which had been investigated and found innocent. Two of the versions spelled trouble for whoever pursued them. In the corridor machinery clattered, people queued to get coffee and rolls, Grishin was shouting for his secretary and a clerk trundled past with a trolley full of files. Kirov scooped up his notes and joined the line by the document shredder, evoking a look of surprise from the assembled secretaries. He filled in the destruction docket against one of Tumanov's cases and fed the sheets into the machine.

The call came at two o'clock. A Major Kolomeitsev, identifying himself as a member of Department 44388 — GRU under another name — asked Kirov to present himself immediately at the Aquarium for a meeting with Colonel Heltai concerning a subject which would be familiar to him. Kirov gave a noncommittal answer, replaced the handset and went to see Grishin.

The office was empty but a smoldering cigarette lay in the ashtray among a stack of dossiers. The top folder was untitled but marked with a departmental code for the Rehabilitation Committee. Kirov flipped the cover open to see if the contents identified the subject of the Committee's current attentions. The top document was a memorandum addressed to Grishin and headed with a case reference and title. The subject was "Unjustified Harassment of Scientific, Medical and Technical Personnel Contrary to the Principles of Socialist Legality." The name of the individual concerned had been masked. Kirov closed the file as Grishin came back into the room.

"Pyotr Andreevitch," said Grishin with a careworn surprise. He invited Kirov to take a seat and asked him how the Bulgarian investigation had gone; was Kirov any closer to establishing a link between the Bulgarian pharmaceuticals plant and the source of the black-market antibiotics?

"No."

"You found nothing of interest?"

"The plant was given a clean bill of health. I checked the records

163

of the cadre's office. If GRU had discovered anything that implicated the plant there would have been changes in the management. The records show no unusual personnel movement. The conclusion has to be that GRU drew a blank."

"Nothing else?" Grishin said this lightly, the words floating on top of something else. Perhaps only the stress of the Committee's inquiries. Perhaps I'm seeing plots and ambiguity everywhere — the worn-out spy's equivalent of senility. Kirov shook off the idea.

"The Resident and the GRU station chief are working together."

Grishin was amused. "It happens. I believe it's called friendship. Unusual, I admit."

"There's an American working in close collaboration with the plant."

"He has an official reason for being there?"

"Yes."

"So? I'm sorry if I don't follow you. There's still some sort of case against the plant? If so, what is it?" Grishin smiled patiently and then repented. "I'm sorry. I wasn't intending to discourage you. Quite rightly there are aspects of the Bulgarian business that disquiet you and, naturally, you are looking for a theory that explains them. A word of warning only: a convenient theory today can become inconvenient tomorrow. But carry on. I think you're on to something. Run with it."

"Thank you, Rodion Mikhailovitch."

As Kirov left the general's office he looked back. Grishin had returned to his documents and was staring at them blankly. The paper reflected in his moist eyes and turned them white.

He went to the Fire Brigade cubbyhole where a female clerk in a faded twinset was on duty. He told her to go and smoke in the toilet. The room was a simple box with a desk, a typewriter, a chair and a waste bin. A secure cabinet was fixed to one wall and held the duplicate file keys kept by the night shift. It was locked. The waste bin contained newspaper chess problems and the remains of someone's supper. Lying on the desk were the roster and the shift log. Kirov picked up the latter.

The last entry in the log was marked by a page torn from a diary and stained with coffee. Scribbled on it were notes written by the duty officer which the clerk had been transcribing into the log in a round schoolmistress hand. The rostered shift was listed by name, the previous night's activities were summarized by quarter-hour intervals, and the security checklist was ticked off. Kirov's own visit was logged in. There was no reference to the presence of Special Investigations in the building.

Kirov looked through the other entries. The duty officer was obliged to sign for any keys taken from the security cabinet, note incoming cables and record the numbers of files taken and the fact of their return. Nothing was entered for the previous night. He turned to the duty officer's jottings and compared them with the fair copy in the log; though not yet completed, the copy tallied so far with the notes and the balance of the draft entries contained nothing of interest. He scanned the back of the rough copy. Five lines of chess notation in a different hand and then more of the duty officer's writing, a series of four-figure numbers with various letter prefixes and no explanation. Kirov made a note of these, inserted the marker back into the log and replaced the latter on the desk as the clerk returned.

He went back to his own office and called his secretary. He gave her the list and asked her to compare it against the key list held by Grishin's department. Next he called Registry for a response to his check on the American, Craig. Registry confirmed that the dossier on the American was held by the First Chief Directorate, but access was restricted: it held joint KGB/GRU material and required two authorizations. The chief of the American desk could sign for KGB. For GRU authorization reference should be made to Colonel F. G. Heltai. Kirov was informed that MVD held no record of Craig, nor was any held by the 7th Department of the Second Chief Directorate which had responsibility for the surveillance of tourists. It followed that Craig had told the truth and he had never visited the Soviet Union.

A curtained Kremlin limousine driving down the official lane of the Khoroshevskoye Shosse passed a line of trucks. Kirov watched it go by, saw the reflection of his own car in the curtained windows, which were normally so anonymous as to defy even curiosity, and for once he wondered about the particular occupant: did he live his life in fear of being poisoned? Was it simply an obscure and irrational dread that had caused the murder investigation in the wake of Andropov's death? In the West they might use analysts, but here it was possible to set the police on the trail of one's nightmares; and with the advantage that they could make them come real, and complete with confessions.

From the highway four floors of barred windows and grimy brickwork were visible and belonged to the GRU factory that took Western equipment apart to see what made it tick. The main body of the Aquarium was lost in the classified installations around the Khodinsk airfield. Access was down a narrow lane by the Institute of Cosmic Biology and through a checkpoint manned by the special guards battalion. Kirov submitted to the searches and the scrutiny and was introduced to the glass palace forming the main building and left to cool his heels in a windowless side room watched over by an armed soldier.

After an hour there was a noise at the door. A lieutenant came into the room with a two-man escort. He invited Kirov to follow and together they took an elevator to the ninth floor, passed through a pair of internal checks and arrived finally in a wide carpeted corridor with pictures on the wall and a small reception lounge complete with club chairs, scatter cushions and magazines. There Kirov was again left alone, but this time with a copy of the *Economist* and the day's edition of the *Herald Tribune*. A secretary offered him a glass of tea and a biscuit and suggested politely that he stay away from the window.

An hour in a bare room and then a half-hour in a lounge that would have done credit to a decent hotel — was Heltai confusing his cues? It was impossible to tell. Kirov wondered if Heltai had made the connection to their common past, the hotel in Riga — indeed if he even remembered the incident of his emergence from the sea carrying a Ruslan and Ludmila cake which had so impressed a fourteen-year-old boy. Like many powerful images it had no fixed meaning. This one had left an adolescent with a sense of the other man's significance yet no thought of what that significance might be. It joined those other images which have importance but no consequences, as if in the press of a crowd his hand had been brushed by a stranger who was there and then gone leaving only the sensation that his hand had been touched by the fingers of God.

"Kolomeitsev," said the major, coming from the office and introducing himself. "I'm sorry you've been kept waiting. General Vlassov is ready to see you."

"And Colonel Heltai?"

"Colonel Heltai sends his regrets. He was looking forward to meeting you. Do you two have some personal connection? I got the impression that you knew each other, old friends almost."

166

"The colonel told you that?"

"Not in so many words," Kolomeitsev answered confidingly as if he too were an old friend, "but one gets an impression. By the way," he added, to broaden the basis of the conspiracy between them, "a word to the wise. Vlassov is inclined to be bad-tempered. If I were you, I'd just listen while he shouts off; and if at the end you could promise to be good—even apologize just a little bit for the trouble in Bulgaria—then so much the better. You don't have to mean it. I'm sure that you had good reasons for doing whatever it was that you were doing there. The main thing is to appease the powers-that-be. At a purely personal level I'm sure that you and I can sort out the basis of our collaboration quite amicably."

"We're collaborating, are we?" Kirov asked.

"I hope so," Kolomeitsev replied slightly more stiffly. "Your escapade in Bulgaria has the makings of a good interdepartmental row. A promise of mutual cooperation could defuse it before it really gets started. If you and I could reach an understanding, I would be able to lend you a bit of quiet support against Vlassov."

"I appreciate that."

"Don't mention it."

Kirov's first impression of General Vlassov was of a man used to getting his own way. He was tall, crop-haired and tight-built; a man who plays tennis at the age of fifty. His skin looked stitched to his face in fine lines and tucks. He remained seated frigidly behind his desk while his languid subordinate made the introductions then draped himself over a chair and watched the action from this ornamental pose.

"You work for General Grishin?" Vlassov began with the sort of pointless question intended to establish the speaker's power since it demanded agreement. Then he got straight to the point: "What the hell were you doing in Bulgaria?"

"I was pursuing inquiries into the illegal trade in antibiotics."

"Why wasn't the local *referentura* informed?"

"General Grishin waived the requirement."

"That wasn't my question. And don't think you can hide behind that Grishin-shit: Grishin violated KGB's own procedures. Your own Resident has complained to his masters in the 11th Department and they've got a few questions of their own about what a purely domestic surveillance department was doing operating in one of their satellites. So forget Grishin. I want to know why you thought a clandestine operation was necessary."

"It was an operational decision. I don't feel obliged to justify it here."

"Not *justify* exactly," Kolomeitsev intervened helpfully. "I don't think that's quite what the general had in mind." His words were directed at Kirov, but his eyes were elsewhere. Behind Vlassov's desk a mirror was screwed to the wall. *"Explain* might have been a more appropriate expression," he suggested.

"Explain will do," Vlassov agreed.

"My investigations are concerned solely with illegal activities here in the Soviet Union. But I had reason to suspect that Bulgaria was the source of the antibiotics concerned in the illegal trade. Since I had no knowledge of how the Bulgarian end of the racket might be working, I was concerned with . . ."

"What?"

"The possibility of some official involvement in the business."

"By KGB?"

"I was referring to official involvement of an informal nature. If it existed, then it might have been unwise to alert the persons involved as to the purpose of my visit."

Vlassov smiled. Kirov thought that the idea of suspicion and a witch-hunt within KGB would appeal to him. Kolomeitsev also gave the appearance of being charmed by the prospect, but his eyes still wandered guardedly to the wall behind the general.

"Did you establish whether the Bulgarian factory was the origin of your illegal supplies?" Kolomeitsev asked.

"I think it's unlikely."

"May I ask why?"

"Because GRU investigated the plant as recently as 1984 and apparently satisfied itself that the place was operating normally."

"How did you learn of that investigation?" Kolomeitsev inquired calmly when Vlassov had left the room ostensibly on other business after expatiating on the operational confusion that could arise if business was carried on by prima donnas who felt obliged to report to no one. The major offered cigarettes from the box on the general's desk.

"Rumors — nothing more. Once people knew I was interested in Bulgaria they told me stories."

"What did they give you?"

"No details, just that GRU had looked over the Bulpharma plant."

"And found?"

"Nothing, so far as I can tell. What was your interest?"

"Not the same as yours. The connection is purely accidental. Our interest was more political."

"I thought that political cases were for KGB?"

Kolomeitsev smiled wryly. "Things change." He produced a piece of frankness as genuine as a magician's card. "Look, I can't promise to be totally open with you—in this business, who can? But on the basis that we are cooperating, I can tell you that our investigation had nothing to do with the economic aspects of the case. Have you produced a report? Why don't you let me have a copy? I could straighten you out. That's fair, isn't it?"

"Where does the economic end and the political begin?"

"That's exactly my point! Now what do you say to a copy of your report?"

"I might be able to arrange that," Kirov agreed, and as an afterthought added: "The American, Craig—is he political or economic? Mine or yours?"

"Mine—but not for any reasons to do with our investigations into the plant." Kolomeitsev betrayed another confidence: "The Bulpharma plant was built to licensed technology belonging to an American company, the Lee Foundation."

"Yes?"

"Well, to tell you the truth, there's a second plant. It was built here in the Soviet Union without the knowledge of the licensor. William Craig assisted us in converting the Bulgarian designs to meet Soviet conditions of production. What can I tell you? Craig is one of the good guys. He's on our side."

They finished their meeting with mutual expressions of goodwill. They exchanged complaints about their respective superiors and made a few imprudent remarks about their services. This proved that they were friends.

Kolomeitsev showed him to the door. The receptionist was gone; darkness had fallen. It was the time of day when people stand at the doors of their offices and make small talk with their neighbors.

"I'll say goodbye then. Till next time. Wait here and someone will come and sign you out."

Kolomeitsev offered a hand. Behind him the door of the next room opened and a figure emerged. "I'll see you as soon as you're finished," the stranger said to the major, and seeing Kirov his eyes registered a slight surprise. "Fix some coffee," he continued, "oh—

and something to eat, a biscuit, a sandwich, whatever is available."
He spared Kirov a stranger's nod. A sparse red quiff was all that
remained of his hair; his face was round and bland; his eyes mild
and apparently without lashes or brows because of his paleness;
his age perhaps sixty and running to fat. Kirov felt a pang of recognition.

"See me as soon as you can," the stranger told Kolomeitsev
curtly and treated Kirov to a more leisurely scan. He said, softly so
that Kirov was scarcely sure he heard the words: "We must talk
some time, Pyotr Andreevitch." Then his back was turned and he
had stepped quickly into his office leaving only a snapshot image.
In his left hand he held a half-eaten cake and on his nose there was
a dab of cream.

15

Kirov returned to Dzerzhinsky Square. It was evening and the Fire Brigade was in occupation. He interrupted their chess game to ask whether there was anything for him from the diplomatic bag or the radio decodes from Washington. He was told no.

He went to his office and there found a parcel on his desk and a scrawled note from Bogdanov. Uncle Bog had listed the bars where he might be found. Kirov pocketed the note and turned to the parcel. It was wrapped in newspaper and roughly taped. He cut it open and threw away the wrapping. What he uncovered was a porcelain figure of a shepherdess.

Taking Uncle Bog's list, Kirov tracked him through the city's bars. Boganov was known at the Zhiguli beer cellar. Someone had seen him talking to a fence called Yuri the Bazaar; they had done some serious drinking and then pushed off in the company of two girls. Kirov followed them, working from Bogdanov's list, to the bar in Stoleshnikov Lane. He ran into Yuri the Bazaar and the two girls outside the Aragvi restaurant. Yuri was looking groggy and applying snow to a graze on his cheek. One of the girls told the story: yes, they had gone to the bar; Bogdanov, the creep, was drooling like a madman and had picked a fight with his companion; the militia had been called, but Bogdanov had squared them and paid for the mess. When last seen he had been heading for the metro and talking about taking a train to Taganka. There was a bar near the theater, the third on the list.

The place had a hanging atmosphere of smoke and sweat. Bogdanov was at a table, sipping morosely at a flat beer. He brushed a hand across his face, smearing it with misery, then, noticing Kirov, pulled out a smile from somewhere and laid it out beneath his old muddied eyes like stones buried in a swamp. "You found my present," he said.

"I found it."

"Want a drink?"

"I'm OK."

"I want a drink." He looked around as if one might turn up. "How was the Aquarium?" he asked. "Red carpet treatment—undying love—did you get to see Heltai?"

"No." Kirov was still asking himself whether it was Heltai he had encountered in the corridor.

"Who'd you see, then?"

"A major called Kolomeitsev. He told me that the American is working for us, and he offered me a deal if I would collaborate with him."

But Bogdanov wasn't listening.

"Heltai—I've been checking out this Heltai," he said, and between the dreamy words yelled out for a drink for anyone who cared to hear. Then: "Hungarian—old hand with AVH in the bad old days—cut his teeth during the purges in the early fifties—ran for cover to us when Imre Nagy and the Fascists took over in 'fifty-six and started rehabilitating the victims. GRU took him up." He shook his head to and fro in long drunken swings. "A Naughty Boy, this Heltai. Definitely!"

"Who's your friend?" a surly stranger asked Kirov.

"Fuck off," said Bogdanov leaving the stranger frozen out with indifference. "Fuck off," he repeated, then leaned forward confidingly and had a couple of shots at resting his hand on his chin.

"How is Heltai a Naughty Boy?" Kirov asked.

"A bogeyman—a widow-maker. He used to globe-trot doing wet jobs for the GRU station chiefs. Bang-bang. Yes!"

"Why didn't I hear of him when I was stationed in Washington?"

"Not his patch. The Western Residents have too much muscle to allow GRU killers in their territories. Heltai worked the Afro-Asian beat, killing coons for his masters. He couldn't look you in the eye without sizing you for a coffin. Specializes in poisons. Has a degree in it—or something."

Kirov did not press his questions. Something had given Bodganov a scare and he was wiping it out with drink. There were tears in his eyes. "Bloody smoke," he murmured and wiped them on his sleeve. "Want a drink?"

172

"Where did you come by the figure?"

Bogdanov put a cigarette to his lips and fumbled with some matches.

"You know Yuri the Bazaar?"

"I saw him."

"Bastard—sell his mother. Ah . . ." Bogdanov inhaled deeply and leaned back so that his chair tottered on the point of overturning. He kept it like that so Kirov had to follow the conversation with a knot of tension in his guts, waiting for the collapse.

"Yuri?" he prompted.

"Yuri—sure. I run into him in Dzerzhinsky Street where he hangs around the club looking for a bit of trade, a chance to do some favors."

"What sort of favors?"

"This—that." Wobble, wobble, went the chair. "Stolen goods. Some of the boys get a little light-fingered when visiting other people's premises. Yuri helps them out."

"He bought the figure?"

"I'm walking down the street and I see him holding it. Hi, Yuri! I say. Nice bit of stuff—where'd you get it? And we settle for a hundred rubles on the spot. I don't have the money on me, but I have an honest face. So I take the pot to your room and tell Yuri I'll settle with him later in the Zhiguli."

"I'll pay you back."

"Forget it."

Kirov remembered the fight in Stoleshnikov Lane.

"So you know about that? Well, I was short of a hundred rubles and Yuri is an arsehole. We had a disagreement. That and maybe I hit him for old times' sake." Bogdanov began to drift off again. Then: "Change! I'll tell you what *change* means! That sonofabitch seriously thought of hitting me back!"

He staggered off to find a toilet and returned with two beers. He sat down and stared at the glasses through eye slits that looked as though they would heal over. Kirov sensed the same incoherent anger and tried to distract it.

"Where did Yuri get the figure from?"

The question shook Bogdanov back from his torpor. "Huh? Oh, yeah, the figure. He bought it from Dyukov."

"Dyukov?"

"He works for an MVD team of burglars, locksmiths and other handy mechanics, doing jobs for whoever asks."

"You're certain?" Kirov pressed.

"Certain," Bogdanov repeated flintily. "Yuri and I talked about it until he was nearly unconscious from the effort." He smiled at his own understatement, thinking about his fight with Yuri the Bazaar. Almost boyish. He looked to Kirov for approval, and Kirov thanked him and told him that he would find them both a cab to get Uncle Bog home where he could sleep it off. He asked if Bogdanov was OK to be left alone and Bogdanov said he was. Kirov left the other man some cigarettes to get on with and stepped out into the street and the cold air to find a cab and to think.

He knew who had broken into Viktor Gusev's *dacha*. He didn't know what they were looking for.

At Romashkovo the next day he stopped the car on a whim and went to study the cemetery. There on the hill he looked over the graves, brushing away the snow to reveal the names of people he didn't know. "No marker, no ceremony when I go," said Uncle Kolya earnestly. "You're not going," Kirov answered thinking the old man was worried about dying. "What sort of crap is that?" Uncle Kolya answered scornfully, then relented. "Just remember: *no ceremony*. I want to go out like your father." My father? Kirov wanted to ask; but the general had had his say. He would explain nothing of the elder Kirov's burial or, as seemed more likely, the secret scattering of his ashes.

Question: what happened to the bodies?

Kirov had never met anyone who knew, with the exception of old Chestyakov, who, in his dotage and over a drink after lectures, confessed to having disposed of a couple, but not the who and the how of it, which was where the secrets lay. Instead the ancient Chekist rubbed his nose and gave his cabalist leer, which said, it is for me to know and you to discover, but maybe when your time of initiation is come, the rites performed and the words spoken. Then maybe . . . When Kirov believed in KGB — when he was in love with KGB — it was possible to imagine that each new operative was gifted with a corpse to bind him to the brotherhood. Chestyakov in full regalia, Chekist, priest and magus, holds it clenched in his left hand (the right hand holds the initiate's badge, the sword and shield of KGB). Here it is, outstretched and secret. "And this is *your* body, Pyotr Andreevitch. Your own special body. Bury it carefully."

He returned to the car, leaving the wind to sweep snow over his footsteps. Bogdanov, nursing his hangover, had stayed in the vehicle and left the engine running to maintain heat. The windows steamed up. The interior smelled of tobacco, the dampness of Bogdanov's coat, his stale body. Kirov took the rear seat and let the other man drive. He examined the mail he had brought with him. Tomsky had brought it in that morning; he was acting as bagman for the Washington Resident in Scherbatsky's absence. He had just returned from the United States and looked like a man who has just visited his mistress. A man could be generous in that mood.

"Could you do me a favor?" Kirov asked as he accepted the canvas pouch in which Yatsin had sealed his letter.

"Why should I do that?" Tomsky reacted suspiciously.

"No reason. Why did I agree to help out Scherbatsky?"

"OK, OK — point taken. What do you want?"

"Information on a company, the Lee Foundation. They're involved in pharmaceuticals."

"I've heard of them. Why don't you simply call up the main file?"

"It's an American corporation. I thought the American desk would know its way around the records and be able to collate the data more easily than I could."

"Ask Bogdanov to do it."

"He doesn't speak English. It's all right if you don't want to do it."

"No, I said I'd do it. But data is all you get — no report, no analysis."

Kirov agreed no report, no analysis. In any case he doubted Tomsky was qualified to produce them. He asked whether Scherbatsky had surfaced again. Tomsky said he hadn't. He'd just vanished.

To: Colonel P. A. Kirov
   12th Department,
   Second Chief Directorate,
   Committee of State Security,
   Moscow
   SUBJECT: ACADEMICIAN I. A. YAKOVLEVITCH

Reference your inquiry as to the present whereabouts of the above person. Academician I. A. Yakovlevitch was granted an

175

exit visa from the USSR on health and compassionate grounds on 2 May 1984. He was suffering from recently diagnosed angina pectoris and wished to visit friends and relatives in the United States of America and Israel. He was already in serious ill health at the time of his departure and died suddenly within twenty-four hours of his arrival in the United States. According to the autopsy conducted by the American authorities, the cause of death was heart failure.

(Signed) General I. A. YATSIN
Washington

The pouch contained a second document, a hastily scribbled letter:

Petya,

I am dashing this off before T catches the plane, so excuse the fist. You should be getting a formal report with this note, and it represents the official truth. We didn't handle the business over here; so the official report is all I know for sure—honest! Except one thing. Yakovlevitch may have had a "friend" on the plane. Draw your own conclusions.

Don't let the bastards get to you!

Vanya

PS When are you coming here again? I'm keeping the vodka cold and the women warm!

See you, pal

V

"Why did you ask Tomsky to get the material on the Lee Foundation?" Bogdanov asked as they drove away from Romashkovo.

"I don't want my name logged against the file."

"Then why did you ask me to pull the records on the American?"

"They know I've met him and they'll expect me to check and confirm his background out of simple curiosity."

"So how is the Lee Foundation different?"

"They'd know I was still digging into the Bulgarian business."

"That's what we're doing, is it?" said Bogdanov sourly. "Wonderful!"

They turned off the road into the woods. The car struggled on the soft ground.

"I've got another job for you," Kirov said. "I want you to check the passenger manifests for all Aeroflot flights to the United States on the second of May 1984. Find which flight carried Academician I. A. Yakovlevitch and get me a printout of the passenger and crew lists and a rundown on every name that appears."

He put down Yatsin's letters and looked out of the car. The birch trees were thin and stood in clumps like bundles of firewood in the shadow of the pines. Here in the depths, the snow hung evasively in the top branches and a clammy mist filled in the gaps.

"Why am I doing this?" Bogdanov asked. Kirov passed the papers from the back seat. Bogdanov dropped his speed to a crawl, laid the papers on the passenger seat, opened the two sheets and glanced over them. He grunted and said: "What is Yatsin getting at? Murder? He thinks that Yakovlevitch was knocked on the head by his 'friends'?"

"Maybe."

"And 'heart failure'—what are we supposed to read into that? Poison? Is that the way we do it these days?"

"It's happened before," Kirov answered, but Bogdanov wasn't interested in history, not the Doctor's Plot or any other plot. And, he had to remind himself, the Doctor's Plot was just a fabrication by Stalin and Beria. There was no plot. There were no poisoners.

They parked like last time in the clearing between Viktor Gusev's *dacha* and old man Dubanov's cottage. The old man's pig was rooting in the trees at the edge. It paused, treated them to its glittering stare, squealed, and its curly-tailed rump vanished into the shadows. They remained for a moment in the car and watched to see if the landscape would suddenly jump. Finally Bogdanov produced some aspirins from the glove compartment and took a couple for his hangover. He offered the bottle to Kirov, and, remembering what happened last time, murmured: "I hope we're alone this time. I'm getting too old for the rough stuff."

They took the muddy path toward the cottage. Around them the forest creaked and crepitated and the invisible pig grunted bad-temperedly. The mist hung in shabby patches. The cottage with its woodpile, chicken run and privy stood in mud and slatternly disorder. Kirov rapped on the door. There was no reply.

Bogdanov went round to the rear, leaving Kirov to peer through the windows. Then from the privy a querulous voice said: "Sod off!"

They waited. The voice repeated, "Sod off!" several times, then after a couple of minutes the door creaked open and old man Dubanov, bagged in rags and furs and holding the seat of his pants, came out grumbling: "Can't even crap in peace and quiet." He identified them and giving a sly grin of welcome said: "What do you know—my favorite Chekists!"

"Hello, grandad," Kirov answered.

"Hello, grandad, hello, grandad," the old man repeated with the same sly amusement. Then: "Where's my present, son?"

"I've got some tobacco for you." Kirov held out a package.

Dubanov showed surprise, then complacency. He murmured: "You're a dutiful boy," and took the gift. He suggested they go inside. "And bring your friend. I don't want his ugly mug frightening the pig."

They entered the crowded room, breathing in the fog of woodsmoke and the old man's pipe. Dubanov cleared the rubbish off a couple of chairs and invited them to sit. He took a position for himself by the iron stove and squatted into his clothes like a frozen pigeon into its plumped-up feathers.

"So," he drawled, "what brings you back? I didn't expect to see you two again."

"Has anyone else been to see you?" Kirov was guessing. The I-know-something-that-you-don't-know look in the other's eyes had to mean something. It vanished and the old man moved uncomfortably and patted his feathers.

"Another couple of Chekists. They wanted to know what you two had been after. I told them to sod off—same as I'm telling you."

"You told them to go away?" Kirov said skeptically. Behind his bluff Dubanov struck him as a frightened man. *Like me.* That was a new thought. Kirov tested it for accuracy.

Bogdanov reached for the parcel placed by his feet and passed it to Kirov. The latter opened it and displayed the contents to the old man. The porcelain figure of a shepherdess.

"One of a pair," said Kirov. He had not previously examined the figure closely and now he could see the coyly modeled girl holding a lamb in a setting of rococo garlands of flowers. It made him think of Mozart, and a snatch of melody went through his head.

"You had the other one," Bogdanov said bluntly. "I saw it."

"You broke it!" Dubanov retorted.

"Let's say my hands slipped."

"But that isn't the point, is it?" Kirov intervened reasonably.

178

"You went into Viktor Gusev's *dacha* before the other . . . Chekists arrived. You stole the companion figure of the shepherd. Why not both? Were you carrying too much to hold both figures? What else, Semyon Kuzmich — what else did you take?"

The old man murmured and grumbled. His face was alive with fear, hatred — memories. He stood up and went to the corner of the room, returning with two empty bottles. He offered them to his visitors. Bogdanov snatched them. They once held perfume.

"Scent! What did you want with scent?"

"I drank it," Dubanov answered crankily. "It's OK. Have you ever tried it? I took the full bottles of booze and when I'd finished with those I drank the scent. Oh, and I also took some cans of food."

"Nothing else?" Kirov asked patiently. He had been fooled once by the old man's cunning. How to get at Dubanov? The old man claimed to be a hero. He had served five years in Kolyma. How? Nobody survived five years in Kolyma.

Except the stool pigeons.

"I have to get something from the car." Kirov stood up slowly. He told Bogdanov to wait. "Talk to Semyon Kuzmich. I'll be gone about five minutes." He turned and moved to the door, lifted the latch and looked out onto the mist and the old man's pig, which was lying belly-down in the mud and grinning philosophically.

"Wait."

Kirov continued to examine the pig. Bogdanov cracked his knuckles.

"Wait!" the old man pleaded.

"Yes?" Kirov let the door close. He turned to Dubanov and assumed again his expression of mildness and understanding.

"Damn you, I'll get it — get it — understand?" Dubanov was on his feet and again burrowing in the litter and rubbish, and complaining bitterly: "I don't know why I took it — don't need it — can't use it." He emerged clutching something to his chest. "I saw it and thought, 'That's Chekist stuff for sure.' Yes. I know my Chekists — goddamned bloody Chekists!"

In his hands he held a spool of movie film.

Anya Dimitrievna was waiting at the office with a typed list. It contained the file and key numbers held by the department compared against the numbers jotted down by the Fire Brigade duty officer on the night that Special Investigations had visited the offices. The list showed that the investigators had called for access to the files of Grishin, Kirov and Bogdanov. There was no mention of Radek.

"Why not?" Bogdanov asked as he fiddled with the projector and tried to focus a light on the screen.

"Because he's clean."

"Clean of what? Ah—there—got it!" The leading edge of the film was fed into the mechanism. "Turn the lights down, will you? Clean of what? Radek used to be a dirty little toe-rag—there better, better . . ." Bogdanov sharpened the focus, "he used to work for Trapeznikov who had some very nasty habits and was never likely to go to heaven. Shit!" The film snapped. He paused to trim and refeed it. This time it engaged properly and Bogdanov grunted with satisfaction. But the subject of Radek still rankled. *"Openness*—that's the new policy, isn't it?"

"So they tell me."

"Sure it is!" Bogdanov affirmed acidly. Then: "But how come in this place *openness* feels like a conspiracy?"

They took their seats. In the darkness of the cinema the screen flickered and swam with images. The room itself was small and stacked with dusty boxes and a debris of spools and broken equipment. Its shabbiness reminded Kirov of the porno houses off New York's Times Square that Yatsin used to favor. Yatsin had his dreams. "Let's go inside, Petya. Just to take the weight off my legs." He wore elasticized stockings that stilled the throbbing of his veins.

The screen flickered. A black and white interior came into vision. The bedroom in Viktor Gusev's *dacha*. Items of clothing strewn on the bed. Pieces of figures—an arm—a leg—people on the edge of the camera's field. No sound. Bogdanov complained: "Why didn't that stupid bastard, Dubanov, take the tapes as well?" Yet without the sound the pictures had their own slow rhythm.

The man appeared first, a bare torso, a forearm, his back to the camera, firm and well muscled. His body was naked but for leather bracelets and anklets. His head was entirely covered in a velvet mask.

"Christ!" murmured Bogdanov. The man's hand beckoned, extending itself toward a figure out of sight. "Please God it's a woman!" The body swayed to unheard music.

The woman was fair and smooth and masked. Her anonymous body was an abstraction, a flow of shapes and shadows and planes

180

of light, infinitely plastic in the imagination. She moved gracefully across the camera and held a pose, her back toward the viewer, the shallow valleys and contours of her flesh hazed and shaded. On her left shoulder blade was a dark mole, and this slight blemish was her only individuality.

"Go on," said Bogdanov to the man. "Get stuck in!" He waited in anticipation.

The man beat up the woman ferociously.

16

The day that Kirov was inducted old Chestyakov gave his speech. It was full of high purpose: the KGB was the active conscience of the Party, the sword and shield of the Revolution. Above all the KGB functioned at the core of the Party's morality.

It was possible to be cynical about such statements, remembering that Chestyakov and a bunch of his retired cronies laid about the food and liquor after their descent from the dais to hobnob with the recruits and told various stories ranging from the salacious to the sadistic once they had a few drinks inside them. But that would be to ignore a part of the truth. Those like Kirov who were there, fresh and green and smart in their new uniforms, were conscious of their own election. They were told—and they knew— that they represented the nation's best. It was inconceivable that they did not exist to achieve something worthwhile.

"Let me give you a practical tip," Uncle Kolya said. After the presentation and the congratulations the general took Kirov to the Berlin restaurant. He had primed the waiters to give good service and they fell over themselves to be helpful. The Berlin was an old-fashioned place with a fountain and gilded mirrors and music to match; and since it was highly rated by foreigners and the waiters spoke English there was a hubbub of foreign voices in the background, so that if you wanted to you could imagine yourself somewhere else. And of course you were. The KGB was somewhere else.

". . . practical tip." Uncle Kolya fiddled with a piece of bread as if the subject were too difficult to broach openly and it came to Kirov fleetingly that the old man wanted to talk about women. He had tried to years before, failed and ended feebly with:

"Always take precautions, Petya—do you understand me?"

"Conspiracies," the general said. "Plots. *Stay away from them!*"

"I will," Kirov promised faithfully, and heard the older man murmur in a dissatisfied way that he was not following the point.

"There are no new conspiracies, only continuations of old ones. New bits get grafted on and old bits seem to die away, but it's all the same story. Nothing new ever happens. Nothing old ever really goes away. It can always come back."

Kirov supposed Uncle Kolya was drunk since what he was saying was largely irrelevant and in any case not true. Uncle Kolya caught something of his reaction.

"You don't understand, do you?"

"I'm sorry."

"It doesn't matter."

"I'm sorry." Kirov reminded himself that it was the day of his induction. Perhaps Uncle Kolya had been thinking of his own. He had joined the KGB on the same day as Kirov's father, which was why they had been friends and loyal to each other. Kirov raised a glass to toast them all, living and dead.

"Don't try to understand," the general said regretfully. "Just remember. You'll never understand what is behind it all. *Conspiracies are not meant to be understood!*"

Those were the words. They were burned on Kirov's memory. He wanted to ask more, but Uncle Kolya brushed aside his question and proposed a toast to his future. Later, when he tried to revive the subject, he found the question could not be raised. The words had become a secret, and had therefore never been spoken.

Kirov was certain that Viktor Gusev was a blackmailer. He was not the man in the film. Viktor was a voyeur not a participant. Despite his illegal wealth he was a spectator of his own possessions, not a true owner; never at ease with them; struggling to acquire a sense of style, to read and understand the books and culture he had access to. Nadia Mazurova was right: Viktor remained at heart a poor boy from the provinces. He had never possessed her except as an ornament, as remote from him as the pair of porcelain figures stolen from his *dacha*.

Which left the question: who was the man in the film?

Who was the girl?

He asked Bogdanov to stay in the office and confirm the trace on Orlov, the former pharmacist at the Kremlin hospital now believed to be somewhere in the north working on a nature reserve. He took Tumanov with him and together they drove to Lyublino where Nadia Mazurova had moved back into the women's hostel. It was a four story dun-colored building in a potholed street of apartment houses with a school and a militia station at the corners. The warden was a fierce elderly woman who kept watch from a booth by the keys and the mailboxes. She stopped the two men and told them that male visitors were not allowed; and, when Kirov insisted, she directed them into a lounge where there was a television set, a table-tennis table and some worn-out furniture scattered with magazines. Nadia Mazurova joined them there.

Her manner was calm and she bade them good morning, but her eyes were bright and her gaze was penetrating. She was wearing a skirt and a striped blouse. Her hair was bundled into a damp turban.

Kirov invited her to take a seat. She accepted and with a show of care folded her elegant legs and placed her hands in her lap while Kirov watched her impassively. He cleared his mind of thoughts to be free for impressions. Contemplating this interview it seemed to him that it had no true agenda, since an agenda supposed some knowledge of the subject. Instead of which he had only facts without meaning and a sense of her opposition.

"I'm surprised to see you again," she began.

"Really? I thought you would have expected me. Our conversations so far have been — unproductive."

"I've tried to cooperate."

"Have you?"

"I thought so," she answered but she didn't look at him. There was music somewhere and the voice of the warden yelling: "No loud radios! What do I tell you? No loud radios! There are people trying to sleep!" Tumanov was unwrapping a piece of gum.

"Why didn't you tell me about Viktor's *dacha?*" Kirov asked.

"His *dacha?*"

"You had a key for it. It was one of the three you had on you when we first met. A key for the hostel; a key for Viktor's apartment — and there was a third key: that was for Viktor's *dacha,* wasn't it? Get me some cigarettes," he said to Tumanov.

"Now?"

"I'll pay you later." And to the woman: "The key — do you want me to try it to prove my point?" He studied her eyes as they followed Tumanov to the door. "He makes you uncomfortable?" He could see remembrance of that first occasion: the minutes locked away with Tumanov, mistaking his stupidity for sinister intent, Bogdanov whispering in her ear. Kirov thought that Bogdanov's hazard at a threat had struck some deep chord in her, but you could never be sure: any woman would react to a threat of rape. It was a suggestion that wouldn't be made again. Not again, he promised himself.

"I told the others when they were here," she answered his question. "Investigator Bakradze and the other one, the detective."

"Antipov. What other questions did they have?"

"You don't know?"

"A different department."

"Ah!" She accepted the answer with quiet disbelief. "They wanted to know the same things as you. What were my relations with Viktor? Who were his friends?"

"And you told them you knew nothing — helpfully, of course," he added wryly and tried her with a small smile that she resisted. He wondered if she had also distrusted Viktor Gusev. Did that explain why they weren't lovers? He offered her a confidence.

"I've learned more about Viktor since we last met."

"Have you?"

He ignored the rejection, the emotional push.

"Viktor was betrayed."

She looked sharply away. He continued patiently.

"Viktor's friends sacrificed him. There was an investigation into the illegal trade in antibiotics and the investigators wouldn't be satisfied until they had an important arrest. So his friends threw Viktor to the wolves to put a stop to the investigation — he was going to be the Total Explanation behind the conspiracy. Why did they pick on Viktor?"

"I don't know."

"Didn't he tell you? He certainly knew that something was going on because I think he tried to protect himself. He obtained a movie camera and some recording equipment and he took a film of one of his accomplices in a compromising situation. That seems to me like the preparation for blackmail. Was he using blackmail to try to save himself, or have I got it the wrong way around? Was Viktor set up *because* he was a blackmailer?"

"I don't know."

"Don't know? Don't know which? That he was betrayed? That he suspected he was at risk? That he was a blackmailer?"

"I don't think he was a blackmailer—not in any bad sense."

There was a good sense?

"I have the film," Kirov told her and he saw Nadia Mazurova's face freeze with the same appalling look of fear he had seen once before although this time no violence had been offered to her.

Tumanov returned with his purchase. He smiled at the woman as if he could win her over, and flipped the pack across to Kirov, who took a cigarette, lit it slowly and let the match burn down so as to catch her attention again.

"There is a man in the film," he resumed quietly, requesting her understanding. "He puzzles me. Who is he? Why did Viktor need to film him? To threaten the man with betrayal in turn if he betrayed Viktor? Even so, why take a film? He could simply denounce his accomplice to the police. He didn't need evidence—it's no secret that MVD are not too fussy, and once in their hands it was fairly safe to assume that he would confess. So why the film?"

There was no response. Tumanov edged forward in his chair, intent on some cheap version of Uncle Bog's style of pressure. Kirov signaled him back. Nadia Mazurova had turned to the younger man in fear, and freed of her attention Kirov could interpret her. Violence was the catalyst to that fear. She knew what was in the film.

"You haven't answered my question."

"I'm sorry. I don't know the answer."

"Do you want to hear my solution?"

"I suppose I must."

"I think you must," Kirov said. "I think that the man in the film used a false identity and that Viktor did not know his real name. I think the man was not supposed to be in Moscow and that the film was the only way he could be proved to have been there. In fact he was a man that Viktor was not supposed to know because their connection could not have been explained. You might say that he wasn't supposed to exist."

He watched her. He willed her to answer, the sensation so intense that it seemed to him that it must be tangible to her. Then the door opened and a girl in T-shirt and trousers came into the room. Behind his concentration Kirov heard her loose mules flipflop across the wooden floor, heard the pages of a magazine turning, the television being switched on, the sagging springs of an old chair sigh as the intruder sat on it. He excluded the distractions, but Nadia Mazurova could not; her attention was stretched and stressed between his gaze and the incidental noise. He could hit her with words like a taut string.

"Tell me," he said. Her eyes said she couldn't. "Tell me," he repeated. "It's important. This stranger is also a dangerous man. He beats women, and some day he'll kill one. You know him, don't you? *You know that he beats women!*"

The girl sitting with her magazine cast a lazy glance in Kirov's direction. Though his tone was low, she had caught the urgent force in his voice. "Get her out of here!" he whispered to Tumanov. The latter got to his feet and sauntered across the room. Kirov returned to Nadia Mazurova. Have I lost her? he wondered. Then: what do I have of her to lose? He delivered up his concern as if he were sacrificing a piece of himself, regardless of whether his concern was authentic: he said: "Is it you with him in the film, Nadia?"

She shook her head, masking her face in the tumbling edge of the loose turban.

"Say it!"

"It isn't me."

"Again!" He could hear the brutality in his voice and in the background the giggle of the girl and Tumanov's amorous encouragements to leave the room.

"It isn't me!" She locked on the words, and now they were staring at each other, the man silent, meditating his next action, the woman trapped in her distress, her face flayed with emotion. Kirov sensed her deep evasiveness and fear. He thought: she has no reason to fear me. And in the next moment he wanted to impress her with his intense dangerousness to her. Then she spoke—a name.

"Zagranichny."

"The man? Zagranichny is the name of the man?"

She nodded.

"Are you sure?"

Her eyes looked up blankly. She was distancing herself as if recoiling from a series of blows. As he pressed her with further questions she retreated from him behind a veil of difference that resisted his comprehension. Then she asked if he had finished, if she might leave; and he agreed. She stood up and faced him as though inviting some formal parting; but turned and walked away without looking back. Her blouse clung to her and the turban trailed across her shoulders. In his imagination Kirov could see the flesh of her back and the dark plaque of a mole worn as a badge on her shoulder blade exactly as he had seen it in the film.

He felt a profound pity for her, and he hated it.

In the car Tumanov chewed on his gum and spoke in the flippant sentences that suited him. He asked why Kirov had been so easy on the girl; why hadn't he pulled her in and really given her the business? He genuinely wanted to know.

Uncle Bog was waiting impatiently at the office. He had news of Orlov: the pharmacist was confirmed as posted to the Darvitsky Reserve. "It's a hell of a demotion after working at Kuntsevo for the Kremlin bigwigs. There just has to be a dirty story behind it unless he suddenly turned into an animal lover. By the way, how was the Mazurova?"

"Someone is frightening her."

"Uh huh? Well, you should bring her in and open her head up. Or don't we do things like that anymore? Remind me."

Instead Kirov said: "I was wrong about Scherbatsky."

"How?"

"He wasn't responsible for giving away Gusev's *dacha*."

"She told you that?"

"She gave Antipov the location."

"That figures: I told you the guy who sold the shepherdess to Yuri the Bazaar was MVD. He must have been working for Antipov." Bogdanov gave a grunt that said I told you so. "And did she have anything else for you?"

"She gave me a name for the man in the film."

Bogdanov pushed back his seat and looked up. "Anyone we know?" he asked cautiously.

"Zagranichny."

"Never heard of him. Any connection with our business or is that just one more thing we don't know? Don't answer. Anything more? Address? First name? Please tell me you got a description, or am I supposed to go around asking every suspect to show me his dick?"

"Try the hotels. Viktor lured Zagranichny into his trap by pimping for him. So if he needed Viktor to supply him with girls, the probability is that he came from out of town."

"OK, I'll buy that. What else?"

"The second factory, the one that GRU say was built here based on the Bulgarian plant; have you managed to trace it?"

"Maybe—I'm still waiting for confirmation." Bogdanov turned to his papers and drew out a slip. "I've got someone working on the problem. He's running through a list of pharmaceuticals produced in Soviet plants and looking for analogues to those produced in Bulgaria. Once he's found his analogues, he can check which factory has the total product slate that best resembles Bulpharma. So far he's got one possibility, but he's looking for others. I'll know tomorrow."

"Who's the present candidate?"

"Pharmprodsoyuz Number One—it's an outfit based in Tbilisi; we have a file on it but nothing suspicious. The plant meets its targets regular as clockwork and its products hardly ever show on the black market, which suggests that any that do are just the result of petty theft, probably from hospitals and pharmacies. The plant management is clean." Boganov paused. Sometimes he got the look of an old dog. Kirov remembered a dog that Uncle Kolya kept for years at his *dacha*. It used to roll its yellow eyes and give a painful stare as if it had some ancient wisdom to deliver but there was no language to express it. Instead it would sigh with a snore through the soft flaps of its nostrils and then scratch itself. Bogdanov said: "Radek stuck his nose in here. If you have nothing to do tomorrow he invites you to go skiing with him. It's a while since you split a bottle together and he's feeling guilty—I'm quoting him—and friends ought to stick together and . . ."

"Why did you change the subject?"

This time Bogdanov did scratch himself. He said: "We'd make more progress if Grishin gave some push to get the American's file out of GRU or whoever is blocking it. Craig helped build the second plant, so he must know where it is. But," he added with something like concern, "these days Grishin is scarcely showing his face. While you were away there was a long session of the Rehabilitation Committee. Grishin was seen sitting for hours, waiting to be called in. The secretaries are smiling behind his back and there's a smell of blood in the air. Me, I don't understand what the Committee has to work on. I thought everybody had been rehabilitated except Trotsky?"

"And?"

"And? . . . And?" Bogdanov had the old dog look again. Mute.

Then with an effort he said: "What the hell is going on in the world, that in this place of all places we're starting to get frightened?"

"Frightened?" Kirov asked. "Is that what's happening?"

"Isn't it?" the other man answered. He placed his pen on the table, giving up all pretense of taking notes. The chair swung around so that he faced Kirov straight on, his back to the window and its view of the sky and the gray courtyard, the snow on the ledges and a melancholy crow flapping around after some meager pickings let fall from the windows. His gestures said: Look at me — I'm an old man. His sparse bones were scattered about the chair like dirty underwear, gray and seamed.

"OK, boss, however you like it. We're not scared. Everything's fine. We know exactly what's going on and we don't have a care in the world."

17

Serebryanny Bor—the Silver Woods. The last time that Kirov had been there was with Lara. They took the river bus from Gorky Park. It was the spring thaw and the boat on its two hour journey nudged through the broken ice floes to the laughter and wonder of the passengers. They picnicked on the beach and hired a pedal boat. The temperature was in the seventies and crowds of Muscovites sunned themselves while the foreigners from the embassy *dachas* watched them, the sunbathers and the ice floes, and concluded that the Russians were crazy.

Now it was winter. Kirov drove to the island by Marshal Zhukov Avenue. Radek, by arrangement, was waiting for him. Around the ski center a crowd of adolescents milled about in a snow fight, breaking the brittle stillness of the day with their shrieks and laughter. The long queue to hire skis showed the same bumping good humor; kids running about talking to friends; passing food and drink down the line; throwing snowballs at anyone who took their fancy. Returning skiers, whose skis would be released to the later arrivals, were greeted with cheers and inquiries as to the state of the *pistes*.

Radek stood apart from the crowd, drinking something warm from a small flask. On the ground beside him were two pairs of skis and a light backpack. He was wearing a fancy ski suit and goggles and his smile was relaxed and indulgent. He waved in Kirov's direction and said warmly: "Hi! Glad you could make it. I was worried—well, like I say, glad you made it."

Kirov looked about. "There's just you?"

"Why not? We don't get much chance to talk. I thought—"

191

Radek hesitated almost shyly. "We don't get much chance to talk," he repeated. "We should do. You—me—we're on the same side, right? We used to be good friends."

Kirov couldn't remember that last part. But friendship was often an uneven arrangement. He remembered Radek only as a caterpillar who had unaccountably changed into a butterfly, a gray-suited *apparatchik* who had discovered that these days style counted and he could wander around the Ukraine with his gang of Hollywood Stars in flashy clothes and fringed boots, busting meat suppliers like a Wild West marshal.

"I suppose Lara is the problem," Radek interpreted. "Look, I'm sorry about what happened at the party. I tried to rub your nose in it—I guess I was drunk."

"It's OK."

"You mean that? It's just that these days—well, we've got to stick together. No one else is looking after our interests, am I right?"

"Let's ski."

"Ski? Oh, sure—ski."

Kirov fixed his skis while Radek stowed his flask and slipped the backpack onto his shoulders. "I know these trails," he said. "Stick with me, Petya, and we can get away from the crowd." He pushed off and was soon fifty yards ahead and calling for Kirov to follow.

For ten minutes they stuck to the tracks running between alleys of birch and pine that shed snow as they passed. Radek kept ahead, not slackening until they were clear of the other skiers. Then he paused for breath, allowing Kirov to catch up, and offered a drink. They stood in a clearing where a forest road cut the ski track. On all sides the trees stood dark and spare and the views disappeared into silvered shadows.

"Here, try this," Radek passed a half-liter bottle of spirit. Kirov refused it.

"What is it you want to talk about?"

"Aren't you enjoying yourself?"

"I'm enjoying myself. Why did you invite me here?"

"It's what friends do, isn't it? Look, have a drink." Radek took a hefty pull from the bottle and offered it again. He smiled beneath the cold glitter of his eyes. Why are you apologizing? Kirov wondered. After his drink Radek was staring about him at the sun and the trees. He began a story about winter when he was a child: it was all gone, where did it go to? Friendship carried its burden of responsibility and guilt which perhaps explained why Kirov preferred the company of strangers. He supposed that Radek was feeling guilty about Lara and found that he didn't care.

"Here, have you seen this?" Radek fished inside his backpack and came out with a newspaper. "Today's — read it — I've marked the article." It was a copy of *Pravda,* and he held it out straight armed as if it were a gun.

"What's in it?"

"Read it." He tapped the page. The apologies were gone and Radek looked as smug as a well-fed dog. Kirov took the paper. It was open at an inner page and an article was ringed. The heading was: "Advances in Soviet Medicine." Three columns of bland prose. Radek pointed out the piece: "Third paragraph from the end." Kirov turned to it and read:

No review of Soviet advances in the techniques of renal surgery would be complete without praise for the achievements of the late Academician I. A. Yakovlevitch. A good Communist, he left the USSR for personal reasons but remained at heart a Soviet citizen. The stresses of his personal problems may have contributed to his death and his loss to Soviet science. One of the benefits of *perestroika* should be the lessening of such tensions so as to allow our men of science to continue their contribution to the modernization of our national life.

"Let's go on," Radek said and he took the newspaper back. He indicated a gap in the trees off the ski track and headed in that direction where the ground was more broken and the going difficult. Kirov followed into the crackling silence of the forest and the cold uncertainties of the winter sun.

They reached another clearing heavily shadowed by trees. The spoor of a fox crossed the sea-gray covering of snow. Radek paused again for breath.

"Well?" he asked. He began to remove his skis. "Take the weight off your feet. Let's relax and have a bite to eat." He removed his backpack and fumbled among the zippers of his fancy ski suit for some cigarettes. In his borrowed glamour he bore an air of adolescent insecurity; if you didn't know his history you could feel sorry for Radek. He fingered the cigarette nervously and then laughed. It was a pitilessly ironic laugh; if he had been asked, Kirov would have said that Radek lacked either the insight or the humor for it, but evidently he was wrong.

"How do you know of Yakovlevitch?" he asked.

"He's on the agenda of the Rehabilitation Committee. That's where this little story got itself authorized. Ah—I see Grishin hadn't told you."

"He mentioned the name."

"But did he tell you that it was up before the Committee?"

"We didn't get around to the subject."

"No? Why do you think that is?"

Why indeed? Kirov tried to think back to that day at Grishin's *dacha*, remembering the other man's difficult, impenetrable mood. He talked about Yakovlevitch but didn't explain that the surgeon had figured in the famous quarrels by which the Committee was known. Why not? Because he thought I already knew? Kirov registered Radek's amusement—not that: there's got to be more. Because he thought I had fed Yakovlevitch's name to the Committee.

"Didn't you think that business went on while you were in Washington?" Radek's voice was taking a sinister tone from his efforts to be friendly.

"Tell me."

"That was when the Great Jewish Antibiotics Ring was being put together—oh no, not *your* version but the other one, handcrafted by Andropov himself. I helped Grishin put together the case against Yakovlevitch. Not that I had responsibility for it— that was Grishin's: it went with the glory and I was only a humble mechanic, if you must know. But it was obvious, even to me, that the Yakovlevitch case was bound to come up again for reconsideration. Given our new relations with Israel and the fact of the next round of arms-control negotiations with the Americans, the rehabilitation of a dead Jew has got to be the cheapest available method of demonstrating the sincerity of *glasnost*."

Kirov nodded as sagely as a drunk. Among the other things he had not expected was that Radek would get smart, but here he was delivering neat analyses you couldn't argue with. Kirov decided he deserved Radek as the price of ignoring him.

194

"Grishin is finished." Radek used the heel of his boot to draw circles in the snow and stared at the results. "He's too old, too tired, too — *implicated*. This Yakovlevitch business will finish him. A sacrifice has got to be made. Someone in the KGB has to assume the responsibility if the point is to be proved."

Where did you get that last bit of piety from? Kirov would have laughed but there was an earnestness in the other man that commanded a perverse respect. He had beaten Grishin. No wonder that the latter had been distracted. He knew the danger he faced once the Yakovlevitch case was reopened.

"You still haven't explained why you invited me here."

Radek looked up sharply. He put away philosophy and turned to business. "Isn't it obvious? Grishin is out. I want his job. I *deserve* his job." He was still shuffling emotions like a deck of cards — slyness, sincerity, sentiment, cynicism. He wants friendship and he hates me. Kirov thought back to the night when he had disturbed Special Investigations in their search of the files. They had not checked any belonging to Radek. He must have already delivered his files on Yakovlevitch to the Rehabilitation Committee.

Radek reached out and picked up a small branch that had fallen into the snow. A twig, sharp as a spine, pierced his thumb but he ignored it and a small flow of blood fell drop by drop onto the white snow. "Grishin is a relic, an old Stalinist. Did you know he cut his teeth working for Beria? Whatever happens, he has to go."

But not without a fight. There was the missing piece. Kirov couldn't imagine Grishin unaware that there was a move against him. It wasn't possible to suppose he had reacted passively while Radek conspired to destroy him. And yet Yakovlevitch was going to be rehabilitated. Because Grishin got the wrong target. He thought I betrayed him to the Committee. And Grishin did what?

He gave me the Great Jewish Antibiotics Ring.

"I want your support for my promotion," Radek said evenly. "I'm not trying to do you down, Petya. I could — but that's not what I want. As Chief I'd still need your help."

"Is that so?"

"I mean it."

"I know you do." Subtlety was in sufficiently short supply that Radek couldn't forgo it by losing him. Not that he'd shown too much of it lately. But then even Grishin had fallen for Radek's simplicity. Which raised the question: how did Radek intend to hold him to this new arrangement?

Radek was strapping his skis back on. He caught Kirov watching him and threw a winning smile in his direction as between pals playing the same game. Still confusing his cues. Doesn't know whether to recruit me or frighten me. Radek said: "I'm heading back." He was standing in his skis and fixing his pack.

"I'll be ready in a minute."

"Sorry, Petya, I can't wait." Radek took a last drink from the bottle of vodka and reached into his pocket for something else. His fingers fumbled and Kirov recognized the other man was drunk. Radek had found what he was looking for, but before showing it said: "You do understand that this has nothing to do with Lara, don't you?"

"If you say so."

"I don't think that sexual jealousy should come into business, do you?"

"Whatever you like."

Radek held out a clear plastic envelope close enough for Kirov to see.

Inside was Scherbatsky's Chinese watch.

"It has your fingerprints on it. We also have photographs of you coming out of Scherbatsky's place in Kavrov on two occasions. Scherbatsky was under arrest for corruption and you had no official business with him. You take my point? There are people who could make a case out of that."

"Then make one."

"You wouldn't like it."

"It gets worse?"

"Maybe," Radek answered thoughtfully. He replaced the envelope carefully inside his pocket. Then, with a sudden show of passion—because they were friends—he said: "But it doesn't have to. I don't want your skin, Petya! Just your loyalty when I'm Chief. Loyalty—it's not a lot to ask, is it?" He stood for a moment looking supplicant and doubtful, then turned and pushed away into the trees. Kirov heard the hush of his skis fading into the distance and was left alone in the clearing.

He made his way back toward the ski center, navigating by the unfamiliar paths. There was a crowd by the hire point and a

196

commotion; an ambulance was parked in full view and next to it a black police Volga; and standing by the car, part masked by the young skiers, two detectives in black overcoats and trilbys standing up to their ankles in snow. They were taking down names and addresses. No one knew why, but the rumor was that the body of a skier had been discovered in the woods.

Uncle Bog was waiting outside his apartment, hanging around the shadows and cracking his knuckles. He cornered Kirov before he could reach the door and said urgently: "What the hell's going on?"

"Tell me."

"Tell me? Grishin didn't show today! He's sick—yesterday he's well, but today he's sick!"

"People get sick."

"Balls! Sick people don't have their telephones cut and a car full of goons sitting outside their apartments. I know because I got worried and went there."

"Why? What worried you?"

"Don't play games with me, boss!" Bogdanov said impatiently. "When Grishin didn't show, the Hollywood Stars came swaggering around the place saying Grishin was finished; he was sick; he was going to retire. And Radek would be running the place. Bakradze called, asking for you. 'Are the *changes* going to affect your involvement in the antibiotics business? Isn't it time that the whole subject was left to MVD and the Public Prosecutor?' Then some guy from the Aquarium phoned: 'Will Colonel Kirov call Colonel Heltai?' No subject mentioned but I can guess. When I left, Radek's boys had taken off to the club and were planning on moving to the Zhiguli to get pissed with the secretaries." He added reproachfully: "And where were you? With Radek! What did he want?"

"Loyalty."

"Jesus," Bogdanov said softly. "Now there's a commodity in short supply. He should have talked to Viktor Gusev. Maybe Viktor would have sold him some."

The call came while Kirov was asleep. It broke into his dreams.

"Heltai—this is Ferenc Heltai."

Kirov had not heard that voice in years, yet it was the same;

197

and with the passage of those years he could still hear its boyish quality, its strange clarity. He must have mumbled his way into an acknowledgment since the caller continued: "Since I saw you the other day, I've been searching my memory. I was sure that it wasn't the first time. Your face rang a bell; I was certain . . . Did you . . . ?" Heltai gave a laugh, the way Kirov had heard it; the laughter of a man who comes from the sea bearing his mysterious cake.

"Aren't you related to General Nikolai Konstantinovitch Prylubin?" Heltai asked.

"A family friend."

"Ah—that was it." The problem was solved. Kirov guessed that Heltai had been searching for and failed to establish any blood connection. Heltai said: "I met the general once, many years ago—when I was younger and more inexperienced." Another tinkle of laughter. "It was in Riga. We were both on holiday. The general had a boy with him. Was that you?"

"Yes."

"Really? Small world. But I'm glad. It makes us almost friends—yes?"

"It was a long time ago. I'm surprised you remember."

"Oh, I remember a great deal. I learned a lot from the general. He was a very clever man. And you appear to have learned too—how to be a policeman."

"I try."

"And also the value of friends? Being a policeman is a lonely business and we need our friends. But I'm digressing—though not too much: the past helps to keep the present in focus, don't you think? Cooperation—my colleagues suggested to you that there might be a basis for cooperation, provided that we each stick to our respective problems and inform each other; and in particular that we don't trespass on the other's areas of activity."

"I remember."

"But have you learned? For example, I believe you have been looking for a man named Orlov, a pharmacist who used to work at the special clinic at Kuntsevo. Who told me? Not you, Pyotr Andreevitch—not you."

"He's involved in your business, this Orlov?"

"He's not involved in yours—of that I can assure you."

"That doesn't answer my question."

"Let's say he *was* involved in a matter of interest to me. It has nothing to do with the antibiotics black market."

"A matter of poison?" Kirov suggested. He wanted to disturb the other man's placidity, which kept him as unreal as the dreams from which the telephone call had snatched him.

"Stay away from Orlov!" Heltai responded with a chilling calm.

He sounded altogether real.

18

Minsk has fallen.

The train traveled northward during the night, repeating *Radek — Radek — Radek* as it rattled over the points. The passengers dozed or chatted or snacked from the paper sacks they had brought with them. *Radek — Radek — Radek.*

Kirov travelled inconspicuously with the ordinary passengers. One of them was an ornithologist interested in the capercaillie breeding program; another was an expert on forest management. Two guards in the frontier service were returning from furlough. They drank heavily and tried to interest their companions in a pea and thimble trick, taking ten rubles from the ornithologist, who became angry and silent until they offered him a drink and returned half his losses because they said they liked the look of his face. The rolling stock was dark green. The night was dark green as the train passed through swaths of forest. *Radek — Radek — Radek.*

Minsk has fallen. So said Uncle Kolya, explaining to him about his father. Kirov stared through the carriage window into the night which threw back the reflection of Uncle Kolya, in appearance like the ornithologist as the latter mumbled in his sleep. As he was sitting there, Kirov told himself, so his father had sat in the main room of their apartment in Bryanska Street, and outside the windows Minsk had fallen. The child was confined to the bedroom and fretted over his toys. His mother supplied his father with tea and vodka and fed him his meals, which now had the chance quality of deprivation. Betweentimes she wandered about the apartment and sometimes stared at her fur coat, which would shortly adorn the back of a colonel's wife in Berlin. Against her will the Germans would arrive and the apartment would refurnish itself in the poverty of war and become a different place altogether. His father sat and decided who he was to become.

In the streets the people clung to the walls like posters. Among them were the Nationalists, who were not supposed to be there since NKVD had been killing them in droves since 1936 but the older Kirov could feel them as a prickling of his skin. Logic said there were not enough Nationalists to fill a telephone booth, but soon they would fill the Opera House to hold their congress and decide upon the constitution of the Byelorussian Republic. Their former tormentor would share meals with them in the Hotel Europa and they would be uncles to his little boy.

But that was for the future. For the present Stalin had allowed the churches to reopen. He was an old seminarist and at this stage of the war he was gripped by a panic and, for all anyone knew, was on his knees in the Kremlin asking God to help him out of his problems in return for which Stalin would kill anyone that God wished. Stalin was well aware of the function of religion, to usher with its rites through the shadows of the changing world and prepare for the final transformation of death. And doubtless he too was looking for that still core of his being that resisted all change. What did he find that represented his integrity?

The older Kirov sat at his table and looked inside himself and found a policeman.

The train halted at Cherepovets. The passengers, mesmerized by sleep and travel, stirred and scrabbled after their luggage and bade each other farewell. Through the coach window Kirov watched the ornithologist embrace a huge bearded type in he-man clothes, remembering Vanya Yatsin and their last meeting at the Marriott in Washington, where the Americans misinterpreted the effusive, unconstrained Russian manner of greeting. The card-playing soldiers were on the platform too, weighing up the prettily elegant station buildings in their sage-green paintwork and cream trimmings, employing their soldier's eye for a comfortable billet and in the end deciding to squat on their packs until transport or orders arrived. Kirov descended last from the train, carrying his overnight bag.

Beyond the station, Cherepovets consisted of gray apartment blocks with shops at street level. A drab green truck with a canvas top was parked in a row of small cars; an official Chaika with an official chauffeur waited for a Moscow bigwig. The two frontier guards were slinging their packs into the truck. The driver of the Chaika watched Kirov as if he might be expecting him. Kirov avoided his gaze and walked away at a moderate pace until he could turn a corner.

He had spoken to Orlov once. The pharmacist had been difficult to reach; he spent much of his time up country in the Darvitsky Reserve. These days he was part pharmacist, part doctor, part vet, and wholly frightened. He did not want to talk on the telephone; he did not want to talk to Kirov. Kirov had to chide him, threaten him, woo him almost with offers of warmth and security. "You've been out in the cold too long, Grigori Dmitrievitch. Things have happened. There are people who want to help you. It's time to get these matters off your chest." He spun a tale of a new Party and a new KGB, the ones we always wanted; and Orlov bought the story because he needed to get rid of what he knew. Living in the Darvitsky Reserve had changed his perspective. Day by day he saw the beauty and simplicity of the landscape and wanted to harmonize with it. He needed some rite of absolution to free him of his past. Or so Kirov supposed.

The bar in Cherepovets was Orlov's idea. He had an amateur's conception of security and on the phone stipulated a series of checks and passwords that seemed to give him some comfort. Then, having decided that Kirov was a friend, he asked him to bring along some medicines he could not get in Cherepovets, and a ham: he hadn't eaten a ham since he left Moscow and had no friends to send him one.

They had a beer together. Orlov turned out to be small and almost bald, the remaining strands of his hair plastered over his scalp. His face was of a nibbling rabbity kind, sallow skinned with eyes like open oysters. He wore a heroic ensemble of blue quilted coat with a fur hood, a red checkered shirt, rough cord trousers and boots; his head nodded on top of this like an ill-fitting appendage. He was a nodding man. "You made it OK"—nod—"no trouble on the journey?"—nod—nod. Kirov liked him.

"You find it all right here?"

"Here? All right? Oh, sure. It's—different. It's how you imagine the country to be. I don't mean Cherepovets," Orlov was looking around the bar, which was like any other, "but out on the Reserve."

"You wanted a job on the Reserve?"

202

"Not *wanted*—but it's OK. Really."

"A change from the clinic at Kuntsevo?"

Orlov nodded but didn't answer. He proposed another drink.

"I've not had much to do with—your lot before."

"We come in all sizes."

"Of course, at Kuntsevo there was a lot of security."

"There would be."

"But they didn't—you know—socialize."

Kirov said he didn't suppose they did. It hadn't occurred to him that Orlov might be flattered by his interest. Interrogating him would be no pleasure; he was so transparent and fragile you would be frightened of breaking him. Kirov offered to pay for the drinks and suggested they move on. Orlov volunteered that he had a vehicle nearby; they could drive out to the Reserve where they could talk in peace. Outside in the street the official Chaika drove past. Heltai was in the back seat.

Kirov couldn't be sure it was Heltai. There was a face and it was gone, like the occasions that happen several times in a lifetime when our paths come across a famous actor in a hotel lobby, a station forecourt or a street where he waits for a taxi. There he is and now he's gone. His size and shape are wrong. We ought to be excited but aren't. Did we really see him? The car that perhaps contained Heltai disappeared. Orlov missed it; he was fiddling in his pocket for his car keys. And then the two men were walking down the street.

The vehicle was a four-wheel-drive truck. Orlov kept a raccoon dog chained in the back. The animal was fat and lazy; Orlov admitted he kept it as a pet. "I get lonely," he said, and Kirov could see that he did. They got into the cab. Orlov had unchained the raccoon dog and it lay on Kirov's lap and sniffled. They took the road out of Cherepovets toward the Reserve. The snow plows had recently cleared it, but the going was still bumpy. Kirov rocked with the bumps and stroked the raccoon dog's long brown fur and wondered about Heltai—had he really seen him?

They turned off the highway onto an unmade village road, struggling through glutinous mud between banks of frozen snow and a horizon of spruce trees. The village consisted of single-story wooden houses, prettily painted, with white gingerbread shutters, neat fences and birch trees growing in the gardens. Beyond the village the road got worse. It led by a frozen lake, which glimmered in the pale daylight. In the trees they heard the tonk-tonk of a capercaillie calling to its mate. The silence and loneliness of the snowbound landscape folded around them.

They spoke reluctantly as if disturbing the sleeping earth. Orlov had a bag of cold boiled potatoes and they snacked on these, speaking between mouthfuls, pausing to suck out the soft hearts and feed the skins to the dog, which chuckled and scrabbled after them. The air in the cab became warm.

"Just before you resigned, there was an investigation at Kuntsevo."

Nod—nod. Orlov reached over to slip a scrap of potato to the dog.

"A team of GRU investigators visited the clinic and interrogated all the personnel. The leader was called Heltai—yes?"

Nod—nod.

"I'm sorry to ask about it—" Kirov said without knowing why.

"It's OK, Pyotr Andreevitch."

"But I need to know. That's why I've come here."

"Sure—why not—it's OK. I don't care anymore. I used to, but now I don't. I miss Moscow a little maybe, some of the things you can't get here, but not much. Hey, did you bring the ham?"

"It's in my bag."

"Let's have a piece."

Kirov fought to retrieve his bag from the floor. The raccoon dog perked up at the smell of meat. Orlov passed a clasp knife and Kirov cut off a chunk which the three shared between them. Orlov chewed slowly, dreamily, and drove on.

"How did it go—the investigation?" Kirov resumed. He phrased the question sympathetically as if he were asking about the other man's sick mother.

Orlov smiled and said with mild enthusiasm: "You should have been there."

"I should?"

"Uh huh. The day Heltai arrived—all the clinic security staff, the guards, the KGB house chief and his men—all in a line like schoolboys—'yes sir, no sir' to this Heltai, and slipping into his office to tell tales. You should have been there."

"Tales—you said telling tales. What sort of tales?"

"This and that. Maybe you haven't been on the end of a security drive. Everything comes out. If it's only a petty crime it's safest to confess first and not wait for the questions."

"Except that Heltai wasn't looking for gossip. He had a purpose. What was it?"

"Who knows? Andropov was dead. That was enough cause for an investigation. We'd seen the same thing before when Brezhnev died. No one was too concerned. Andropov died from natural causes."

"Did he? Is that what Heltai thought?"

Orlov shrugged. He struggled with the truck as it slid on the compacted snow. "You couldn't tell what Heltai thought," he answered. That didn't help. He tried to expand, tried to help the stranger sitting next to him. "He was angry. Andropov was dead and you could feel the anger as though he was supposed to live forever." Nod—nod. "Yes, he was dead, so someone had to be guilty of something."

"Heltai treated it as if it were a murder inquiry?"

"Yes—no. It wasn't like that. It was—like the difference didn't matter. We were all guilty. Administration, security, doctors, pharmacists, nurses, cleaning staff—Heltai and his men went tearing into us. They split the departments up and interrogated us separately so that we couldn't compare stories. But afterwards we found out that they'd taken the same line with everybody: we were all personally responsible. If you were a doctor they accused you of a slip of the knife or a wrong diagnosis. If you were a theater sister, you'd run the place like a pigsty and allowed infection to creep in. Do you understand what I'm telling you?"

"And you?"

"Me? I kept a sloppy inventory; I used out-of-date drugs; I dealt on the black market. There was no truth to any of it, but who cared? We were all in the same boat. Do you see what I'm getting at? If Heltai was running a murder inquiry, where was the *theory?*"

Where indeed? Kirov turned away and watched the road. The raccoon dog looked up, licked its chops and nudged him with its muzzle for more food. There was no theory. Instead there was a fear, a sense of shock and of panic. Something had happened. Something had been learned. And then panic. Kirov stroked the dog behind its ears and looked distractedly out of the window at the frozen lake and the trees, thinking: Neville Lucas would understand. This was the Englishman's terrain, formless and treacherous, deep in drifts of fact and illusion. You could stick your hand out of the window and touch mystery; and it would feel like snow.

He tried some names out, looking for cues to fit Orlov's story into the competing versions of events. Viktor Gusev — Nadia Mazurova — William Craig — the jeweler Ostrowsky — the unknown Zagranichny who appeared masked and naked in a pornographic film. Orlov recognized none of them. He was naïvely puzzled at the idea that these people he never knew were somehow bound up with what had happened to him. He had never heard of the Great Jewish Antibiotics Ring and the name amused him — why *Jewish?* Was that what all of this was about — a black market in pharmaceutical drugs? Despite Heltai's questions, the thought hadn't occurred to him. He had assumed it to be something else.

"I thought — you know — *it's all happened before!*"

"Heltai said that? He told you this wasn't the first time?"

"No. It was — an impression. Despite all the questions, they didn't really know what had happened. But they were frightened, *that* was the point. As if something had gone on in the past and they were thinking: *is this the same?* And they didn't know, and it scared them. I couldn't put my finger on it. I thought: has Andropov been poisoned? Is that what they want to know?"

"They were asking you about poison?"

"About contaminated drugs. Other people they asked different things — to keep us guessing, maybe. I knew only my part and it came back to that: had Andropov been poisoned?"

Orlov let his explanation fall there. His manner was flat, strangely indifferent to it. He kept his eyes fixed on the road, which appeared to be going nowhere. The truck continued to rock and bump. The cab lulled the senses with warm air. The raccoon dog crooned as it was stroked.

Kirov focused on the dog. He asked a few questions about it and Orlov gave some story about raccoon dogs being native to eastern Asia and Japan and their being introduced to western Russia for their fur, which in the event proved useless. He talked about other things, about ham and capercaillie and had Moscow changed recently so you would notice, and in the same tone he continued: "I wondered — after it was all over and I came here — I wondered was there anything to it all? Had GRU and Heltai been chasing their tails? After all there hadn't been any murder."

"Hadn't there?"

"Of course not. We were all alive. What better proof could you get?"

"What did you do?"

"What could I do? I couldn't ask Heltai, could I? I talked to

206

people—wrote to people. I wanted to find other cases of deaths by contaminated drugs. I wasn't thinking about murder, about poisoning. But maybe there was something to learn, something we were doing wrong. I'm a pharmacist and I wanted to know whether there was a problem connected with the drugs."

Kirov looked up from the dog.

"And was there?"

"There were deaths," Orlov said. "Not many—perhaps half a dozen in the two years before Andropov died. Not much of a problem, eh?"

"No."

"No—" thoughtfully. "That's what I thought."

"But?"

"It was the names. They were all officials—nobody really important, Party chiefs from out in the republics, a couple of economists from the ministries. But the point was: *they shouldn't have been.* The deaths weren't random enough. There was a pattern. I have the names and I found out who they were and what the connection was."

"What was the connection?" Kirov asked.

"They were all Andropov's men."

A freshly fallen tree lay across the road, its top buried in the bank cast up by the snow plows. Orlov nudged the truck against it, got out of the cab and inspected it. The raccoon dog leapt off Kirov's lap and followed its master.

"We can't go on and we can't go around it," Orlov said equably.

"What do we do?"

"Wait. There are tracks on the other side of the tree. Someone has been here already. My guess is they've gone for chains. Give it an hour and they'll be back to shift it. Stretch your legs."

Kirov stepped out into the snow. He scanned the empty road in both directions and looked up for the position of the low sun. From the trees there was silence. The snow lay in still waves on the lake.

"Smoke? Drink?" Orlov was already getting them. In the open he seemed to grow to fill out his clothes. He was no longer sparse and scrawny.

"Andropov . . ." Kirov began.

"I don't want to talk about Andropov," said Orlov evenly. He laughed and shook his head. "Bugger Andropov—bugger all of them. Once I used to care. Now I don't. They're not important. They don't affect any of this." He swung out an arm to take in the earth and the sky. He spoke with a dignity that made Kirov want to laugh with a deep and bitter laughter: the other man was too simple to be alive. Orlov said: "Who cares if they kill each other?"

I care, Kirov told himself. If not about them, then about something else: about the truth, with all its elusiveness.

Orlov started chatting about other things: the animals, the trees, the Reserve and its conservation program. "I didn't give a damn about it until I came here—but now . . ." He was full of homespun philosophy about nature, as trite and tedious as you could get, and Kirov still liked him for it. They continued like this for a quarter of an hour while the cold day dozed and the treetops nodded and the raccoon dog pursued its interests skipping about in the snow before settling in the driver's seat of the truck. At the end of that time a second vehicle appeared a way off on the road behind them. "Company!" said Orlov, who was pleased.

They waited. The other truck struggled on the road, approaching slowly, visible across a spur of the lake. They could hear the thrum of its engine, taut and brutal in the still air. A kilometer away the newcomers stopped. A man dismounted from the cab and stood, peering in their direction. He got back into the vehicle and it came on again, slow and laboring. In the trees the tonk-tonk of a capercaillie rose and fell.

"What are they up to?" Orlov asked. The dog smelled nervousness and jumped down from the cab. The strangers had halted again, three hundred meters away. Their truck stood dark and compact between white snowbanks. Orlov shot a glance in Kirov's direction. It spoke innocence and betrayal. The strangers leapt out of their truck and began firing.

They had automatic weapons. That first burst took the raccoon dog and flung it up in the air. The same volley hit Orlov in the arm, spun him round and left him alive and in shock to collapse against the truck. Kirov flung himself onto the bank to the thud-thud of bullets burying into the snow. He scrabbled over the frozen crest and tumbled into the shadows of the trees.

He heard them—four voices, tense but relaxed, like hunters on a spree. And Heltai with his high clear voice giving orders which he called suggestions—"Wouldn't it be a good idea to fan out to look for him?" and a single shot, which put an end to Orlov.

Kirov crouched in the cover of some spruce saplings. Behind

him the trees went on forever into darkness. Ahead the sun lay low over the lake and cast long bars of light through the margin of the forest and the snowbank glittered. Heltai was calling indulgently as if to a naughty child.

"Pyotr Andreevitch! *Petya!* I know you can hear me. Let's not be silly now. Come on out and we'll talk things over."

Figures were climbing over the snowbank. Kirov retreated, covering his tracks by moving over the sheltered spots where the snow was thin and his prints were lost in the leaf litter. Heltai continued to give casual instructions to his team then resumed: "Petya, what we have here is a misunderstanding. I'm sure that we can reestablish cooperation if only we talk things over. Otherwise there's likely to be—an unfortunate accident."

The accident he had in mind came as a burst of gunshots. Their direction was random. They were trying to draw his fire. Heltai wasn't to know that Kirov didn't carry a gun.

He retreated further. The sun disappeared and the road was now hidden. He heard footfalls off to his left and hunched in the cover of the trees. Heltai was still calling. Now more faintly. "Petya! Petya!" His mother calling. Uncle Kolya calling. "Petya!" The cold biting into him as long as he was motionless. More shots, sticks breaking, the sound of Heltai's men, driving him back to avoid encirclement. As long as Heltai controlled the road he was trapped. The trees would envelop him forever. If he lost the road he was a dead man. "Petya!"

Tree by tree he fell back until the cover ran out. Behind him a gully cut through the forest. The slope fell away sharply in rocks and a few stunted bushes to a frozen stream, and on the farther side a dark wall of trees. To his left the shape of a man broke from this side of the gully and the figure scouted the slopes. If Kirov tried to cross to the other side he would come under the hunter's field of fire. Back along his trail the noise of the others grew closer. He hugged the cover. Closer, closer. A man emerging suddenly not two meters away from him—looking away from him—looking ahead—looking at him—*now!*

Kirov dived for the other man's legs. The man buckled at the knees, his gun went off and he was flying backwards. Kirov leapt onto him, his hands grappling for the other's throat. Wrists around his own. A strong man, holding him off by strength, mouth open and yelling murder and other people hearing and running but Kirov didn't dare to look: will his strength never run out? Butt him!

The man stares back, wide-eyed, bloody-nosed and determined — you bastard! — butt him again, and again until he goes slack and his gun can be grabbed and smashed onto his head. And he lies back. Behind the anger and the blood he now looks pitiful.

Kirov gripped the gun and dropped over the edge of the gully, slithering on his side down the slope through the rocks and scrub. Bullets pinged off the rocks. Farther up, from the crest of the gully, one of the hunters was firing. Kirov skidded into the shelter of a boulder, rolled over and loosed half a clip at his pursuer. He sprang to his feet again and ran flat- and slither-footed across the bed of the stream across the shivering crackling ice. More shots and the thwack of bullets into the scrub on the far side. He turned and emptied the magazine into the figure behind him, ditched the gun and threw his body onto the far slope, scratching and clambering through the stone debris and the dried berry bushes. No shots. He felt like a spider on a wall. No shots — and the tension of their absence was almost as killing as the bullets. His hand yanked at a root and dragged him upwards so that he reached the top of the gully. He pulled himself to his feet and his limbs ached and were torn with the effort. Slowly — but whether it was slowly he couldn't tell since time was meaningless. And stretch, crucified against the trees.

He didn't hear the shot. He was flung bodily into the trunk of a tree. His left arm was limp. His body was bruised to depths that didn't exist. He was on his back, lying face up to see the sky through the treetops. Frozen in shock. Motionless and cold.

I'm dying, he thought. And it felt peaceful.

19

They found him sitting with his back to a tree. He felt their warm breath on his face as they stooped to examine him and heard their impossibly distant voices. They carried him, head and foot, his face looking upward at the sky breaking through the pine tops, and laid him on the snow while they opened their vehicle. They placed him inside and covered him with a blanket, but even so he was cold and it didn't hurt; no pain, just a frozen peacefulness.

Somewhere he lost track of time and consciousness. He was in a room, the wooden interior of an *izba,* with a stove burning and the air warm and still; lying in a bed, buried under bedclothes. People came and went: a man and a woman; the woman bringing him bowls of soup and holding him gently upright to feed him; the man standing framed by the door, a watching presence like the eye of God. They didn't speak to him.

Then Uncle Bog turned up.

"I thought you were dead for sure," he said in a jolly manner. "You didn't come back and I thought, that's the end! But I said to myself: why should Radek have it all his own way? Why should he be king of the castle? So I came looking for you, and here I am!"

"It wasn't Radek," Kirov answered, and fell asleep.

When he woke up Bogdanov was still there, talking to the man and woman. He noticed the movement and came over to perch on the end of Kirov's bed.

"Concussion, shock and exposure damned near killed you," he explained cheerfully. "Fortunately no damage done. Cuts and grazes and your arm is bruised and may hurt for a while." He had no idea how Kirov had been injured. There was no bullet wound.

Perhaps a branch had hit him, or he had fallen in dodging the shots. Bogdanov was unconcerned as long as the outcome was OK. But Kirov had seen his own death – or an incomplete version of it, like the bodies sometimes fished out of the Moskva with the evidence rotted from them. Murder, suicide, accident? Bogdanov was still speaking and Kirov gathered that the occupants of the *izba* had found him when they went to remove the fallen tree from the road. "Friends of Orlov. It gave them a shock. Bodies all over the place and you freezing to death and unconscious. They figured you for another friend of Orlov – don't ask me why – and took you in. I think they're cut up about Orlov being dead, he was a nice fellow by all accounts. Still that's probably what saved you from Radek. If they hadn't showed he might have finished you off."

"It wasn't Radek."

"No? Whatever you say. Don't you have enough enemies? Tell me about it another time." Bogdanov patted his arm and told him to take it easy. "Oh, and here's some reading matter, selections from the American desk's dossier on the Lee Foundation as requested from Tomsky. I've read it. They make pharmaceuticals. It's no big deal."

Night came and went in restlessness. The wooden house creaked. The wind rattled the shutters and a fall of snow, driven by a gale, crackled across the roof. An oil lamp burned smokily in one corner of the bedroom and threw shadows across the wall.

Kirov was feeling better the following morning. He woke early and his eyes fell upon the papers that Uncle Bog had left by the bedside, the file on the American company. He picked them up and perused them. They were much as Bogdanov had described. The file was thin because the KGB had a minimal involvement in the secrets of foreign pharmaceutical production: drugs were not strategic, and technically they were often harder to copy than electronics. Someone had once explained this difficulty to him. It wasn't enough to have the recipe, you also had to know how to cook. That was why William Craig had been of interest: he knew how to cook. Most of the file consisted of financial data and market rumors that could have been gleaned from the press. None of it was secret. Some of it was even funny. The Lee Foundation was heavily enmeshed in lawsuits against distributors of bootleg versions of its products. They had their origin in Taiwan. Like Scherbatsky's Chinese watch.

Bogdanov appeared at breakfast.

"How goes it this morning, boss?"

"OK."

"Fit to talk? I don't want to rush you, but there are a lot of bad men after your blood and it doesn't do to stay anywhere too long."

"I'm OK." Kirov struggled to a sitting position. His injured arm was still weak and throbbed when he used it. Bogdanov took a seat and waited patiently.

"Why did you think Radek tried to kill me?" Kirov asked at last. He heard the tremor in his voice. He told himself it would soon be all right.

"I've got bad news for you."

"What?"

"Scherbatsky is dead. They found his body out on the trail at Serebryanny Bor the day that you went skiing with Radek. Bullet in the back of the neck, straight out of the department textbooks. He was wearing his watch—you know the watch. There are no prizes for guessing whose prints are on it. How did they fix that?"

"Scherbatsky offered it to me as a gift. I must have touched it." Kirov thought back to the occasion he had visited Scherbatsky. The pleading and the nervousness. Radek must have promised a deal to tie Kirov to the housing fraud.

Bogdanov sighed and asked to sit down. "However he did it, Radek has you tied to Scherbatsky on the housing fraud, and now he has a case for murder. It's a neat frame—who would have believed he could pull it off? And he wouldn't have if you hadn't got your eyes fixed on this *Jewish* thing instead of watching your back."

"Forget Radek."

"Radek wants you dead!"

Kirov shook his head. "He just wants my loyalty while he takes over from Grishin. He wouldn't go through all the complications of his scheme if he intended to have me killed."

"Uh huh—then who was it?"

"Heltai."

"Heltai?" Bogdanov hesitated short of surprise; then: "I told you he was a Naughty Boy. But it makes some sort of sense."

"You've discovered something?"

"Something—but God knows what it means. I did what you suggested, checked the manifest of the flight that took Yakovlevitch to America. There was an extra crew member on board, a flight attendant. The name is bogus but the description fits Heltai. I say he was on the plane and that he made sure our friend the

Academician wasn't going to survive the journey. Poisoned him, I guess: something to simulate a heart attack. First Yakovlevitch, then Orlov and an attempt to kill you. GRU are taking care of anyone who could throw light on what happened when Andropov died. What are they hiding? Murder?"

"No—or at least not Andropov's murder."

"Orlov told you that?"

"Orlov didn't know."

"Then what was so special about him?"

"He was too curious," Kirov answered. Like me, he thought. Orlov was innocent enough to want to know the truth. He looked at Bogdanov who didn't give a damn about the truth and who was hanging on to this business only because they were in so far that the safest course might be to see it through. That and maybe loyalty. Uncle Bog should throw in his lot with Radek, or make an arrangement with Heltai.

"What was he curious about?"

"Medical poisonings. He made some inquiries and found another half-dozen cases where patients had died of contaminated antibiotics or something similar. The victims were all Andropov supporters."

"Terrific," Bogdanov murmured. "I love it. But doesn't that mean that someone was trying to kill Andropov?"

"It was meant to."

"Then who was responsible if it wasn't Chernenko and the rest of the old Brezhnev crowd?"

"Andropov himself."

He was tired. His head was spinning with images, speculations, possibilities, his sense of time adrift; the present like flotsam washed up by the tide of the past onto an empty beach. If only things would stay still!

Bogdanov could be heard in the next room; now a low murmur, now a burst of laughter as he entertained the man of the house with a dirty story. Between times he patrolled the outside of the *izba* and scanned the expanse of snow with binoculars or sat in a corner of the room fretting over a pack of cigarettes.

"So where are we, boss?" he asked with a fake smile, as he offered some bread and a bowl of soup. "Sure, I remember. Andropov is bumping off his own supporters. Tell me that again, how does it go? You don't want the bread?" He took it himself, gnawed at the sour rye, smiled between bites and let his old, dead eyes look anywhere but at Kirov. Waiting for an answer he talked about his wife: he couldn't call her; she'd be going crazy. He riffled through his knuckles like a deck of cards. "The bit about Andropov—tell me again how it goes. How are you feeling? OK to go on? No? OK, let me tell you one. About Zagranichny, you remember Zagranichny, the guy who flashes his dick at the girls in Viktor Gusev's *dacha*. You were right about him. He is from out of town.

"I searched the hotel records and came up with some names and dates: F. T. Zagranichny, from Sverdlovsk, stayed at the Kosmos for four days in April—another one: Yu. A. Zagranichny, from Kubishev, spent a week at the Mezhdunarodnaya in June—one more: D. S. Zagranichny, from Volgograd, three days at the National in July."

"The same man?"

"You can bet on it. The forenames may have changed, but the handwriting is the same. Also the hotel security logged two incidents during Zagranichny's stay at the Kosmos and the Mezhdunarodnaya. A couple of the local girls who work the bars were badly beaten up. No names, but it's just our man's style, right? This guy is incredible!"

Zagranichny. The name had dull echoes. Kirov could hear them and tried to register them. Another day maybe, and he would feel better and understand. He asked: "Why didn't he change his surname?"

"Good question." Bogdanov chewed it over. "Why does he beat up girls in the same hotels he's staying at? How is it that the hotel security doesn't nail him on the evidence of the two girls? Answer: Zagranichny thinks he can walk on water! He can change his identity papers every time he comes to town and even though the surname's the same no one can touch him; he can get the MVD boys at the hotels to shut their traps and forget what they've heard; he can get our hotshot Viktor Gusev to lay on girls for him whenever he wants them; in short he has *friends* and he doesn't care. Boss, this Zagranichny is totally crazy, but he is very important to some very important people."

"He's playing games with us."

"Damn right he is! Why 'Zagranichny'? Why does he stick to the same name?"

They stood outside the cottage. Bogdanov studied animal tracks in the snow. "What do you think they are, boss? When are we going back to Moscow?" In his city coat and overshoes he was out of place. "All these trees give me the creeps. My guts are killing me. Every time I go outside for a leak, I seize up. When do we go home?"

"Where are the others?" The cottage was empty, the man and woman gone.

"I did them a favor and sent them away. I have a set of papers for you and some tickets for Moscow. One of these days Heltai is going to be back to check that he's finished the business. He'll have some very bad-tempered people with him and we're in no condition to face them. Boss, we've got to get out of this place."

Kirov agreed. Apart from a dull ache in one arm he had recovered. There was nothing to keep him here except the tug of the empty snow-covered spaces, the appeal of that unencumbered clarity.

Bogdanov took a cigarette and flung the empty pack on the ground. He lit the cigarette philosophically and made a few remarks about the traveling; they would go separately; meet in Moscow. Then: "You were going to tell me about Andropov, what he was doing having his own people killed."

"Was I?"

"You may as well let me know the worst." Bogdanov stared at the bitter stub of his cigarette and threw it away.

Kirov stared at the snow and a bird flying across the horizon, black against white. "Andropov was a sick man," he said. "That was the root of his problem. He knew that he hadn't long to live, and he had only reached the top after a close run-in against Chernenko. He still had enemies."

"So?"

"So he wanted to clear the old Brezhnev crowd out of the Politburo and vacate the ground for his successor — who wasn't going to be Chernenko. He was in a hurry. He couldn't wait for the old men to die since he was likely to die first. He had to provoke a crisis, one that would give him the leverage to get rid of Chernenko and his supporters. His answer was the Great Jewish Antibiotics Ring."

"He invented it?"

Kirov shrugged. Not "invented," he thought on reflection. Although from a strictly logical point of view it was not true, it seemed to him that no one had invented the Great Jewish Antibiotics Ring. Certainly no one had ever fully defined its shape; indeed even now its shape was unfinished, still changing. It grew by accretion, by metamorphosis, in the way that archetypes have an appeal that forces successive generations to take them and shape them to new purposes. Perhaps.

"I don't think that Andropov invented the whole thing," he said. His eyes were still fixed on the bird, which was now hovering low in the sky. "My guess is that there was already an idea floating around in the KGB. Fabricate a plot to implicate the Jews in the antibiotics shortage and solve two problems at once. It was — a conspiracy looking for conspirators." He turned to Bogdanov to see if he understood. The words maybe, but not the meaning. He carried on with the explanation. "Andropov learned what our people were doing and recognized that Academician Yakovlevitch and his supposed ring of corrupt Jewish doctors and peddlers of black-market drugs could as easily be made to look like a gang of medical poisoners. And by creating victims for the murderers among some of his own minor supporters, Andropov could make the object of the plot appear to be his own death. The obvious beneficiary would have been Chernenko, so, when Andropov exposed the plot he could calculate on the Politburo swinging behind him to expel Chernenko and all his followers.

"Except that Andropov died too soon."

"He died too soon," Kirov conceded.

"You think Chernenko learned about it? Jesus, it must have scared him stiff!"

"That's why the GRU investigation was set up. Andropov had been head of the KGB and the KGB had fabricated the plot. GRU were the only people Chernenko could rely on to find out exactly what had happened and then bury the answer. The answer still frightens them because it reminds them of the past, the way that Stalin used to do things. They thought they'd put that behind them and they could sleep safely in their beds knowing that the worst that would ever face them was retirement and a pension. But if Andropov had pulled off his plan, he could have used it as the basis for a purge and there would be no telling how far it could go."

There was a pause while Bogdanov took in the explanation. Kirov watched him from the corner of his eye, still distracted by the

217

distant bird. The older man looked slightly ridiculous, shabby and solemn like a pauper at a funeral. In the end he asked: "And that's it, boss? That's what this is all about?"

"It's how it started," Kirov answered, and even then he could never be sure. Conspiracies weren't meant to be understood. All that could be grasped were versions of the truth.

"What do we do? Tell someone?"

"Tell who? The KGB doesn't want to know: it wants to forget its own part."

"Then maybe we should forget too. That's all that Heltai is asking, isn't it?"

"I don't know. I don't think so." The bird dropped suddenly from the sky, falling onto some small rodent struggling through the snow, making its clinical kill. Kirov admired the simplicity.

Bogdanov was saying: "What is 'I don't think so' supposed to mean? If Heltai's interest is in suppressing the Andropov story so as not to frighten the children, then we go along with him. We put an end to the Great Jewish Antibiotics Ring."

Kirov turned and examined the other man slowly then proposed they return inside. He added in answer to the question: "I don't think it's that easy. I think that the Ring has changed: it's become something else and I don't know what." He smiled and gave Bogdanov an encouraging pat on the back as they went through the door, meaning that everything was going to be all right. Watching the bird he had experienced something of its clarity. In these days of convalescence his exhausted mind had had a vision of the underlying pattern of events. He knew he could take apart the fabric of the Great Jewish Antibiotics Ring. He would go back to basics: the circumstances of Viktor Gusev's death. He would talk to Bakradze.

The Gorbachev Version

Only people who like people should join the police.

YEVTUSHENKO

20

They returned to Moscow. Kirov traveled on new papers with the general passengers, his identity masked by the stubble of a mustache. Bogdanov made his own journey public; he called the Center from Cherepovets and asked for a car to meet him off the train. Kirov spotted Tumanov in his leather jacket waiting at the barrier. Bogdanov hailed him, made a fuss long enough to attract attention, and then left with his deputy. Two men broke out of the crowd in the hall and followed them.

Kirov waited on the platform for the next arrival and walked out in the new influx of passengers. He took a regular taxi across town to the Paveletski station, bought a ticket there for a local destination and, just before the departure time, quit the line and picked up a lift in a Zhiguli that was operating as a fly cab. He had the cab drop him on Volgogradski Prospekt. There he took the metro back through the center to Pushkinskaya and collected another fly cab outside the *Izvestia* complex. The driver took him all the way to Babushkino.

Kirov halted the taxi short of the *dacha* and paid off the driver. Since the last time he had been there the snow had come to stay. It was compacted in the lane; it creaked underfoot as he walked toward the house, carrying the small case with which Bogdanov had provided him. It carried tracks. In the ordinary way Uncle Kolya had few visitors. Tatiana Yurievna went up and down a couple of times a day between the village and the *dacha*. Dainty even in her felt boots, she left only small footprints. From one week to another no car would call on Uncle Kolya except the doctor in her blue Zhiguli. But now there were tire marks from a large sedan and two sets of men's prints.

The trail left by Tatiana Yurievna as she went up and down to the village was sharp and crisp. It crossed the marks left by the car and its occupants. Fine snow had drifted across the tire tracks though today there was no wind. Yesterday? The day before? Kirov stirred the footprints with his toe and took the path up to the cottage.

Smoke was issuing from the stovepipe. The window to Uncle Kolya's bedroom was shuttered. Kirov gave the door a light tap and heard the footfall of the housekeeper as she moved her bulk on her impossibly small feet. The door opened and Tatiana Yurievna stood in the space.

Kirov put a finger to his lips, took her by the arm and led her toward the woodshed. She offered no resistance. She was amused and offended at the same time: giggly and nervous. "Pyotr Andreevitch! What are you doing? Let go! Don't be silly!" He tipped the door open and gently pushed her inside into the darkness and the smell of shavings and cut logs. She was still squeaking.

"You've had visitors," he said.

"The doctor."

"Not the doctor. Two men—one short, one tall. They were here yesterday."

"Oh, them! They were nobody, a couple of people with papers for Nikolai Konstantinovitch to sign."

"Did you know them? Have they been here before?"

"No."

"Were you expecting them?"

"Not particularly. They phoned yesterday morning."

"Listen carefully—" Kirov began; then, seeing the tension, he framed his question affectionately, as if asking after grandchildren, "When they were inside the house, was there any time that either of them was left alone?"

"No."

"Think about it."

"No—really—I'm certain. They weren't in the house above five minutes. I took them straight in to see your uncle Kolya; he signed the papers and they left right away."

"Good, good." Kirov blessed her with a hug and a flirtatious kiss on the cheek. She put her head on his shoulder and called him her good boy. He nodded and, speaking into her hair which lay against his lips, said lightly: "And did they ask questions, these two men, questions?"

"Not to me."

"To Uncle Kolya?"

"Sign here — that was all. They didn't even tell the poor man what he was signing, and Nikolai Konstantinovitch wasn't interested. I asked them. 'Papers, grandmother,' they said. That was all. Cheeky devils."

She pulled away to look at him and frowned at his thin smile. "Don't worry," he told her. He put his arm around her waist as he opened the door of the shed and let in the daylight. "I may be staying two or three days. Can you make up a bed for me? And laundry — my clothes are dirty."

"Oh, Pyotr Andreevitch!" she laughed; then with surprise said: "You've grown a mustache!"

"Do you like it?"

"Well . . . you're grown up, and if you think it suits you then it suits you. But why do you want to stay here?"

"Uncle Kolya isn't well. I worry."

Tatiana Yurievna eyed him suspiciously, but didn't voice her disbelief. Years of living with the general had taught her that some things were best not inquired into. After a flicker of hesitation she was asking questions about the amount of washing needed and how did she expect her to feed him when he turned up without notice? They were back at the cottage. Kirov asked her to wait outside and be quiet. He opened the door and went inside.

The room displayed Tatiana Yurievna's sense of order, everything clean, folded, put away. Her interrupted needlework lay on the table. Kirov moved silently, running fingers along the underside of surfaces, checking the light fittings, entering the small kitchen, the bathroom and the housekeeper's tiny bedroom. From the invalid's room a voice said: "Old Woman! Who's that with you?"

Kirov tapped the door and answered: "It's me, Nikolai Konstantinovitch."

"Why so secretive?" The general was sitting in semidarkness on an old chair. He was wrapped in rugs. Age and grayness hung on his face like rugs. By his chair the small table was stacked with medications.

"I'm being careful," Kirov answered.

223

The old man took the statement at face value. His eyes clouded and his lips sucked at the thought.

"You've had visitors," Kirov suggested.

"Something to do with my pension," the general answered shortly, and, before the younger man could ask, elaborated: "Papers to sign."

"Tatiana Yurievna wasn't sure."

"The Old Woman is a moron," was the curt response. "I wasn't going to sign something without knowing what it was. It might have been a confession, eh?" Uncle Kolya smiled briefly; a precise smile you could lift and put in your pocket. "So, these days you need to be careful, huh? That doesn't sound good." The sight of the other man hesitating at the doorway made him cross. "Come on in. Take a seat and let me see you. You've grown a mustache. Don't like it. Makes you look like Him—you-know-who." The recollection dislodged a thought. "Careful, you say? I used to be careful, and so was your father. Much good it did him."

Kirov sat down as invited. The old man watched him, half in pity, half in annoyance.

"Who's after you?" he asked.

Kirov let his eyes wander in the dimness. He detected a slight smell of camphor. Hearing the question a second time, for a moment it seemed impossible to answer; as if his enemies were a nameless and bodiless legion.

"Radek," he volunteered. "He's the—"

"I know who Radek is. I'm not senile. What's he up to?"

"He wants to replace Grishin. He's used the Rehabilitation Committee to reopen an old case and maneuver Grishin out."

The old man found that appealing. "That's rich! And you, what does this Radek have on you?"

"A circumstantial case that I was involved in the Moscow housing fraud."

Uncle Kolya wrinkled his nose: "Everyone's involved in the Moscow housing fraud. There isn't any other way of getting a roof over your head. What else does he have?"

"A murder," Kirov admitted.

He expected a pause or some indication of surprise, but the old man merely commented sorrowfully: "A frame-up—and you walked into it?" Then: "What does he want? Don't tell me—loyalty!" Now it was Kirov's turn to be surprised into silence.

The odor of camphor seemed stronger. Tatiana Yurievna busied herself noisily. Uncle Kolya's lungs crepitated like hailstones.

"How did you know?" Kirov asked. He looked up from studying the accidental hanging together of objects in the room, the still-life quality of bottles on the round surface of a table and the contrast of glass and wood. The general's face was set, burying him in the past, in old plots and dead men. Conspiracies never die, as he had once confirmed.

"It's what they always want. It's what Stalin wanted, but he could never get enough of it. You could grovel at his feet but even then he could never be sure. That's why he destroyed those closest to him — Yagoda, Yezhov — Beria, if he'd lived long enough." The old eyes had a charitable look to them. "Your friend Radek has been taking a leaf out of the Old Man's book."

"Because he betrayed Grishin?"

"No."

"Then what?"

"Because he's trying to bind you to him by your crimes. That's their version of loyalty." He groaned at some discomfort and edged himself on his chair. Seeing Kirov's interest he began to explain. "How do you think Stalin kept Yagoda loyal? Answer: he had the goods on him because Yagoda had murdered S. M. Kirov and betrayed the Leningrad Party. For the same reason he had a hold on Yezhov, who was Yagoda's accomplice."

"And Beria?"

The old man laughed. "Beria was easy meat! He was a treacherous little shit. During the civil war, when things were looking a bit rocky for the Reds and Beria was working in Armenia, he played fast and loose with the local Nationalists, the Dashnaks. Stalin knew all about it, and he didn't care — his own past wouldn't stand too much scrutiny — except that the story gave him a lever. Beria! Hah!" After that moment of enjoyment the general fell silent. His eyes, which had been alight with the recollection, grew dim. He said tetchily: "Who cares? It's all in the past. You have to figure out a way of turning the tables on this character Radek."

"You didn't mention my father."

"Give me a cigarette."

Kirov held out a pack of Belomors. The old man took one, spun it in his fingers as if he suspected its authenticity and snapped for a light. Kirov proffered his lighter and the old man took his wrist and held the hand and lighter in front of him, peering at the younger man across the flame. "What does your father's case have to do with anything?"

"Was he — loyal?"

"To whom? To what?" There were real tears in the old man's eyes, the kind you get when crying about the past. "Don't you think I've asked the same question? Your father betrayed Yagoda to Yezhov and Yezhov to Beria. And in 1941, when the Germans took Minsk, he betrayed *everybody.*"

"Then why did Beria accept him back?"

"Because he recognized that your father was a policeman. Do you understand? There was never anything personal in your father's treachery. He spied and betrayed people because that's what he was trained to do. The Germans knew it, and Beria knew it too. And in Beria's case, when he found your father in jail in 1945, he had the advantage that here was a man who was *totally* compromised, vulnerable, naked. He looked at your father and saw a man who would be completely loyal."

"He had my father shot," Kirov pointed out.

"Nobody is ever loyal enough," Uncle Kolya answered.

Uncle Kolya dozed. Tatiana Yurievna came into the room. For a second she stared affectionately at the sleeping figure, then busied herself and asked Kirov to sort out his washing. The old man woke grunting out of the dreams he claimed he didn't have.

"You still here?" he said, fixing his visitor with a one-eyed stare while he wiped the sleep from the other eye. "What now? More questions about your father? I'd have thought you had more than enough on your plate without digging into history."

"Is it history? You once told me that old conspiracies never die."

"Did I? Bloody rubbish — I must have been drunk. Here, make me comfortable."

The general had slid down the chair. Kirov lifted him into a sitting position. The old man had lost weight. The bulk of his years of splendor was gone and he had become an insubstantial thing.

"Do you remember a man called Ferenc Heltai?" Kirov asked.

"No."

"We met him on holiday in Riga. I was a boy, maybe fourteen years old. Heltai was a Hungarian. He" — Kirov hesitated — "came from the sea carrying a cake in a box."

"I remember a creepy Hungarian, was that him? I don't recall the cake."

"It's the sort of thing that children remember."

"Possibly. He was in AVH as I remember. He worked out of the headquarters in Andrassy Street; he was heavily involved in the purges. Now I can see him, I remember that he came running to us because in fifty-six the Fascists were in power for a time and it was unhealthy to be a policeman. He didn't go back when we liberated Hungary. What does he do these days?"

"He's still alive and poisoning people for a living."

The old man was indifferent. "Someone has to do it. What does it matter?"

"Tell me about the Doctors' Plot."

The general did not want to talk about the Doctors' Plot. It was history, all dead and buried; a relic of Stalin's time, the last of his magician's concoctions, all poison and illusion. Kirov reminded him that it was at that time that his father had been shot. Didn't that mean something? Or was it all coincidence? Never mind whether it signified now, Uncle Kolya had a duty to tell him.

"It mightn't have happened if Zhdanov hadn't died." With that lapidary statement the old man began. He halted at the end of this first sentence to catch his breath, but it seemed to Kirov that he was offering an opportunity to withdraw; then, when Kirov refused it, he continued: "He was an old crony of Stalin, one of the few he didn't kill. Or maybe Stalin did arrange his death—when you think what happened later, maybe he did. I don't know, so don't expect a complete explanation.

"Stalin's doctor was a Jew, name of Academician V. N. Vinogradov. There were a lot of Jewish doctors in those days. Stalin didn't like Jews."

"He was Zhdanov's doctor too?"

"Who?"

"Yakovlevitch—sorry, Vinogradov."

"Search me. Probably. It didn't matter: it was always possible to make a connection between Vinogradov and Zhdanov even when none existed. You're missing the point."

"Go on."

"Go on! Go on! Yes—OK. Next—what? So Stalin decided that someone had poisoned Zhdanov. The Jews, naturally—who else?—creeping around the Kremlin with bottles of God knows what in their bags; poison their mothers, they would. Stalin called Beria in. Arrest them! If they killed Zhdanov, *who would they poison next?*"

"Stalin?"

"That was the theory. Beria had to set up the facts to fit it. And it scared him. You see, he knew his Stalin. Back in 1934 or whenever, Stalin had asked Yagoda to bump off S. M. Kirov, and Yagoda like a good boy had done the deed. Then, come 1938, Stalin used the same murder as an excuse for purging NKVD and getting rid of Yagoda. So Beria could see what was coming. He could arrest Vinogradov and a bunch of other Jewish doctors, but that would only be the beginning. If Vinogradov was planning to poison Stalin, who was he working for? Since the plot was a pure fabrication, the answer could be *anybody!* The answer could be Beria himself. That was what frightened him."

"What did he do about it?"

"Nothing—nothing directly. Once Stalin had invented the plot, Beria was trapped. He couldn't refuse to arrest Vinogradov otherwise he would be accused of complicity. Yet once he had arrested him, Vinogradov could be forced to implicate anybody that Stalin had a grudge against—and you've got to remember: *Beria was Jewish!* Beria had one slim hope. If Stalin really was moving against him, the Old Man had to have in mind a successor. So, if Beria could outguess Stalin and identify his own successor, he could drag him into the plot as a potential accused and Stalin could do nothing about it without revealing his own hand. At the least it would gain time."

"And that's what he did?"

"Yes," said Uncle Kolya and he lapsed into silence. He stamped on the floor to call Tatiana Yurievna, and when the housekeeper arrived he pointed mutely at the bottles and she tut-tutted and dosed him with the stuff. Kirov sat passively through the little scene. He accepted Tatiana Yurievna's complaint that he was tiring the general, and her reproach that it was foolishness to keep talking about the past, as she gathered they were doing, when these days things were so much better. Satisfied with this she left the two men alone. When she had gone Kirov resumed.

"Who was Beria's successor to be?" he asked quietly.

"Your father," came the answer as Kirov had expected. And his memories of the photograph of his father and Beria at Sochi, and

228

of Uncle Lavrenti bringing him presents were all explained. "And now you know," said the general. "The rest doesn't matter. Stalin died not long after Vinogradov's arrest, and Beria moved immediately to wind down the Doctors' Plot and release the prisoners."

"Except my father."

"Except your father," the old man admitted. "He was different. In Beria's eyes all the holds he had on your father fell away to nothing. Instead of being causes for loyalty, they became grounds for resentment. So he had your father shot."

"And replaced."

"If you like."

"By you?"

"What are you getting at?"

"You were my father's deputy and his successor, weren't you?"

"I —" the general spluttered but Kirov would not allow him to speak.

"What hold did Beria have over you? How did he propose to keep you loyal?" He was searching for some sign of anger within himself, but could find nothing except, perhaps, a small measure of pity. The general was staring, eyes open and tearful and a trickle of spittle dribbling down his cheek. He rolled uncertainly to one side and reached for a bottle of vodka that he put roughly to his mouth and then held out as an offering. Uncle Kolya bearing gifts. Uncle Kolya standing at the apartment door with his smile and his swagger and his presents for the beautiful widow and the unfortunate traitor's child.

Kirov stood up and told his host that he had to leave. He had to go into the city on some business and would be back later that night.

"I shot your father," the old man replied pathetically. "I pulled the trigger. That was Beria's hold on my loyalty." Kirov had opened the door and was speaking to Tatiana Yurievna about his laundry and the next meal and where to make up his bed. The general could see only his back and interpret its rigidity. He shouted: "Your father was glad it was me! He knew I was loyal to him! That I loved him! I love you too, Pyotr Andreevitch!"

21

Bogdanov arrived in the late afternoon, alone and in an unfamiliar car. From the window Kirov watched him struggle along the snowbound path. His black angular figure appeared thin and frail. He's getting old, Kirov told himself.

Bogdanov explained the car. "I got it from the Sluzhba pool." He greeted Tatiana Yurievna coyly like a girl met at a dance and made a flattering reference to her cooking, which he had sampled on some past occasion. Kirov guessed he had something to be pleased about.

"You shook off a tail to get here?"

"A couple of goons were watching my place," Bogdanov replied off-handedly, "and Heltai has the Center staked out, but nothing to get excited about. How is Uncle Kolya? Can I see him, pay my respects?"

"He's all right. He's sleeping. What about Radek?"

"Your guess is right. His interest is in replacing Grishin and he doesn't know about the other thing. At the moment he's busy counting his winnings. Until they find you or you show up and kiss his arse, I'm reporting to Radek's deputy, Petruk."

"Petruk was Scherbatsky's case officer."

"Was he now? Then this must be his reward for keeping quiet about where the bodies are buried. It makes things a bit more tricky. Radek may want you alive and well as a loyal soldier, but Petruk is likely to be less enthusiastic. It means you're on your own. You don't really have a case against Heltai, and, if you try to take what you do have up to the Director, Petruk will kill you before you get through the door: with Scherbatsky's blood on his

230

hands, he has to. Radek can go hang himself if he tries to stop him."

"What about your position?" Kirov wasn't used to Bogdanov when he was full of life. His deputy carried his personal raincloud, and anything else wasn't normal, particularly this brittle good humor.

"Me?" the other man answered with a hint of self-mockery. "I'm safe until they settle accounts with you. What would they want with a toe-rag? They figure that any move against me would only scare you off. They still hope you'll come in with your hands up." He dropped the pretense. "If you want my advice, you should accept their offer. Radek has you stitched up for the housing fraud and Scherbatsky's death. There are times when you've got to recognize that you're on the losing side; and Radek's backside can't be any less tasty than Grishin's. And with Radek's support you can maybe do a deal with Heltai: kiss and make up and promise to forget."

"It's going to be OK," Kirov told him. "Trust me."

"The last time someone said that, I got pregnant."

They waited in darkness. The office workers spilled into Pushkin Street from the Public Prosecutor's Office, carrying their briefcases and shopping bags. Bakradze wasn't in the crowd. He had his little Zhiguli, so clean and neat you could spot it anywhere, and behind the wheel the lawyer looked as dapper as always. Bogdanov, hunched and shabby, watched him like a visitor from another country.

A couple of vehicles apart, the two cars slipped into the evening traffic. Bogdanov fiddled with the radio, searching for something to fit his mood, but the bad-tempered station wasn't playing. Kirov hummed the tune to "Moscow Nights," the way they played it in the hard-currency bars to remind the foreigners that they were taking part in a mystery. Neither man speculated where Bakradze was heading. Follow the traffic. Let it play out. Let the thread unravel through the darkening streets. Register the fact dumbly when the other car drove into Sadovo-Sukharevskaya, where the MVD Fraud Squad ran its operations away from the other CID base in Petrovka.

The lawyer parked outside the old mansion. He showed his ID to the militia guard and went inside. Five minutes later he reappeared with Antipov and the two of them talked on the pavement for a while. When they were finished the detective went back into the building and Bakradze returned to his car and set off again. More roads seen through the enveloping evening. Trucks with the name of the enterprise stenciled on the side; official limousines with the curtains drawn; Volga sedans used as taxis; convoys of Army wagons with soldiers hanging over the tailboards whistling at the girls. Bakradze was heading for Lyublino.

The lawyer began to weave among the streets between the factories and the apartment blocks. For a moment Bogdanov thought that he had been spotted, but quickly realized that Bakradze was simply lost: the industrial sections of the city were bandit country to him. Then he seemed to find his bearings and this time moved directly, cruising past the façade of a large public hall. He stopped a couple of streets farther on, parked and removed the wiper blades from his vehicle.

Kirov ordered Bogdanov to halt the car. Bakradze was on the opposite pavement retracing his route toward the public hall where a queue trailed out of the entrance and into the street.

"Do you know this place?" Bogdanov asked.

"Komsomol use it," Kirov said. He had noted the kids in the queue and guessed at a concert, though that didn't explain why Bakradze was there. The lawyer had some sort of deal at the door; he went to the head of the line to the catcalls of the crowd.

"It's a Pamyat meeting." Bogdanov pointed out a sign, a handmade poster. He looked about and spotted a posse of militia loitering by a Black Raven in the next street. "There's your proof — and there." The MVD men in official plain clothes stood out in the line. "Do they look like conservationists to you?"

They filed in with the crowd and found a place standing at the back of the hall with the latecomers and the MVD snatch squad who felt they could handle trouble better if they kept in a bunch and on their feet. The hall was laid out with benches and stacker chairs and packed all the way to the dais. Bakradze was at the front, showing no interest in the audience. On the dais someone was fixing a screen and a slide projector and testing the microphone.

After ten minutes the hall doors closed and the audience settled in a detectable mood of expectation. The sound system gave a quick blast of Tchaikovsky. Three men trooped onto the stage to vigorous applause from the crowd including the MVD watchers. The chairman, a small character in a cardigan and a hairy suit, took the microphone and delivered a quick eulogy of the guest speaker. He praised the speaker's contribution to conservation, to culture, to the maintenance of Russia's traditions, and, not least, to Pamyat. He invited the audience to give a warm welcome to the poet and sage, Feodor Nikitich Valentinov.

Kirov had seen Valentinov once before—at Yelena Akhmerova's party, where the poet had mixed easily with the film crowd but had insisted on speaking Russian. His appearance had not changed. He still wore soft leather boots and a belted peasant blouse. He still glowered at the world through an Old Believer beard. Above all, his face expressed the same inspired ferocity. As he spoke now, his piping voice had a seductive quality. He was a speaker who made love to his audience.

He began slowly, speaking without notes, reciting with nostalgia and satisfaction Pamyat's history of successes. He caressed his listeners with the warm assurance that they were the ones who had accomplished these achievements, and that not he but *Russia* through all its countless generations was grateful. Through them the ancient churches of Russia were saved; through them the vandalism of Moscow was prevented; through them a halt had been called to the hideous Victory monument, which would otherwise have violated the beauty of the Poklonnaya hills. Yes, Russia was grateful. Applaud! Applaud *yourselves!*

But what was Russia? he asked; and, not too seriously, he praised the democracy and prosperity which Marxism-Leninism had brought to the land. He adopted a tone that caused a *frisson* of seditious delight to trouble those who understood. Russia—ah Russia!—he told them, letting his tongue fill the word with emotion, Russia was more than a society, an economy, a political territory bounded by frontiers. Russia was the first repository of the transcendent values of humanity, the successor to Rome and Byzantium, the home of spiritual truth, of an Orthodoxy that went beyond any narrow church creed or mere doctrine. Love, loyalty, fidelity to friends, discipline, honest obedience, more, more, list the qualities that we treasure, for look around and here in Russia they are all visible, because Russia in every real sense *is* humanity.
But!

Valentinov trembled at that fateful *But,* and his face, which had been a vision of triumph, turned to sadness—not an ordinary sadness but one of deep compassion and wisdom that chilled and silenced his audience with a sense that they were sharing in that pain though they did not understand its cause, nor did their sharing help him because he had taken the burden of suffering from them. So they could remain only mute and awestricken as the speaker changed from Valentinov to something ineffable, something truth drenched, truth imbued, truthful beyond the merest contemplation of doubt. And they knew that he was going to explain to them why that paradise which we — yes, you, me, we all — deserve is so clearly not in existence though we are aware of our own truth, virtue and beauty.

What is it that frustrates their expression? Can it be that there is — let us say it and not hide it — a counter-truth, a sham of virtue, a beauty which consists of meretricious ornament? Yes! And their names are Cosmopolitanism and Liberalism. Cosmopolitanism is a mongrel culture, a mishmash of borrowings without history or integrity, driven forward by the forces of capitalism, freemasonry and Zionism. Its ideology is Liberalism, an attempt to seduce humanity from its roots with nigger art, a cacophony of sound masquerading as music, and the relentless pursuit of novelty. Whereas true humanity longs for stability leavened by a process of organic growth tapped to our wellspring of being, humanity's counterfeits, the henchmen of Liberalism, are in the thrall of change.

And so on. Valentinov drenched his audience in words, elevated them, angered them, soothed them. With his hands he conjured them out of their seats. By a wave he conducted their applause. With a sideways gesture, palms down, he dismissed them to their places.

Kirov heard the MVD man next to him say: "He's right. It's the truth."

"What is?" asked his colleague.

"It's all the fault of the Jews."

In the crescendo of clapping and hooting that terminated Valentinov's speech Kirov saw Bakradze slip away. He ordered Bogdanov urgently to bring the car to the rear of the hall then looked back to the stage where the air was dense with sweat and smoke and Valentinov was standing with his arms open to receive his supporters and his face bathed in glory. By Kirov's side the MVD men were becoming twitchy and nervously alert for any sign of trouble. Kirov brushed past them into the aisle between the rows of seating, which was now filling with people stamping and whistling their approval. Where was Bakradze?

234

He fought his way forward. The crowd was good-tempered but resisted any attempt by those at the rear to get close to their hero. At the front the marshals were holding people back from the dais. Across ten rows Kirov caught a glimpse of Bakradze in a press of Pamyat officials and journalists making his way toward an exit door. Kirov shouldered his way harder, ignoring the objections, and followed.

When he reached the exit, Bakradze was already gone. Kirov pushed against the opening bar and found himself in a short corridor with a storeroom on one side and an office on the other. He checked them and found both empty. He returned to the corridor and tested the external door at the far end. It yielded and he was outside in the cold night air.

The door gave onto an alleyway cluttered by trash cans and broken crates. The alley opened into a loading bay and then onto a patch of snow-covered ground criss-crossed by footpaths. A couple of cars were parked on the empty lot, otherwise at first sight there was no one. He looked around for any sign of Bogdanov but saw none.

His eyes were still unadjusted to the darkness and the sudden cold after the overheated hall smacked his face. He stood shivering with his back to a wall and listened while his eyes allowed for the change. Between the dull sounds of traffic he heard footsteps cracking the frozen earth. Darkness stood above the pale glimmer of snow. No moon. The clouds, reflecting the lights of the city, were darkly yellow and sick with snow. A heavy night and sharp as a guillotine blade, it rustled and creaked with cold and somewhere voices murmured.

Standing on one of the paths a pair of lovers talked. The man faced the woman, holding her a body's width away, his two hands clamped on her arms. Kirov could see them now. The man was talking, shaking the woman to punctuate his points. She was resisting and unresisting: her limp body registering her dissent. Not lovers. From the left a set of bright headlamps threw the scene suddenly into relief. A car came spinning over the ice onto the empty lot. Bakradze turned from the woman and his face was caught frozen in the light.

"Hold him!" Kirov yelled as Bogdanov threw open the door of the car. He set off at a run. The lawyer had released the woman and was hesitating over which direction to take. The woman had no uncertainties. She had turned and was running frantically toward a cluster of buildings at the farther edge of the open ground. Kirov chased her.

She wore flat shoes and fear lent her speed as she sprinted across the snow. Kirov followed, trying to close the fifty-meter gap between them. She stuck to the paths. Kirov struck an angle across the unbroken snow but stumbled into a tangle of potholes and junk and she gained on him. Then she reached a wall.

Who are you? Her head was wrapped in a scarf, but her shape and movements were familiar. For a second she faced him and he glimpsed small features and a pale skin. He shouted: *"Nadia!"* But the face was not hers; it lacked the intensity, the mystery. Instead a fierce little face examined him briefly, and then the woman clambered over the wall with Kirov only meters away. And she was gone.

He followed, but it cost him time. His quarry had found some convenient grip on the brickwork that he missed in the darkness. When he finally found himself on the other side in a small yard, it was empty. The ground was cleared of snow and there were no discernible footprints other than at the base of the wall. Kirov searched the confines of the yard but the woman was gone. He found a gate and went through it, finding himself on a familiar street and next to him a building he knew. It was the women's hostel where Nadia Mazurova lived. Yet the woman had not been Nadia but a stranger, or rather someone whose ill-formed image haunted a corner of his memory. Where had he seen her before? He tried to grasp the recollection but it evaded him like the woman herself and he was left with his anger and bewilderment.

He returned to the disused lot to look for Bogdanov.

22

The car was still parked with the engine running and the headlights blazing. Bakradze was spreadeagled over the front with a cut to the head and Bogdanov's gun jammed in the small of his back. Seeing Kirov approach, the lawyer offered a plaintive: "Pyotr Andreevitch!" Kirov told him to shut up and get into the car. He took over the driving, leaving the other two men in the rear seat.

They left Lyublino and headed north. Bakradze passed the long silence in nursing his head; Bogdanov put his hands through cat's cradle exercises and jabbed his hostage in the guts if he showed signs of recovering his aplomb.

"Stop him, can't you?" Bakradze complained.

"Promise to be good," said Bogdanov.

"Whatever you like."

"Say it! 'I want to be good.' I want to hear the words."

"Jesus! OK—OK—I will be good. All right? Damn it, you've hurt me! Pyotr Andreevitch, what's this about? What have I done?"

There was no answer.

"The Pamyat meeting? Is that it? The KGB are investigating Pamyat?" Bakradze tried a laugh to establish if they were still friends. "This is all a mistake! I was *supposed* to be there! The Department is conducting its own investigation of that gang of Fascists. You don't think I was there on my own account, do you?"

"I was watching you," said Bogdanov. "Every time Valentinov opened his mouth you were eating his words."

"It has nothing to do with Pamyat," Kirov answered.

237

"He's telling you to shut your face," Bogdanov explained helpfully.

They drove a while longer. Bakradze grew restless. He tried another approach. "Does Radek know about this? He's running your show while Grishin is sick, isn't he?" This amused Bogdanov.

"I think he's trying to frighten us, boss. Going to tell the grownups about us, are you? Get our wrists slapped? Nasty KGB is carrying on like in the Bad Old Days, using violence and all the other things we don't do anymore. I'm upset."

"I just wanted to know."

"Ah! We're only making small talk? The weather—shall we talk about the weather, hnnh?" Bogdanov took hold of Bakradze's wrist and gave it an affectionate squeeze.

They crossed the Ring Road, still heading north. Bakradze asked where they were going.

"Electric Corner," answered Bogdanov.

"Why there? There's nothing except a rubbish dump."

"And what else are you? You think your shiny suit gives you a bit of class?" Bogdanov had let slip one of his obscure hatreds.

Kirov intervened soothingly: "It's somewhere quiet where we can talk."

"Talk? What's to talk about? I don't know what you want."

"Then keep quiet!" Bogdanov snapped, and pushed his fist into the other man's abdomen again.

By Electric Corner a glow of flames broke the dark horizon. Bonfires were dotted over the broad expanse of the dump. The *bomzhi* who inhabited the place and the nearby woods between police raids had built them. Kirov swung the car off the highway and onto the approach road, then followed the frozen tracks made by the garbage trucks through a silent avenue of cardboard shanties and fires encircled by empty-eyed tramps. He pulled up in a broad, beaten turning spot and switched off the engine and the lights. The car and its occupants rested silently in the middle of a ring of fires from which the tramps had now disappeared. Kirov turned to his unwilling passenger. It was time to begin.

"I'm—disappointed with you."

"Agree with the nice man," Bogdanov contributed. He straightened the lapels of Bakradze's topcoat and smoothed it down as if sending a child to school. He beamed and said kindly: "Let's not piss about, eh? You know the score. He's the nice one with the questions and I'm the one with the bad temper and the nasty

238

habits—got that? Now answer the questions and we'll get along fine." To Kirov he said: "Fire away, boss. I think our friend understands us."

"I simply want to know the truth," Kirov said with a hint of apology for the manners of his companion. "No stories. Just the truth."

"No stories," Bogdanov interpreted. "Remember that."

"I want to know about Viktor Gusev."

"About Viktor," said Bogdanov.

"About Viktor," said Kirov and he let Bogdanov repeat the words again, knowing that by denying Bakradze an opportunity to speak he would force him to.

"Well, cat got your tongue?" Bogdanov asked. "I think he's shy, boss. Well, he's got a lot to be shy about, hasn't he—haven't you, huh? Don't worry, we don't kiss and tell, I say we don't kiss and tell. Go on—trust us."

Bakradze looked to Bogdanov then to Kirov. The look told Kirov that he had been right in his speculation, and he felt the relief that went with drawing back that first veil.

"What do you want to know?"said Bakradze.

"Why was Viktor killed?"

There are as many ways to interrogate as there are human types and human circumstances. This is not true, but the KGB psychologists earned their bread by telling cadets that it was so. Then they met old Chestyakov who told them that people gave information because of brutality, omniscience, affection and cooperation, and also for money but since the students had no money they must consider the alternatives. At bottom interrogation was a deal: information in exchange for the cessation of pain, for sympathy, for the photographs and negatives of the embarrassing occasion we don't talk about—even for love. But in every case the first question establishes the currency of the transaction.

"Why was Viktor killed?" Kirov repeated, meaning that he knew the answer already and that it was not fundamentally important. After all, Viktor's trading had made him into a mere commodity to be bought, sold and disposed of without particular regret. No one could get too excited over the death of Viktor Gusev. Someone had done the world a favor.

"It was an accident," Bakradze answered.

"No—not an accident," Kirov said firmly but quietly.

"I mean it wasn't supposed to happen that way—not *that* way."

"Viktor was expecting you that morning, wasn't he?" Kirov had stood at the window of Viktor's apartment overlooking the street where the MVD circus was gathering. Viktor had drawn back the curtains and seen what awaited him and done nothing to hide the evidence that would incriminate him.

"We called him the night before."

"We? You and Antipov?" Bogdanov interjected. Bakradze nodded, which only annoyed his questioner. "Telling him what? That he was going to be arrested? That he had run out of protection? Why should Viktor wait around for that to happen?"

"Because that was the deal, wasn't it?" Kirov suggested. "And Viktor knew all about deals."

Bakradze cried out: "It was your fault!" Just as quickly he apologized. "You wouldn't leave the Great Jewish Antibiotics Ring alone. Week in, week out you wanted a result—a name. We kept feeding you pimps and pushers and it was never enough. You wanted the total explanation, the Big Man."

There was a tone of admiration in the lawyer's voice, a tribute to Kirov's relentlessness in pursuit of the investigation. Yet Kirov did not remember the facts that way. The Great Jewish Antibiotics Ring had been dumped on him by Grishin like a burden of sin, by its nature insoluble. Why *Jewish?* Evidently Bakradze had seen it differently; but, then, the lawyer had had to live with the fear and uncertainty.

For the moment Kirov changed the subject from Viktor's death. The other man was keyed to answer charges relating to the latter, and out of relief at avoiding that subject would answer questions on another without reflection.

"You were providing Viktor's operation with protection."

"Me and Antipov—Antipov mostly."

"Of course: Antipov had the soldiers out on the street harassing Viktor's people if they weren't paid. And you, I suppose you sidetracked the KGB investigation."

"I told Viktor which way we were being forced to move."

"You told him when it was necessary to make a sacrifice, to give up one of his dealers."

"Yes."

"I understand," Kirov said consolingly. "Cigarette? Drink? Uncle Bog has a bottle somewhere. I'm sorry about all this—really."

"It wasn't as if there was anything wrong in what we were doing," Bakradze pleaded.

"Here's your drink." Bogdanov shoved the bottle into the other man's hand.

"We were dealing in antibiotics not opium, for God's sake! People who needed them and couldn't get them through the usual channels — we helped them out. There's nothing so bad about that, is there?"

"That's an interesting point. I can see your argument. Come on, have that drink."

Bakradze took a pull on the bottle. He wiped his mouth and then said carefully: "There's a way out, yes?"

"Maybe," Kirov offered. He glanced out of the window at the fires burning in the darkness and the skeletal shapes of the tramps creeping back through the smoke. "I'm not seriously interested in this end of the case," he volunteered. "There are other aspects — maybe — if you could help."

"Well . . ."

"Bugger his help!" said Bogdanov. "No deals!"

"Pyotr Andreevitch . . . ?"

"Uncle Bog is more excited about this than I am. Remind me about your meetings with Viktor, the ones you used to hold at the Kosmos. Viktor used to drag along his little jeweler, Ostrowsky."

"I don't know what you're talking about."

"Liar!" Bogdanov shouted furiously. "Kick this shithead out of the car, boss. We know all we need to know. We don't need him."

"Calm down." Kirov addressed Bakradze: "All of this doesn't help. I've spoken to Ostrowsky. He used to meet Viktor at the Park of Economic Achievement and trade dollars for diamonds. Viktor was with his friends. Two Georgians, says Ostrowsky. One of them was you, wasn't he? Do you want me to confront you with Ostrowsky so that he can make an identification? He'd do that. Viktor's drugs killed his little girl. His loyalty to the Ring is all used up."

"All right, all right!" Bakradze agreed wearily. "Viktor and I used to have lunch at the Kosmos. We'd talk things over — the investigation — things."

"Why was Viktor buying diamonds?"

"Honest to God I don't know."

"Not for you?"

"*Please,* Pyotr Andreevitch — what use were diamonds to me?"

"You were paid in certificate rubles."

"Yes. Me, Antipov, Ostrowsky—we got certificate rubles and dollars. Ostrowsky was saving for his daughter's future—that's what Viktor said."

"And Antipov?"

"He's a sick man. Bad heart, cancer maybe. He worries about his wife's future."

"It sounds like Viktor was running a charity," Bogdanov commented laconically.

It was too much for the other man. Despite being intimidated he rejoined sharply: "What do you expect? Do you think these things aren't done by real people? Pyotr Andreevitch, you understand!"

"Let's go for a walk."

They stepped out of the car onto the frozen ground. The chill was taken from the air by the fires lit by the *bomzhi*. Seeing the two men the tramps backed away except for those who were sleeping at the edge of the flames. Kirov held his hands out for warmth. Bakradze fiddled with his fly and then urinated into the hot ashes.

Kirov stared into the flames, conjuring up pictures, breathing in the woodsmoke from the crates and debris that the tramps were burning. "I haven't been to a bonfire in years."

"No? No, me neither," Bakradze answered regretfully. "My grandparents used to have a place . . . bonfires on the ice in winter. Shit, how do we get into these things?" he asked. Why am I not somewhere a thousand kilometers away and as many years? But you could never tell how you got where you were. Change slipped a knife between your ribs and you felt only the pain. He glanced over his shoulder at the car, where Bogdanov sat hunched like a ghost behind the misted windows.

"I thought we could talk better out here," Kirov said with a show of understanding.

"Thanks."

"Uncle Bog gets too—excitable."

"He should retire. He's out of the Ark."

Kirov turned and studied the fugitive image behind the glass. He caught Bakradze's suggestion that they were now allies against the old man.

"I have to work with him."

"I know what you mean. These old fellows get dumped on you."

"That's how it is. Have another drink and we'll finish the business. A few more questions and we can wrap up. It's no big deal."

Kirov held out the bottle. An old woman who lay near their feet dozing in the debris stirred and turned over. Her seamed face looked up vacantly and she began to hitch up the hem of her ragged skirts to expose herself.

"A drink," she murmured hoarsely. Kirov passed her the bottle. "Go to sleep, grandma," he said softly and returned to Bakradze. The smoke was beginning to sting his eyes and he proposed they move.

They walked a way into the shadows, blind from the effects of the fire. Some of the tramps moved with them, pausing with them to stand in a haunted circle.

"It wasn't supposed to be like this," Bakradze said, still puzzled. "Viktor was like a friend. Antipov and I were just doing a few favors. How did it all turn into this *Jewish* thing?"

"It isn't Jewish," Kirov corrected him mildly.

"No? Don't you believe it. Just because you don't see them doesn't mean they aren't involved."

"Perhaps," Kirov assented. "Who was the second man, the other Georgian who used to meet with Viktor?"

"I don't know his name — that's the truth."

"What did you call him?"

"Sergei — Mikhail — Georgi — Dmitri — take your pick. He was Viktor's contact, not mine, and Viktor had a thing about names: he used to change them all the time, a joke, I don't know."

"How did you meet him, this Sergei?"

"At a party. Viktor knew a lot of artistic types — writers, actors, painters. They did something for him. Ordinarily he was a joker, a real storyteller, you should have heard him joking with all his women. But put him in front of a writer and he'd shut up and listen."

"It was at a writer's party?"

"An actress — Yelena Akhmerova, have you heard of her? She has an apartment at the Visotny Dom. Viktor used to go to her parties with his special girlfriend, Nadia Mazurova. I think he had a sideline in dope and kept that crowd supplied, but I can't be sure. He introduced me to Sergei — I don't know what name he was going under at that time."

"Sergei was Viktor's supplier?"

"How did you know that?"

Kirov threw in a winning smile, part of his mask of total knowledge. "The antibiotics came from Tbilisi, and Sergei is a Georgian. It fits."

"Tbilisi? Now you know more than me. I thought the stuff came from Bulgaria—the labels on the packages say Bulgaria."

"That's just a cover for the operation. Have you heard of Pharmprodsoyuz Number One?"

"No."

Kirov looked at the lawyer pityingly, increasing Bakradze's sense of discomfort.

"It doesn't matter," he continued charitably. "The Bulgarian plant was built to an American technology. We built a duplicate in Tbilisi."

"I'm sorry. I can't help you."

"It's OK. But you can see that I know the whole story. I just want to confirm points of detail."

They strolled a way farther. The vast span of the garbage dump offered a barren and broken landscape, spectrally lit by the fires and sweet with decay.

"So you used to meet with Viktor and Sergei. Lunch at the Kosmos."

"And sometimes at the Mezhdunarodnaya," Bakradze amplified with a lawyer's exactitude.

"*And* the Mezhdunarodnaya—a bite and a drink in the German Bierkeller, very nice. Why? What was the purpose of the meetings?"

"Viktor and Sergei talked over the state of the market. Not just the antibiotics."

"No?"

"Viktor had a dozen rackets, I don't think that the Jewish thing was even the biggest. Sometimes I got the feeling he ran the operation as a favor to someone."

"So why were you invited?"

Bakradze shrugged his shoulders and kicked at a piece of rubbish. "I was there to keep everybody honest when the money and the diamonds changed hands. And maybe Viktor wanted to impress Sergei."

"Impress him?"

"With his contacts—his 'family,' that's what Viktor called us. Does that surprise you?"

Kirov remembered Nadia Mazurova trying to explain the ways of Viktor's circle—the gifts, the parties, the girls. There was something desperate in Viktor's generosity.

"That was the way Viktor was," said Bakradze, becoming sentimental for a moment. "He spent money like water for the sake of his friends. If you were a writer he'd give you the shirt off his back. 'Real Communism,' he called it. I don't think he kept a fraction of what he was making from his deals."

"I don't suppose he did," Kirov agreed. He paused at the edge of darkness where the glow from the fires ran out. Beyond their vision they could hear the dim, scurrying life of the dump: groans, laughter, abuse, the barking of a dog. He suggested they walk back, and when Bakradze slipped on some tricky patch of ground he held the lawyer up and asked carefully if he was all right.

"But there was a price for Viktor's friendship, wasn't there?" he continued as if he were merely talking aloud. "For example, you had to take care of Zagranichny. That must have been difficult."

"How the hell did you ever learn about that bastard?" Bakradze said vehemently.

"Bastard — yes, I suppose that's what he is. Staying in the best hotels and beating up the girls, leaving you and Antipov to provide him with new papers and clear up the mess he left behind. Paying off the girls he injured and squaring the hotel security to forget all about these incidents. He's pretty special, this Zagranichny."

"I wouldn't know. I don't know who he is or what he has to do with Viktor's business."

"But you met him."

"A couple of times. Other times we'd get a call from Viktor in a panic, telling us that Zagranichny had been up to his tricks again. Antipov was in a cold sweat every time he heard that Zagranichny was in town."

"He was different — he wasn't 'family.' "

"Viktor hated him."

"Hating people? That doesn't sound like Viktor."

"It was the violence. Viktor was always good to his girls; they couldn't do enough for him. 'Why can't all men be like Viktor?' They used to say that all the time; it was a sort of joke between them, don't ask me to explain it. I don't know why we weren't all like Viktor; I don't claim to understand him. Take the art and the writing — Viktor knew nothing about them, but he couldn't get enough. He took up reading: books, books, he was always asking whether you knew any good books. I think he tried his hand at painting too."

"I see," Kirov said studiously.

"Anyway, that's why he hated Zagranichny."

"Viktor knew he was beating up girls."

"It wasn't just the hotels; he attacked a girl at Viktor's *dacha* too. Viktor was in tears about it. We were having a meal at the Aragvi when he told us the story."

"Us?"

"Antipov was there. He went crazy. Viktor, what the hell do you think you're doing? Don't attract attention! But Viktor wouldn't listen because of the girl."

"Which one?"

"He wouldn't say. He just cried. I think that's what turned Antipov against him."

Kirov asked a few more questions about the girl but Bakradze had no more information. "Did Viktor provide you with women?"

"Please, Pyotr Andreevitch, is this relevant?" Bakradze answered with a sudden stuffiness as though an improper question had been put to the court.

"I'm trying to identify a girl with a mole—here, on her shoulder." Kirov pointed as he remembered from the film of Zagranichny and his victim. Viktor had been watching. He had stood behind the one-way glass and let the camera roll and the tears had streamed down his face, then and again at the Aragvi in front of the prim young lawyer and Antipov who was jaded and annoyed by other people's emotions. Bakradze understood none of this. He was applying a handkerchief to the cut on his forehead.

"Zagranichny," Kirov remarked casually. "What game was Viktor playing?"

"I don't understand you."

"Yes you do. Think about it. Zagranichny was a game, a play on words. What does the word mean—*Zagranichny?*"

Bakradze laughed. It was his most unrestrained gesture so far. "You're crazy!"

Kirov lit a cigarette and let the lighted match spin off into the darkness. "If you like," he said equably. But he had upset his companion who kept repeating *Zagranichny, Zagranichny* and finally pronounced: "I think you must be wrong." Bakradze reassembled himself behind this certainty. His air now was curiously offended: Kirov had broken a rule that said you shouldn't tell lawyers anything really appalling; their delicacy wouldn't stand it.

Kirov returned to the matter of Viktor's death. "One last subject," he apologized, "and we can call it a night. Everybody goes home and no harm done."

His companion was fidgety. He stared at the stars, the fires, the thick coils of smoke from burning tires adding to the magic of the night.

"I'll help you," Kirov volunteered.

Viktor had become disposable, hadn't he? The investigation into the Ring demanded a sacrifice to appease KGB — not of some token small fry, but of someone who could be the Total Explanation. And Viktor, so thoroughly implicated that he would inevitably be caught sooner or later, Viktor, who was losing his sense of proportion because of Zagranichny's inconvenient habits so that he embarrassed the police and the customers at the Aragvi restaurant by bursting into tears, had outlived his usefulness.

"And I imagine that Sergei approved since Sergei was concerned to protect his precious Zagranichny and Viktor's behavior in that direction threatened to be compromising."

So what had they done? Kirov asked. After all, Viktor was not without power. He had protected himself by buying a large packet of diamonds from Ostrowsky and it was anybody's guess what he had done with them. And he had filmed and recorded Zagranichny's violent escapade at his *dacha*; and even if Viktor himself didn't know Zagranichny's real identity, he could be fairly certain that KGB would thank him for the information.

"You must have offered Viktor a deal," he concluded.

Bakradze nodded.

"What was it?"

"We told him that, if he cooperated, he would get off with only a couple of years and we would take care of him afterwards."

"And he believed you?"

"He had the diamonds and the film."

"But you didn't intend him to keep them, did you? Once Antipov and his men had Viktor in the cells that would be the end of the story, wouldn't it? How does it go? One more prisoner dies under interrogation but not before he has said enough to satisfy KGB without naming all his important friends?"

"Something like that." In one of his prissy gestures Bakradze played with his fingers and looked for the moon. He was aggrieved that his pretty, even elegant scheme was so transparent. "I don't know why you're asking me all these questions. You seem to have all the answers."

"Not all the answers," Kirov assured him, thinking that there were questions that Bakradze did not even know existed. About

Andropov's death for instance. Or Heltai. "Have you heard of Academician I. A. Yakovlevitch?" he asked.

"No. Is he important?"

"Not particularly." Kirov had been momentarily struck by the parallel. In their different versions of the Ring, the Kremlin surgeon and the racketeer Viktor Gusev had both been groomed as the sacrifice to provide the Total Explanation that was so urgently needed if life were to continue without the truth intruding. "Not particularly—but let's talk about Viktor's death," he added just when his companion thought the subject had gone away. And even now he couldn't be certain; Kirov looked on the brink of forgetting everything. "Viktor must have had quite a shock when I turned up at his apartment."

"We all did."

"I imagine so. At all events it's obvious what went through Viktor's mind."

"Is it?" Bakradze was genuinely curious.

"Look at it from Viktor's point of view. KGB was his insurance policy. If he didn't like your deal—if he had his suspicions—he knew he could hand over the film to the KGB. If you wouldn't protect him, then we would—that's what Viktor thought. Right up to the moment when I interrupted your friendly conversation. And then what was Viktor to think?" Kirov remembered that moment of panic when Viktor had concluded the KGB was working with MVD and the Public Prosecutor's Office. Suddenly Viktor had his Total Explanation and he saw himself naked before his enemies. And in that same moment of panic Antipov had shot Viktor before the latter could reveal anything. Poor Viktor. No more tears in the Aragvi or anywhere.

They could see the car. Bogdanov was lounging by it, passing out cigarettes to the tramps. Kirov put a hand out to halt his companion and asked as an apparent afterthought: "Who was the girl you were with tonight?"

"She called herself Vera. I've never met her before."

"Not one of Viktor's girls?"

"Maybe—there were so many. Sergei asked her to call me."

"Why?"

Bakradze had a pleading look. "I want to get out of this business. It's starting to frighten me."

"I understand. But why did Sergei get in touch?"

"Now that Viktor is dead, he wants to reorganize the network. I told the girl I wasn't interested. I've had enough — that's the truth, Pyotr Andreevitch! You've got to believe me!"

"OK, I believe you. Keep calm." Kirov looked away. He was exhausted with confessions and Bakradze was now an empty husk. What Chestyakov had never mentioned in his lectures was this final taste of disgust when the interrogation was finished and the relationship between interrogator and subject was revealed to be as fraudulent as a brief affair and sometimes as poignant, even if not on this occasion.

"What happens to me now?" Bakradze asked pathetically.

"What are you going to do with him?" asked Bogdanov who had come over with his entourage. "Clear off, boys," he said, dismissing them, and the three men waited while the *bomzhi* disappeared into the smoke.

"I need to believe in your good behavior," said Kirov.

"Kill him," said Bogdanov. "Nothing personal," he explained to Bakradze. "Boss, we can't afford to trust this guy."

"Have you told me everything?" Kirov asked the lawyer.

"Jesus Christ — I — *please,* Pyotr Andreevitch!" Bakradze begged.

Don't! Kirov thought. "I think we can trust you," he said consolingly.

"You won't regret it."

"We're going to be friends?" said Bogdanov. "Fair enough." He held out a hand to Bakradze, who took it gratefully. Bogdanov grasped him firmly and pulled him forward onto his other hand. Bakradze gasped and fell back holding his hand to his chest. Blood leaked between his fingers.

"We can't carry on the way we used to," Bogdanov said as he returned with Kirov to the car. "My head's on the block as well as yours. It makes a difference."

23

They drove to Babushkino by country lanes past woods and collective farms and fields deep in snow, its crust speckled with star glitter. The land slept and the air shivered and cracked with cold, you could take it apart like shards of glass if you only tried. But you never did. The radio played a current affairs program. A meeting with the West Europeans in London. Disarmament talks in Geneva. With one mighty bound the Great Gorbachev frees himself from the shackles of the past and leaps into a brave future of peace, prosperity and away with armaments. And for my next trick — Truth!

The village is silent, the houses closed in behind their delicately carved shutters. The wheels of the car snap like elastic bands across the compacted snow. The engine purrs warmly as they creep along the silent street, bringing presents, so don't wake the children. In the lane beyond the village, where it forks and a branch goes off between the trees to Uncle Kolya's *dacha*, they turn off the engine and sit with their thoughts.

"What is it between you and the old man?" Bogdanov said. He pushed the words out as though darkness and silence were objects. "When I called on you earlier you could have cut the atmosphere with a knife. Is he frightened? That doesn't sound like Uncle Kolya. Or have you had some sort of argument?"

"He shot my father," Kirov answered. He couldn't hear his own voice or judge its tone or even guess what message he had tried to convey. Bogdanov received the remark with a grunt.

"I'm sorry," he answered at last. His eyes remained focused forward, searching the road for ghosts. After a minute he added:

"That's the way those old characters used to carry on—" meaning that we don't do things like that anymore and the death of Bakradze is altogether a different case, so forget about seeing the crowd of grinning tramps circled around the lawyer's body and the old woman stealing the lawyer's pants. "I don't suppose it was personal."

"It wasn't personal," Kirov agreed. "It doesn't matter."

They got out of the car and inspected the ground where a set of tire tracks was visible. Kirov thought of the doctor who was pretty, with long pale wrists and a habit of stroking her face while she made diagnoses. She drove a Zhiguli with small tires and a deep cut in one of the treads. The prints impressed in the snow were from a large sedan, a Volga perhaps. They went one way, up to the General's *dacha* and didn't return. The car was up there with its invisible freight of bogeymen.

"Heltai," said Bogdanov, nudging the edges of the tracks with his toe. "Amateurs. No technique. Some trap!" He turned around and started walking back to the car. Kirov delayed long enough to look up at the house and wonder if Heltai had come along in person to take up a conversation begun so long ago in a hotel in Riga.

"Where do we go now?" Bogdanov asked from behind the steering wheel. "I'd like to offer you a bed for the night, but, if Heltai isn't watching my place, for sure Radek is."

"What about Tumanov?"

"Forget him. First, his place is like a whorehouse: five in a bed and take your turn. Second, he's started cleaning his teeth and smiling at Radek. Face it, boss: we're on our own."

"Take me to Neville Lucas."

"Lucas? OK, sure, why not. You can always rely on a traitor when the going gets rough."

"So where have we got to?" Bogdanov asked as they drove through the city's emptying streets and Kirov stared half dreaming into the shadows. "Bakradze and Antipov were working hand in glove with Viktor Gusev. OK, fine, that I understand: Viktor needed protection for his operation and MVD provided it. Am I right?"

Kirov nodded. He wanted to sleep. Open his mind and let the pieces ease into their slots.

"OK. What next? Viktor is getting his supplies from Sergei, who isn't called Sergei but something else. Sergei has a source in a factory in Tbilisi and it seems he's calling the shots. This is all clear. And it's clear that Sergei introduced Zagranichny into the operation and loves him and mothers him like his own child, making sure into the bargain that Viktor and his paid policemen do the same. But what Zagranichny actually *does* for Sergei is a mystery."

"A mystery," Kirov agreed.

Bogdanov paused. "Are you taking the piss?"

Kirov snapped out of his speculations. He opened his eyes and caught the old man's withered glance and knew that Bogdanov understood well enough what there was to be understood and that this recitation was just for reassurance.

"OK, OK," Bogdanov said. "Let's forget about *who* exactly Zagranichny is. He's special and Viktor knows that he's special and that no one else is supposed to know about Zagranichny, which is why Viktor plays tricks with names. The point is that when his friends started to turn cool, Viktor tried to strengthen his position by getting compromising material on Zagranichny—the film and the tape—which he could use if Sergei or MVD put pressure on him. By the way, where is the tape?"

"Antipov has it. He found it when his men raided Viktor's place."

"I guess that's right. Tough luck on Viktor. He didn't realize that pressure wasn't exactly what his friends had in mind. They wanted him dead as a sacrifice to KGB to take the heat out of the investigation into the Ring and because his hatred of Zagranichny had become a dangerous embarrassment to Sergei. This is wonderful," Bogdanov said unenthusiastically, "and so far I understand it."

"Good."

"Yes—good for me, I'm really smart, I should learn to read and get an education. If I'm so smart, why don't I know why all the cash from this racket was being converted into diamonds? More to the point, if this whole business of selling antibiotics is being run out of Tbilisi and the Bulgarian thing was just a cover story, why are Heltai and his GRU death squad after your blood? What's the death of Yuri Andropov got to do with anything? Or Academician Yakovlevitch's murder? Where's the connection?"

"I don't know," Kirov told him. Conspiracies are not meant to be understood—but that was something he couldn't admit; the old man needed simple, violent certainties. To take Bogdanov's mind off the mysteries he put a request to him. "I need help from your friend, the computer wizard."

"Krapotkin?"

"The American desk shares a closed file with GRU on the American, William Craig. I want access to it."

"That's a tall order."

"I need it, damn you!" Kirov said fiercely.

"OK! OK!" Bogdanov agreed quickly. He concentrated on the road so that he didn't have to look at Kirov and after a few seconds repeated in a pained voice, "OK," and again after a lapse, "OK."

"Craig set up the factory in Tbilisi," Kirov explained.

"Terrific," Bogdanov responded moodily.

"I'm going to Tbilisi."

Nadezhda Dmitrievna answered the entryphone in her fat sleepy voice. She was a fat young woman with a small, smooth and very pretty face. Neville Lucas, peddling the last scraps of his physical prowess and the fading charm of his dubious past, chased other women before the night closed on him and treated her badly if fidelity was a measure of performance. Nadezhda Dmitrievna appeared to accept this and exercised a mother's patience, knowing that her perpetually adolescent son would always come home for her food and her fat embraces and because she washed his socks.

She met Kirov at the door, wearing a voluminous nightdress and a long woolen dressing gown.

"Don't get him drunk," she said skeptically and let Kirov in.

Behind her Lucas chimed in English: "Peter! Super! Get a bottle, woman!"

"He's been to the National. Drinking with his friends. With Jack Melchior and one of his wives."

"A birthday!" Lucas justified himself. "Got to celebrate birthdays. Traditional. Where would we all be without tradition?"

"Make some coffee," Kirov suggested gently. "I'll take care of him. What ho, Neville!" he selected from Lucas's repertoire of dated slang, heard and remembered in a hundred bars. He allowed Lucas to clasp him warmly.

"I'm feeling splendid. And you? What brings you here? Pull up a pew." Lucas took a seat on an old chair and pulled a frayed pajama jacket across his vest to make himself respectable. He was still wearing trousers. His feet were bare.

The center of the room was occupied by a long trestle table. It held a model train set with a green engine and carriages in a brown and cream livery. Lucas had laid out the scenery of a West Country branch line as he remembered it from the holidays he had taken as a child in Torquay. The layout represented a decade of favors from visiting English businessmen who were short-changed with Lucas's doubtful contacts in the foreign trade organizations — his little men who would always do a good turn for a pal.

"I need a bed for the night."

"My humble abode is yours. What's wrong? Has Lara locked you out?" Lucas had forgotten that Lara had returned to the ballet and was sleeping with Radek. Nadezhda was used to the Englishman's impromptu generosity.

"I can't make up a bed," she said. "I didn't know you were coming."

"Anything will do."

"Anything will do — see?" Lucas agreed. "And don't forget to bring that bottle. Oh, and some cheese."

"No cheese. He has an ulcer," she explained to Kirov.

"Bloody old hen," said Lucas equably.

"She's probably right. You should take care of your health."

"*My* health is fine." Lucas made a point. "From what my spies tell me, though, Grishin's is none too good. Retired to his *dacha*, to Mummy and that idiot wife of his. Outmaneuvered by Radek, so they say. Set up by the Rehabilitation Committee to take the blame for the disgrace of some surgeon or other, so they say. Funny, that — I had thought that if anyone was going to do for Grishin it would be you."

"Why me?"

"Because you were Grishin's loyal subordinate. Who better to stab him in the back?"

"Is that the way it works?"

"Isn't it?" Lucas answered indifferently. "I thought it was a fine old Soviet tradition. All that stuff about medical poisoners plotting to kill Stalin — wasn't that Beria's doing? Or was Stalin plotting to kill Beria? I forget sometimes which way around these conspiracies are supposed to work."

Nadezhda Dmitrievna padded into the room with a bottle of vodka and a plate of dry sausage cut into slices, which she placed on the table. "Don't keep him up too late," she said to Kirov. "You can sleep on the couch."

"Thank you."

"You've grown a mustache."

"Yes."

"Neville keeps wanting to grow a beard."

"Go to bed, woman," said Lucas good temperedly.

"Don't drink too much," she answered. Her little-girl face frowned as if with a little-girl problem, the multiplication tables or a stain on her party dress. Kirov sensed her relentlessness. Women had it in a way that men rarely did, perhaps in compensation for their lack of power. Power allowed men to fantasize about its use. Its absence demanded that women wear away at intractable reality with a chilling persistence if the world were to resemble what they wanted.

"Cigarette?" Lucas offered. A pile of cartons in their duty-free wrappers stood on the floor. Obscure English brands. "Help yourself, I'm giving up."

"Why are you collecting them?" It was a joke that Lucas importuned travelers at every opportunity to provide himself with their cigarettes.

Lucas shrugged. "A way of keeping the score? So long as they keep giving me their smokes, I know that they remember me. That's important. Did you know that some old codger in MI5 published his memoirs not long ago? About Philby and Blunt and Hollis and all that old crap, MI5 spying into their navels and finding nothing but fluff."

"So?"

"So I didn't even rate a footnote! Bloody offensive, I call that!"

He poured two glasses of vodka and nibbled at a piece of sausage, closing his eyes as he did so. His pajama jacket was too small. His trousers exposed his bare ankles. Finding clothes in Moscow to fit his large frame was a problem. His face relaxed to a deep and sleepy sagacity.

"Which side are you on?" Kirov asked.

Lucas's slow eyes opened. He spoke lazily.

"Sides? You've come to the wrong shop to talk about sides. I'm not on anybody's side. I'm a *traitor,* Peter. It may not be much, legging over the Turkish border with a few out-of-date codebooks and nobody on my tail except a couple of traffic cops and a divorce lawyer, but I've learned to be proud of it."

"Why are you dealing in antibiotics?"

"Not me, old son. At my age aphrodisiacs would be more in my

255

line, and I'd even swap those for a reliable hemorrhoid cream. Where did you get that idea from?"

I'm too tired for this, Kirov thought. Interrogation by the long route. He had a vision of taking Lucas by the throat and shaking the evasions out of him. Never interrogate a friend — quote: Chestyakov to all the spotty kids who wanted to be spies.

"You've grown a mustache," said Lucas, forgetting that the point had been made. "Taking a leaf out of Tomsky's book? He's growing one, or has he just shaved it off? I forget."

"How did you get to know Yelena Akhmerova?"

"A friend introduced us."

"Who?"

"A friend — I don't remember."

"Viktor Gusev?"

"Gusev? Gusev? You've got me there, Peter. Someone you know? Someone from your Jewish antibiotics thing? Why *Jewish,* by the way, did you ever get an answer to that?"

"I'm surprised you don't know Viktor. Everyone knows Viktor. He hangs around all the best places with his gang of friends from Georgia. A regular customer at the Aragvi — isn't that one of your favorite restaurants?"

"Now *you're* being offensive, Peter. Casting nasturtiums. Not nice." Lucas threw back his drink and took another piece of sausage. He was old and wily and played out; and dangerous as an ancient tiger turned man-eater for the easy meat. "I think I want to go to bed. The good boy needs his bye-byes."

"Why did you invite me to Yelena's party?"

"Just as you guessed. I wanted you and Lara to get back together again."

"That's what I thought at first."

"At first?"

"And then I remembered that, during those two or three days, you called me several times. Yelena wasn't giving a party every night, was she?"

"I was lonely."

"You were quite insistent."

"That's a matter of interpretation. I don't know what you're getting at, Peter."

"No? Well, let's say that all those calls were intended to create an opportunity for someone to meet me. Who would it be? Not Lara. She was as surprised to meet me as I was her. And she wouldn't have been with Radek if she had wanted to see me."

"Ah!" Lucas defended himself. "Got you there! I never said that Lara *wanted* to see you. It was all my own idea. I knew Lara would be at Yelena's party and the thought just came to me: Peter—Lara—friends and former lovebirds. I'm a sentimental old thing."

"And the day before? You knew where Lara would be the day before when you suggested we have a drink together? Is that the story, Neville? You would have arranged another casual meeting? I'm surprised you know so much about Lara's movements."

Lucas turned sour. "You have a cruel intellect, Peter. Full of nasty and suspicious thoughts. Not the way to make friends—no, not at all." He stretched his arms and yawned beneath his wide-awake eyes. "Sleepy times," he said. "Yes, definitely. I'll say good-night to you, Peter. Sleep well. Hmm—yes—time to give Teddy a cuddle."

Lucas and his woman slept in the next room. Nadezhda Dmitrievna snored. Her soft breath made a trilling noise like a caged bird. Kirov sat in the main room with the model railway and the piles of cigarette cartons, and dozed fitfully in the darkness.

Sometime in the early hours Lucas came padding into the room wearing his pajama jacket, long underwear and socks. He regarded Kirov doubtfully, then grinned and said: "What, still awake? I've got a sodding headache. Trying to remember where I left the aspirins." He poured a drink and fiddled with the record player. He fanned himself with an old black disc, big as a dinner plate, then placed it on the deck. The strains of "In the Mood" broke the stillness.

"Not Glenn Miller," he said, and added with cautious pride: "My dad. Just as good, don't you think? Bum-bum-bum-dee-diddle-dah. Duggie Lucas and His Big Sound. During the war the old man used to knock them dead in the fleshpots of Morpeth and North Shields except when the American army bands were in town. He could do that since he didn't have to fight. Reserved occupation essential for the civilian war effort—he was a black marketeer. I suppose your old man was in the war?"

"In Minsk."

"Bit of a hero, eh?"

"Maybe."

"Ah—not sure, eh? I understand. In this country it's never clear who the heroes are."

They sat in opposing chairs. Lucas stared at his feet while his fingers took a walk around his glass.

"Look—about your business," he began slowly. "I'm sorry to have buggered around. Old habits. You won't hold it against me?"

"No."

"Only I did know Viktor. It's just as you say, except that it wasn't at the Aragvi I met him, it was that restaurant in the television tower, place off Prospekt Mira near the Park of Economic Achievement, I forget the name. Otherwise you have the picture: Viktor and his smiling crew straight off the morning flight from Tbilisi, buying everything in the restaurant and generally up to no good. And not to forget the girls, one for everybody and a couple of spares to hand out like tips. He liked his style, did Viktor.

"I was invited to join the party. It was embarrassing—me with a tart on each knee and my Russian none too special. Tongue-tied, that's the expression. I had a few too many, you understand."

"I understand."

"And I told them I was in the KGB—gave them my rank and all," Lucas went on guiltily. "Well, I thought it would impress them. And it did! The following morning I'm sitting at home nursing a thick head and there's a knock on the door and a character outside with a bouquet of flowers you wouldn't believe. With Love From Viktor—I must have told him about Nadezhda Dmitrievna—at least, I *hope* they were for Nadezhda Dmitrievna—yes, they must have been. All those women—Viktor couldn't have been . . . And there's a letter. We must have talked about books; Viktor wanted to know if I could lend him some. He was a fanatic for books." Lucas paused. "I behaved bloody silly really."

"I understand."

"Do you?"

"Viktor began to ask you for favors."

"No." Lucas shoved back his drink, poured another and turned the record over to play "American Patrol." "No," he repeated, "it wasn't like that."

"How was it?"

Lucas searched for a word and came up with: "Different." But it was unsatisfactory and he wrinkled his brow before trying to explain. "I think Viktor liked influence for its own sake. Not to use. Maybe it gave him a feeling of security, just knowing that people owed him something."

"That's unusual?" Kirov answered skeptically. He thought of

where Viktor's influence had ended. He had lain on a slab in the Butyrka, and the doctors, on the instructions of his friends in MVD, rummaged in his guts for diamonds.

"Viktor was unusual," Lucas answered. As an afterthought he added: "Someone told me that one night at dinner he burst out crying. Now I call that unusual."

"Who told you that — George Gvishiani?"

"I see you've guessed about George," Lucas replied ruefully.

"Did he tell you why Viktor created a scene? Perhaps he mentioned someone called Zagranichny?"

"Zagranichny? Never heard of him. Not that I would. Viktor used to make up names for his friends; even George Gvishiani was known as Sergei. Viktor said he was a relative of Kosygin's son-in-law and an authentic big cheese, but I think that's all balls. The only favor I ever did was for George, and there wasn't much to it. He wanted to meet you — to size you up, he said — I mean honest, Peter, where was the harm? George was pissed off with Viktor, thought he was cracking up after the crying business. Frankly he was glad when Viktor died. But *you* worried him: he wasn't happy at the thought of a KGB investigation. 'Neville,' says he, 'I want to meet this Kirov and see what he's made of, see whether he's *friendly.*' 'Bollocks to *friendly,*' say I, 'Kirov is straight' — that's the truth, I told him that — but he wants to meet you, and no one is to get hurt. You know the rest: I asked you out for a drink and invited you to Yelena Akhmerova's party. George Gvishiani was there by arrangement. It was a coincidence that Lara turned up."

The last bars of the record expired. Lucas got to his feet and shuffled around the table with its railway layout. He set an engine going and studied it with morose distraction. Without shifting his eyes, he asked: "Are you in trouble?"

"Someone is trying to kill me," Kirov answered.

"Uh huh," Lucas murmured dully. He watched the train go clickety-clack all the way to his childhood. After a moment he said: "In that case it would be better if you only stayed one night."

"Have you heard of a man called Ferenc Heltai?" Kirov asked.

Lucas looked up. He was tired and uninterested. "No," he answered. "Is he important?"

The apartment slept. A clock chimed. Kirov smoked a cigarette and looked out of the window into the inimical street, wondering if Heltai was keeping watch. Spying involved a playful malice when the victim was ready to be taken. Why not hang on a little longer for the kill? You never know who else may turn up. One more for the pot! But he knew that Heltai was not there—not yet. Heltai was at the Aquarium, still speculating whether he had left Kirov dead at the Darvitsky Reserve and husbanding the limited resources GRU disposed of for internal surveillance. For the moment circumstances dictated an economy of force on both sides, but that could easily change. In the meantime, sleep and thoughts of treachery.

Neville Lucas was bemused by treachery, by how easily it had come to him and by the way it left him with a longing for friends and loyalty with the pain of an amputated limb. "It's a matter of security," he explained as the train went around and around hypnotically. "Here—so far away," but he didn't say from where or what. From Torquay with its mackerel boats and penny arcades and its station on the Great Western Railway forever beyond the reach of his toy trains? In a lucid moment he explained that treachery changed everything. The ground beneath your feet crumbled and never became as firm again: not friends nor a new home ever gave you the same old certainties. So, if the *quality* of friendship did nothing for you, try quantity. Peddle your stories around the Moscow bars and buy new friends with an old tale, a photograph of a more-or-less famous spy and a bogus promise to use your influence with the legion of little men who will always do a favor for a pal. Not all that different from Viktor really. Later, when Lucas slept, Kirov checked the bedroom to make sure that he had not slipped treasonably away to buy the love of some more friends—Ferenc, have I got a tale for you! Lucas and the woman were folded about each other in a ruck of bedclothes, each stealing comforting body heat from the other so that you could watch them and envy them.

He dreamt of holidays, of the rainswept promenade in front of the hotel in Riga where he had sat drinking mineral water with Uncle Kolya and Ferenc Heltai. He wondered if Torquay were like that. He worried about what to do with Neville Lucas and Nadezhda Dmitrievna.

In his dreams Kirov went into the bedroom and massacred the couple as they slept.

24

Bogdanov met him in the departure hall at Vnukovo in the lively crowd of Armenians, Azerbaijanis, Georgians, Ossetians and other free-spending southerners who had just unloaded their goods in the Moscow private market and were now happy and looking forward to warmer places. He brought tickets, money, identity papers and clothing. He explained sourly: "I paid for these from my own pocket. I could hardly bill Radek for them."

Kirov asked him: "How good are the papers?"

"They look OK but for all I know they could have been lifted from a stiff. Don't flash them around too much in case they ring a bell."

"Where did you get them?"

"From Yuri the Bazaar—we're friends again. He tells me they're kosher but there are some people who say he's not an honest man."

"What about Craig's dossier?"

"I've got Krapotkin working on it. Crashing into a closed file on the First Chief Directorate's system isn't easy. I can't make promises."

"I know that," Kirov said comfortingly. He thought that Bogdanov looked exhausted even if he wore a glued-on grin that said he wasn't. Why does he stick by me? When Kirov was gone, Bogdanov would be left to field Radek, nod and agree with him that it was a mystery where Kirov had vanished to. And then there was Heltai; but Heltai was unknowable. "Good luck," Kirov said, and grasped Uncle Bog's forearm.

The passengers boarded the plane, bundled their warm clothes and their parcels into the racks and settled into the cramped seats. There was an atmosphere of good humor in the cabin except for the tail section where most of the Russians were sitting. Kirov found himself next to a cheerful Georgian who had done good business in the city and pressed him to share a bottle of Ararat brandy. His companion was still talking business and hospitality in equal proportions after takeoff when a stewardess emerged from the crew cabin to check the passengers.

At first Kirov paid her no attention. She walked the length of the plane, disposed of the passengers and turned to walk back. She found a hand in her way. "Please, comrade," she said and her uninterested face looked down.

"Hello, Nadia," said Kirov.

She stood for a moment without expression, barely appearing to register his presence. Then two pale flush spots showed beneath her makeup. Her eyes looked uncertainly aside before focusing on his, and her mouth, which had been limp with boredom, hesitated then formed a faint smile.

"You gave me a surprise, comrade investigator."

Kirov had forgotten the lies he had told her about his role and it seemed for a second that she was talking to someone else. He glanced away reflexively but saw only his fellow passenger who had blanched at the mention of his rank. "You surprised me too," he said at last.

"Did I? After all, this is my job: I'm supposed to be here. And you . . ."

"Pyotr Andreevitch."

"Pyotr Andreevitch . . . You have business in Tbilisi?"

"Something like that. Do you fly this route often?"

"Fairly often," she answered calmly, as if to annoy him.

He returned her even tone: "Is that how you met Viktor?"

"I met Viktor in Moscow. I've told you that already."

"You said you were introduced to him by someone you met on a plane. That someone—he was a passenger on this route?"

"I forget. Why do you ask?"

"I may know him."

"There are a lot of people. It's not likely."

"No," Kirov agreed. "Unless, of course, he was one of my friends. Georgi Gvishiani—do you know him? He often flies between Tbilisi and Moscow."

Nadia Mazurova hesitated. Kirov saw the lie in her eyes and

her lips taste it. She prepared herself for a glib answer, then something held her back and in avoiding him she looked down at his hand which rested flat against a panel of her skirt.

"I have things to do," she said, picking the hand up and delivering it back to him. She disappeared into the crew cabin and reappeared only at the end of the flight when, passing down the aisle, she left him with a note on which was written one word: *Tamara.*

He took a bus from the airport to the central bus station and a cab from the Verei Bridge to Rustaveli Prospekt where he was deposited under the sycamores and the damp Georgian sky outside the small Intourist hotel. He checked in at the desk and asked the clerk if there was a hotel in the city called the Tamara. The clerk was impatient and superior and said in accented Russian that there was such a hotel in the Avchala district, an industrial area where you wouldn't want to stay unless you had to. Kirov carried his bags to his room and drew a lukewarm bath. He unpacked, shaved and bathed, then took a short walk to ease the tension of traveling and had a snack in the Nargizi café. The atmosphere in the café was light; the cinema next to the Intourist was showing *Iron Harvest* and the diners were talking excitedly about the seasonal sensation and the moving performance by the film's star, Yelena Akhmerova.

He left the café and found a phone booth. He telephoned the hotel and asked for his room. The connection timed at fifteen seconds. He left the phone booth, walked along the boulevard past the park and picked up a cab at the Hotel Tbilisi. He asked the driver to take him to the railway station where he found another public telephone and called the hotel again. This time the response time measured twelve and a half seconds. He took a further cab, this time across the river to Plekhanov Road and had the driver drop him by the film studio on the corner of Chelyuskintsev Street. By now it had begun to rain, a fine drizzle, not too cold. The shift workers on the tramway system were returning to their apartments opposite the studios. Outside Ordzhonikidze Park children were standing on the pavement and pointing at the parachute tower, which was faintly visible through the rain. Past the Dynamo Stadium Kirov turned into the Didube district of the city.

He followed a road running parallel to the river and flanked by apartment houses. In the gaps he glimpsed the steep hills of the

263

old town and once, as the rainclouds shifted, the Metekhi chapel up on its height. The light was almost gone by now and the people were streaming with the rain into the buildings. Cross streets ran at right angles to the main route. They held factories and more apartment blocks, the occasional dimly lit shop, the occasional queue and rattling tramcar. At a junction a traffic cop stood bored in his covered booth and noted car numbers as if it were a hobby. Kirov took a right and followed a winding road up an incline with factories on both sides.

The placard said: Pharmprodsoyuz Number One. The plant was isolated by a high wire fence and stood across a tarmacked yard. There was a single entrance with a cabin, a military guard and a pivoted barrier backed by gates, which for now were open. The place appeared to be laid out in two complexes of steel-frame structures with cladding over a brick base to single-story height. The main complex opened directly onto the yard with an office entrance and a canopied loading bay. The smaller section was in its own compound, fenced and guarded, blank walled with its face turned away from the road so that the entrances were invisible. As Kirov walked along the main fence a series of fixed spotlights on the fence to the inner compound was turned on and he saw a dog patrol come around the corner of the building and pad across its face.

He walked the length of the site where it bordered the road. At the corner a narrow muddy lane divided it from the adjacent plot which was occupied by a run-down engineering works. The lane was in darkness and cluttered with scrap and oil drums. At the far end it terminated in a patch of scrub and bushes growing wild against the plant fence. Kirov scaled one of the bushes and dropped from it over the fence and into the yard.

Wooden pallets and empty crates had been stacked in this corner of the yard. They gave cover to survey the terrain. The yard was empty of people; only the guard post was occupied and the guard was sheltering from the rain and visible by the light of his cab. Kirov came out of cover and moved one of the packing cases closer against the fence as a precaution for an easy exit. He ignored the shriek as it scraped across the tarmac. He told himself that no one was around to hear, and nobody was. He tested his weight on the crate, and, satisfied, crossed from the shadows of this deserted corner toward the building.

The near side was offices. By now most of the staff had gone home and they were empty and unlit but for the cleaners who could be seen flitting by the windows. The storage and production areas were dark walls into which a couple of doors were let. Cracks of light shone around the edges of the doors and a low hum of operating machinery was vaguely audible. This part of the compound also held an electricity substation, a generator house and a locked store. Two trucks were parked alongside the store.

From the shelter of the trucks Kirov got a good view of the second smaller complex. The fence was higher and the insulation pots clamped to the posts indicated that it was electrified. The building had an independent power supply and, sticking out above the roofline, an oversized heating and ventilation unit. A smaller structure stood behind the main part. The shingle on the door described it as the emergency medical and decontamination center. It was lit and manned.

Although this second compound intrigued him, Kirov decided against any immediate attempt to enter it. Apart from the electric fence, the place was floodlit and he counted two armed dog patrols and two stationary guard posts with good fields of vision over the yard. He turned to matters nearer to hand, the trucks and the store. Examination of the trucks gave only their origins: a transport enterprise from Batumi on the Black Sea coast and another here in Tbilisi. The doors were easily forced but the cabs yielded only log books, a goods manifest for a shipment from Batumi without much detail, some fuel coupons and small effects belonging to the drivers. A check of the store confirmed that it was padlocked and the windows barred but apparently not alarmed. Kirov found it curious that the store was not open for business when the plant was operating.

He returned to the corner of the yard where the junk had been piled and rooted in the scrap that was littered among the crates. The search was interrupted by the sound of voices, and two men came out of the main building and ran through the rain across the yard toward the store. Kirov stood motionless in the shadows while the pair busied themselves with the trucks, intent on their work for a few minutes; then they were finished and ran back to the main building without giving attention to his direction. He resumed his search and found what he needed, a flat iron bar, rusted but not so bad as to be unusable.

On the far side of the store, away from the main building, a single window overlooked the fence. The security bars were let into the brickwork. The builders had skimped on mortar and it was patchy and crumbly to touch. Kirov used the piece of iron to chisel into the joint at the first course of bricks beneath the window. After five minutes' work he had exposed the base of the bars and removed them. He took off his coat to cover the pane and gave it a sharp tap, enough to crack the glass without shattering it, then forced the shards apart and pulled them out of the frame. He climbed through the gap.

The interior was in blackness. Cardboard cartons were stacked against the wall below the window. Kirov clambered over them and felt his feet touch the concrete floor. He decided to chance his torch and shone the beam down the length of the aisle, which led to a door fifty meters away between rows of pallets piled with various sizes of drums and more of the boxes. By the door was a storekeeper's office, a bank of light switches and a junction box. A stacker truck was parked to one side and wired to charge its batteries. Kirov crossed to the next aisle and shone the torch again. More rows of boxes stacked on metal racks, each hung with a bin number and a stock control sheet. Another aisle and more of the same plus a sluice, mops and cleaning agents. There were five aisles.

He tried the storekeeper's office. Two desks, a filing cabinet, a manual typewriter and a dozen box files holding goods-received notes. He leafed through the latter and found nothing of interest except an omission: there was nothing to show any deliveries from Batumi—which could have meant no more than that the truck in the yard was a one-off. He searched the desks and the filing cabinet for the main stock record and drew a blank; then looked for a safe but found none. He was still searching the office when the light came on.

The source of the light was the main store. The external door was open and the two men he had identified as truck drivers had come in and were standing with their backs to the office window. A third man in a khaki overall and carrying a clipboard joined them. The three went into a huddle, the man in khaki tapping the clipboard and gesturing at the aisles. The drivers followed his directions and disappeared behind a row of bins. The store clerk stood for a moment writing notes, then turned and approached the office. His hand rested on the door handle.

Kirov flattened himself against the wall in the angle of the door and gripped the iron bar he had used to jimmy the window. The door opened slowly. Then a voice shouted out and the hand released its grasp on the handle and the door swung lazily. Footsteps sounded across the bare concrete. Kirov breathed out and chanced a glance through the doorway. He saw the clerk disappearing in the direction of the two drivers. Kirov slipped after him and took shelter behind a stacked pallet.

The light in the store was poor. The three men were grouped dimly by one of the bins; the taller of the drivers was resting his arms on a small trolley; the other held a large box cradled against his chest; the clerk was gesticulating and trying to take notes at the same time. They talked for a few moments then the clerk helped the second driver to load four of the boxes onto the trolley. They walked back down the aisle trundling the loaded trolley and passed Kirov's position crouched in the shadows. The drivers took their load outside and the clerk retired to the office that Kirov had just vacated.

Slowly Kirov emerged from his hiding place. He felt the cramp in his legs, the tension of his muscles, the sweat of his palms making slippery the rough surface of the iron bar. The physical discomfort went with a sense of mental clarity that was almost elation. Kirov knew enough to distrust his body's unreliable chemistry. He moved cautiously down the aisle to the bin from which the boxes had been taken. He slit the lid on the next box in the stack, removed some of the loose packing and exposed a row of smaller cartons each labeled in Russian and Bulgarian. The labels stated that the drugs inside had been produced by Bulpharma. Kirov repacked the box and closed the lid.

"Stay where you are!" The taller of the drivers was by the door. His hand held a service automatic pointed at Kirov. He had stepped into a patch of light from a pale fluorescent strip and was clearly visible though his appearance meant nothing; a thousand drivers could look the same, in oil-stained clothes, rough handed, with knuckles like nuts. He looked more or less comfortable with the gun, which meant that he would probably use it. "Who are you?" he asked. "What are you doing here?" He approached guardedly down the aisle. Kirov let his hand slide from the box to grip one of the metal stanchions forming the bin.

"I was checking something."

"Don't give me that crap." The driver's eyes shifted as he tried to identify what had been disturbed. "You've been messing with our stuff. What's your game?" He was closer now but too cagey to come within striking distance. Behind him the store clerk and the other driver appeared in the doorway.

"Careful with that gun!" shouted the clerk. The driver hesitated with the distraction. Kirov yanked on the stanchion and from the higher level of the bin a cascade of boxes and cans tumbled into the aisle. The gun fired and a bullet buried itself into a box.

"Jesus!" yelled the driver. A can hit the hard floor, bounced, the lid sprang and he was doused in fluid.

"For God's sake, don't shoot in here!" chorused the storeman. Kirov's antagonist pressed the trigger again.

The muzzle flashed and for an instant the man was transfixed in mute horror. And then he was gone. In his place there was a wall of flame, a light so bright that Kirov was dazzled and staggered backward, dragging more boxes from the bin. From within the flame a core of fire the shape of a man stumbled forward and careened from the sides of the aisle then collapsed at Kirov's feet. With a roar the fire spread backward across the spill of liquid and leapt upward across the face of the bins on each side of the aisle until it formed an arch under the roof trusses. The first cans began to explode.

Kirov threw himself to the ground with that first blast. He crawled away from the wave of heat to the shelter of the end of the aisle, his lungs heaving with smoke and the superheated air. Behind him the bins and their contents buckled and crashed, feeding the source of the fire. Belatedly a sprinkler system came into operation and added steam to the mix of smoke and gases escaping from the fire.

He sat for seconds only but the flames were spreading with incredible rapidity. Despite their brightness he could see nowhere except into the fire itself. Elsewhere the smoke billowed down from the roof and blacked out his vision. He crawled along the floor where the fumes were least, and in the darkness, intermittently lit by flashes as another bin or pallet caught fire, he searched desperately for the window by which he had entered. He found it—but the second driver was there.

The man was on his feet, blinded, doubled over and staggering between piles of boxes, but as Kirov approached him he glimpsed him through eyes that were blackened and angry with tears and gave a roar of anguish. He came flailing at Kirov with the force of insanity. Kirov blocked the first blow but the impetus threw him onto his back. His assailant recoiled then swung a steel-shod boot at Kirov's head. Kirov rolled away but felt a jarring pain as the toe cap glanced against his shoulder. He tried to get to his feet but his injured arm gave way and he collapsed. The fire meantime was still sucking oxygen out of the air; his lungs were pumping fiercely and even then he could feel only an exploding breathlessness and a growing dizziness. He braced himself for the next blow. His body was tense, awaiting the breaking of bone. *Now!* But there was no blow. His eyes peered through his own tears and he saw the body of the other man, made unconscious by the smoke, spreadeagled on the floor with the flames licking at his clothes.

His next conscious sensation was of his face lying on the cool tarmac. He was outside, lying at the foot of the window. The air was alive with yells and sirens, the roar of flames and detonations, and a great crash as a section of the roof gave way. He did not know how long he lay there. Perhaps it was seconds only, but he was detached from a sense of time. At one point feet came hammering past and someone reached down and turned him over, but seeing the blank eyes gave him up for dead. The air was cool. He wanted to embrace it. The chaos of noise had become music — Mozart — he could hear it.

Slowly he got to his feet. He ignored the fire, which was happening in another world. Everywhere there were people, but he didn't belong to them and they paid him no attention. He focused on the corner of the fence where he had provided for his escape, and walked fixedly in that direction, brushing aside the watchers, stepping over the coiled hoses and avoiding the fire-fighting equipment. He reached the fence and found the packing case he had positioned to climb it, and painfully he scaled the wire and dropped to the other side. All the while he hummed the theme of a clarinet concerto. It told him he was alive and sane.

He found himself sitting on a bench. He was by the river, in one of the parks along the Kura Embankment. The rain had stopped, clear starlit patches broke the clouds. He stood and flexed his limbs, and it seemed a miracle that they worked. He examined his clothes; they were torn and stained with mud and smoke. The backs of his hands were burned red; he touched his face and winced with pain.

A search of the park turned up a small pool. Kirov knelt beside it and saw his reflection, dim and haunted, in the still water. He dipped his hands into the water, held it cupped in his palms and slowly anointed his face with its sharp coldness. He stayed like this a few minutes in a position of prayer, then got to his feet and began to walk.

He walked without a sense of time or place. Mentally he told himself that it was shock: shock from the fire, shock from his injury, shock from giving and receiving violence. He had no business being on his feet. He said as much and stifled a laugh, but not so well as to avoid the stare of a pedestrian who regarded him as if he were a creature from hell, and maybe that was how he looked; he could smell the smoke clinging to his clothes. He came across a public telephone, almost stumbled into it. In his pocket he found some coins, and for a long moment he held them in his palm where they seemed bright and improbable. Then he made his calls.

He rang the hotel. The switchboard answered. Kirov checked his watch and asked for the room next to his own. The operator tried the connection and reported that the occupant was out. Twenty seconds. He replaced the receiver and then redialed the call, this time asking for his own room. After forty-five seconds without an answer he left the handset hanging and the line open. He crossed the road and took shelter in the doorway of an apartment block. Five minutes later a black Volga sedan pulled up, two men wearing overcoats and the indifference of professionals got out, checked the phone booth and then left in their car.

The rain had stopped but the sky looked unconvinced. Kirov remained in the doorway until a voice reminded him that he was alive and ought to be doing something. It seemed a good idea, he told himself consciously, as if advising a friend. He walked a while, took a bus and a couple of tramcars, and did another stretch on foot through the narrow hilly streets lined by sycamores, and at the end of this, according to his pocket map, was in the Avchala district. He stopped a local and asked for the Hotel Tamara. The man gave him the answer furtively and shook him off.

The hotel was a narrow entrance let into the face of a row of small shops: a place that repaired typewriters, and another with a window of empty bottles and an unhelpful sign in Georgian

270

script. There was an alleyway wide enough for a vehicle and an Aeroflot van was parked there. The street lighting was faint; the lamps in the hotel lobby were bright by comparison; the emptiness and brightness gave it an intimidating air. By now the strange elation that had held Kirov together was entirely gone, leaving only weariness and pain. As for fear, Kirov told himself he could hold off fear by not thinking about it. And here he was not thinking about it; instead he was shivering because the night was cold and his body was mending itself.

He took off his raincoat and reversed it. On this side there were no smoke stains, just dampness and traces of mud around the hem. He checked his appearance again in the window of the typewriter repair shop and his withered face stared back. He pulled the raincoat close and turned up the collar to hide the rest of his disheveled clothing and pushed his way through the hotel door.

The lobby was bright only by comparison. A clump of lights like a bunch of grapes hung from the ceiling, but only three of the sockets were loaded and two of these were duds. The single uncovered bulb lit up an old *babushka* who was minding the desk and eating her supper from a battered zinc bowl. Kirov gave her a flash of his KGB badge and demanded the guest registration cards, which she passed over without query. He riffled through them and found a batch with the names of the Aeroflot flight crew. Nadia Mazurova was in room 102.

The keys to the first floor were held by an aged *dezhurnaya* who sat wrapped in woolens at a rickety table in the corridor at the head of the stairs. She grumbled at the intrusion: the keys were out and she had only the spare; but when Kirov insisted she handed it over and indicated a room at the far end. Kirov said he wouldn't trouble her to let him into the room; he promised to return the key to her, and she left it at that. He approached the room alert for any discordant sign but detected only the silent shabbiness that went with the hotel. He tapped lightly on the door.

There was no reply, no sound save the hollow rattle of an old woman's cough from the direction of the *dezhurnaya*. She was sitting in her faint pool of light, ruminating and paying him no attention. Kirov knocked again and drew the same silence. He tried the handle and as expected found the door locked. He examined the lock itself and saw only old scratch marks made by fumbling guests. He tried the key and it engaged stiffly with the wards then with a click freed the bolt. He pushed the door gently open and turned on the light.

Nadia Mazurova was lying on the bed. She was naked, brutalized and dead.

25

To experience grief requires involvement. Shock demands only surprise. Kirov did not know which it was that he felt: just a numbness on top of the numbness of the night's other events, scarcely a feeling at all. His reflexes worked so far as to tell him to close the door and then he waited for something to happen, an idea to come to him from the dulled and vacant recesses of his mind. The woman's body lay unmoving, the face buried in the pillow with the end of a garrotte trailing like a necklace and her buttocks stamped with bloody palm prints.

Her left shoulder bore the dark blemish he had seen in Viktor's film. Viktor had recognized where things would lead. He had burst into tears in the Aragvi restaurant during dinner with Bakradze, Antipov and his fellow racketeer, Georgi Gvishiani sometimes known as Sergei. Kirov searched for his own tears but there weren't any. Perhaps they would come later when his capacity for emotion had revived; but he doubted it. Grief required involvement, instead of which he was an observer of strangers, a connoisseur of their abstract fascination. Only occasionally, as with Nadia Mazurova, did they touch him with a secret policeman's remote idea of love.

As he sat peacefully the room came into his consciousness. The air held a heavy dreamy scent of cloves, trapped between the narrow walls. There were two beds, barely a meter apart, a washstand with a pitcher of water, and a curtained-off space for hanging clothes. Two flight bags stood on the floor, two pairs of briefs and nylon tights hung to dry over the curtain rail. A magazine was unfolded at the head of the bed where the body lay, and an ashtray with the stubs of some unfiltered cigarettes was posed next to the water jug.

Zagranichny—Kirov supposed that Zagranichny was the killer—had not been an angry man. The furniture and effects were undisturbed; the bed itself bore few signs of a struggle; from this angle even the body appeared unmarked save for the bloody palm prints, and they seemed to have been deliberately planted as if in fulfillment of some obscure rite.

Kirov rose from the bed. He began a methodical search of the room. The cigarettes showed no trace of lipstick, but the stubs were speckled with faint grease spots. He picked one of them up and his nose caught a strong whiff of clove oil that had impregnated the tobacco. He turned to the flight bags and found a change of clothing, photographs, makeup and indications of the owners' identities: Nadezhda Aleksandrovna Mazurova; Vera Sergeievna Kuznova. Kirov went through every detail of the bags and clothing, cut the linings and inserted his fingers to search out coins and hairpins, examined the photographs and tried to identify the people and the backgrounds. And all the while the body said: *Search me too!*

He turned at last from the bags and clothing and looked at the bed. His eyes led him slowly from the bedclothes to the object lying on them. She was pale and beautiful and the pity of her welled up in him with a force that shocked him as if he himself had been left naked, and he couldn't look anymore—couldn't look because he was appalled, perhaps as Viktor had been appalled. He rejected the sight and buried his face in his hands. When he drew them away the palms were wet.

Abruptly and coldly he returned to the corpse and flipped the head over so that he could see the face. He recognized it, but it was not that of Nadia Mazurova. Instead it was of a woman he had seen once before, in a vacant snow-covered lot near the women's hostel at Lyublino when she had fled from him. Bakradze had said that her name was Vera, and so it was. She resembled Nadia Mazurova only in the way of women of the same age and style. And for all that, the sense of grief and pity did not leave him.

He scanned her back and then turned the body over. The front was devoid of marks except the blood clotted in the pubic hair and the pinched line of the ligature which Zagranichny had used to throttle her; a pair of her own nylons. On closer examination the face revealed faint bruises beneath the makeup and the sign of old cuts on the jawbone and in the eyebrow, the remnants of old encounters with her killer, maybe even of the session in Viktor's *dacha* which he had filmed. So Vera had known Zagranichny and gone back. She still didn't deserve what had happened to her. The contrary idea was a lie put out by violent men. Perhaps she had gone back because she loved him — God help her.

There was a noise at the door, a key being inserted in the lock. Quickly Kirov switched off the light and took his place behind the door. A woman stepped into the room and her hand reached for the light switch. Kirov grabbed the hand and pressed his own palm over the woman's mouth. He kicked the door closed.

"Nadia!" he whispered. His hand released hers and slipped to her waist so that he could grip her invisibly to him. He could read her body and it spoke of terror even though she had recognized his voice. "Listen to me!" he urged her. *"Listen!* I'm going to let go of you and turn on the light. Something terrible has happened here, but you are going to pay no attention. You are going to concentrate on me — *look only at me.* Do you understand?" She nodded; her hair brushed his face. He turned her bodily, still clamping her by the hand around her waist so that now she was facing him, the upper part of her body resisting him while the prow of her pelvis was pressed against his. Cautiously he released the hold over her mouth and let his hand stray to the light switch. She made no movement but the release of a sigh which he felt as the stroking of his cheek. The room filled with light.

They stood for a second, each dazzled before the other. He felt her body relax slightly as the sight of him confirmed his identity; but her expression remained fearful, her eyes fixed on his as though the slightest deviation would be into horror.

"Your face . . ." she said uncertainly. He felt the burning of his skin.

"It isn't serious."

"You've been injured."

"It looks worse than it is."

She nodded acceptingly at this and asked simply: "Can I look around?"

"No."

"Why not? What's happened?"

He hesitated to tell her but he had no choice. "Your friend Vera is dead. Zagranichny was here tonight. He went crazy and he killed her. Her body is on the bed. I'm going to turn you slowly so that you can see her, but you won't make a sound, just look and it will all be over. Your own life is in danger, but I'm going to help you. Is that all understood?"

"I understand."

"Good," he said gently. "Now—quietly." He let her body slide in the cradle of his arms and her head pivot away from him slowly, slowly, until her eyes were looking away and he heard the cry catch in her throat. And then she was back to him, her arms around him and her face hidden in his breast. Her body shuddered and his own voice was saying: "I thought it was you—I thought it was you!"

He held her closely and comforted her; and he thought to himself: "She betrayed me," which was the explanation of the police at his hotel, intercepting his calls, since only Nadia Mazurova of all his enemies knew that he was in Tbilisi. Yet the point seemed immaterial as he felt her warmth and softness.

She was finished with crying. She pulled away from him and her expression was cold. "I'm sorry," she apologized.

"It's OK. I understand. Now we must get away. When Zagranichny comes to his senses or his friends learn what he's done, then they'll try to kill you too—is that clear? They won't be able to trust you now that Zagranichny has murdered your friend. Remember that he is indispensable to them. You aren't. You've been an embarrassment ever since Viktor was arrested. Viktor's girlfriend and his courier between Moscow and Tbilisi: you represent the link to the operation here. My guess is that only your connection with Georgi Gvishiani has kept you alive so far; and not even Georgi can save you now—you must believe me!"

"What do we do?"

"Good—good." Kirov held her at arm's length. Whatever her fears and suspicions, her calmness appeared complete. "I need a change of clothes. Can you get them for me?"

She nodded. "The copilot has the next room; he is about your size. If the *dezhurnaya* will let me have his key I can find something."

"And vodka—if he has any vodka, get that too."

She left him alone, closing the door behind her; left him to trust her. He returned to his search of the room. He reexamined Nadia's flight bag, recalling a small cardboard box that held cotton wool and some pieces of jewelry. He looked at them again. A pair of earrings. They answered in part the mystery of Viktor's diamonds. The junk stones that represented his commission on the deals with

276

the jeweler, Ostrowsky, had been converted into presents for his harem. Kirov checked the hands of the dead woman. Sure enough there was a ring mounting several cheap diamond chips. He felt a dull satisfaction that he was right.

She came back into the room carrying a change of clothes over her arm. "I'm afraid it's a uniform. Will that be OK? And the only drink I could get was this." "This" was a bottle of bootleg *samogon*.

"They'll have to do. Put the clothes on the bed." Kirov began to strip off. He washed himself at the handbasin and examined his face in the small mirror. One side was scorched red by the fire but looked as though it would heal well enough. In the reflection of the glass he could see her studying him with her impenetrable gaze. He took his trousers off and exchanged them for those of the copilot.

"The *dezhurnaya* is asleep," she said, anticipating his next question. "What next? Where do we go?"

"Do you know where Georgi Gvishiani lives?"

"Yes, but you can't want to go there."

"Have you got some cream?" Kirov indicated her flight bag. She delved into it and produced a pot of face cream. He applied a dab to the scorched skin and trusted it would work. "Zagranichny is there," he told her. "After tonight, he'll have gone running to his protector." He glanced at the woman. "I need to see him. I need to know for certain who he is."

She didn't recognize his necessities. "There are guards at the house."

"I'm not after trouble. But I need to see Zagranichny with my own eyes."

"And then?"

"I don't know."

"Your people will arrest him?"

"I don't have any people."

Her eyes showed surprise, but it was brief and followed by intelligence. "I see. I knew that Georgi had a lot of money to buy people. I just didn't realize how many people he had bought."

"Now you do," Kirov answered. He finished packing one of the flight bags, bundled up his clothes and handed them to the woman to carry. He wiped the surfaces to remove any prints, then turned off the light. The darkened room was still headily scented from the clove cigarettes, and he wondered why.

* * *

277

The street was broad and hilly and lined by sycamores. It lay near the university clinics off Ilya Chavchadze Boulevard, a block away from the river Vere. The house stood in a walled garden with a wrought-iron gate. It had a stuccoed façade and shuttered windows, a swimming pool in the garden, a patio and a mass of shrubbery. Gvishiani paid well to have it maintained. The pool was lit with a radiant blue light, and the still water invited the observer to drop a body into it.

"How many people does he have?" Kirov asked.

"There's a gardener and his wife, a cook, a manservant and a bodyguard."

"And militia? The police chief is in his pay, isn't he?"

"Sometimes there are militiamen there too."

"And what else?"

"He keeps guns."

"How many?"

"I don't know. In his study there are rifles on the walls. He likes to hunt."

"And the guard—he carries a gun?"

"A pistol. I've seen it under his coat."

"Describe the house."

"There's a hallway: the study is on the left and the dining room on the right. Behind the dining room is a kitchen and there's another room behind the study but I've never been in it."

"What about the upper floors."

"Four bedrooms, two bathrooms and an attic room. Georgi uses the bedroom above the study. The bodyguard sleeps next to it and the servant sleeps in the attic."

"What about the cook and the gardener?"

"The cook lives in the city. The gardener and his wife have a small house in the garden; you can't see it from here. What are you going to do?"

"Do the militia normally have a car?"

"Yes."

"There's no car there now."

The grounds of the house were empty, the garage doors closed. A light shone through a crack in the shutters at the study window. Kirov assessed the terrain and measured its distances in seconds to scale the wall and cross the open areas. "I'm not looking for trouble," he assured her. "I'm not trying to be a hero."

"Aren't you?" The remark was ironic, but she appeared indifferent to whether he caught the irony. It came to him that she regarded men with contempt. Except for Viktor who was somehow different. Among other things, Viktor wasn't a hero.

"Wait here," he told her. He tested the wall for footholds and in a few seconds had climbed it and dropped onto the soft earth on the other side. Without pausing he ran to the shelter of the nearest bushes, from where he could see to the far end of the grounds and the tiny house occupied by the gardener. A shaft of light spread from the main building across the grass and the gardener's wife was crossing from the rear to her home, carrying a covered plate with food from the kitchen. She halted and cast a glance in Kirov's direction then calmly resumed her course to the door of the cottage where she knocked and was admitted. The lights went out.

He crossed the twenty meters to the shadow of the main house and pressed himself against the wall under the dripping eaves. On this side a pair of french windows with heavy shutters gave onto a patio. The shutters were firmly locked and the dining room behind them was in darkness. Kirov edged to the corner and the well-lit façade and paused there. He had to decide whether to traverse the exposed front of the villa in order to check the study window or to try to gain access from the rear. He told himself that Gvishiani's security arrangements were more apparent than real — no dogs or electronic intruder systems; the racketeer had never needed them. He had the comfort and security of his friends, and the rest was all for show. He told himself it was an easy decision, but he felt the intensity of his fear and its absurdity. He was tired of being frightened; his body was stressed and weary with it; he wanted to lie down and sleep away the remnants of the night.

For half a minute Kirov remained in the comfort of the shadows. Then he roused himself and took his first step across the open façade under the brightness of a white lamp hanging at the porch. He crossed the grass on soft footsteps, crunched the gravel of the path immediately before the door, then grass again; and in open view he crouched before the study window and peered through the crack in the shutters. He looked into a large well-furnished room where two men were in conversation with a table between them and on the table a cut-glass decanter and a couple of tumblers.

He recognized Georgi Gvishiani. The Georgian was talking vigorously and smoking from a box of cigarettes that stood on the table. He was on his feet, pacing, standing now with his back to the window and his hands resting on the chimney-piece of a log fire while he considered the wall, now turning sharply and pointing at his companion and his face lit with anger. The person he was with was buried deep into a club chair, a naked leg stretched out and visible from the knee, an arm clad in a red velvet dressing gown lying limply on the arm rest, the fingers of the hand clenching and unclenching. The room was in darkness but for the firelight. The forms of the two men were mingled with shifting shadows. Their voices were inaudible.

Kirov tried to follow the conversation by the gestures and identify the elusive figure in the armchair. Gvishiani was inconstant, at one moment berating the other man, then taking a seat and silently pouring a glass of spirits while his face showed incomprehension and his eyes wandered to avoid the gaze of his companion. He was angry, puzzled and fearful, reduced by Zagranichny to mute fury. Kirov was certain that the stranger in the room was Zagranichny, masked as he had been in the film, but this time by the wings of the deep leather chair.

Nothing. No movement. The two men silently contemplating each other. Squatting outside the window Kirov felt the cold of the night eating into his muscles. He glanced around from time to time, and to his night-adjusted vision the garden seemed as bright as day. Lit by the lamp above the porch, he saw his own long shadow cast upon the grass. He forced himself to stay calm and watch the two men. Long minutes and then Zagranichny rose slowly from his chair, a tall, stooping figure with a large head that lolled listlessly, chin down on his breast. He gripped the arm of the chair for support and in his other hand he clutched a drink. He turned and faced the window. Two large eyes under a powerful brow gazed vacantly toward Kirov, who was transfixed by the bottomless blind-eyed stare. Then Zagranichny shambled toward the door and was gone.

Kirov got slowly to his feet. He moved quickly and softly to the shadows of the side of the house and then across the darkness of the lawn and the bushes to the wall. He found Nadia waiting for him as he had left her. She seemed guardedly pleased to see him, but he could not register the impression in competition with his recollection of Zagranichny, of the violence, desolation and emptiness in that pair of eyes.

"Well?" she asked.

"Well?" he answered sparkishly, wearing optimism like a suit of clothes because she needed it.

"Then it was all right," she said with relief.

"It was fine," he reassured her.

"You found out what you wanted?"

"Yes." He was thinking of Viktor, who used to play games with names. Zagranichny, for example. It was obvious really. Zagranichny meant *from abroad*.

"Did you see Zagranichny?" Nadia pressed him.

Kirov nodded. "I saw him. He's an American. His name is William Craig."

26

"How do we get out of here? Where do we go?"

She had worked that one out for herself. Georgi Gvishiani controlled the police. Now that he had got the story of the murder out of Zagranichny, he would be arranging the clean-up operation. The militia would be watching the hotels, the airport and the railway stations. Nadia knew better than Kirov how powerful the gangster was in the city. There was no point in approaching the local KGB: Gvishiani had long ago bought and sold the director with a villa in the mountains and a taste for the good life on a scale that a KGB officer could not match even from KGB's special resources. Besides, the man was a Georgian and he would stick by his own when it came to handling a Russian who was acting without formal sanction from Moscow.

"I've got to sleep," Kirov told her. He could feel his mind becoming dissociated from his body. The fight and the fire at the factory, the discovery of the woman's corpse, the risks of checking Gvishiani's villa—he had been storing up the effects of shock and was coming apart under the strain. "Do you have any friends in Tbilisi?"

"No."

"We can't use the hotels," he said abstractly.

"No."

He looked around for answers in the glittering sky and the pinpricks of light on the city's hills. "Let's walk," he suggested and offered her his arm.

They walked. They took a tramcar and stood among the sleepily nodding passengers like a married couple returning home from the theater. They strolled along the Kura Embankment and stared at the puddles of light in the darkly rolling river. "Where do we go?" she asked again.

"I need to sleep," he repeated. They entered one of the parks along the embankment and found a sheltered spot in the darkness of the trees and Kirov beckoned her to sit close to him for warmth.

"You're hurt," she told him with surprise in her voice as though she had not believed it.

He nodded and explained that he intended to sleep; he was trusting her to keep an eye out for any militia patrols. "I have to trust you," he told her again, reminding himself that at another time she had betrayed him to Georgi Gvishiani.

"That's all right," she said, and she allowed him to rest his head on her treacherous shoulder.

"Why Batumi?" she asked when he told her his plan.

"Because they expect us to head north to try to return to Moscow." Batumi lay on the coast to the west. It would be possible to pick up a train there.

"And how do we travel?"

"We hitch."

At the third attempt they stopped a truck going to the city. The driver accepted the bottle of *samogon* in payment. He was carrying spare parts for a tea factory; the wagon was only half loaded and it suited him that his passengers slept out of sight in the back.

Ten miles from Tbilisi there was a roadblock on the highway, a car and four militiamen who checked the driver's papers and made a cursory examination of the outside of the vehicle without any sense of purpose. Two miles farther down the road the driver stopped again and opened the back of the truck, letting in the bright daylight.

"Was it you they were looking for?" he asked.

"No," Kirov told him.

The driver weighed up the answer skeptically. "Fuck them," he said finally, and closed up the truck again.

The road descended from the Georgian highlands toward the coast through hills covered in hornbeam and oak, gray in the winter sun. They drove through kilometers of tea plantations and, as evening fell, the land gave way to orchards and the smell of fruit trees pushing through the damp yellow earth, then the fragrance of camphor and eucalyptus and the strange unintelligible

283

shoutings of a road gang working along the highway.

It was nighttime when the truck dropped them in the city just outside the port area. The sky was black and cloudy and patched with flashes from the flare stacks of the oil refineries. A mild breeze blew from the direction of the sea, ruffling the palm fronds.

"Tomorrow we take a train to Moscow," said Kirov. To lift her morale he added: "For now we'll find a hotel and a bed for the night."

"Is that safe on my papers?"

"I have papers," Kirov answered. He didn't mention that the papers carried the security of a money-back guarantee from Yuri the Bazaar. Instead he said: "I'll smuggle you into my room," which made them both laugh since it sounded like a student stunt. And with the laughter, Nadia Mazurova seemed to him for a second to become totally beautiful as her unemphatic blue eyes shone openly instead of with evasion. But as soon as she recognized this dangerous intimacy it was gone, leaving a space between them across which he offered his hand. Together they set out into the warm night, the palms and the eucalyptus, through the streets of a city that was another Russia.

After a couple of tries and some negotiation Kirov found a room at a small hotel. It was shabby and smelled of fish and bad plumbing, and held a single bed with grimy coverings. Nadia sat on it and looked bleakly at the wall while Kirov smoked and studied her and smoked while ideas and reflections drifted in and out of his consciousness. Where had Craig come by his clove-scented cigarettes? Was it important? Who would know the answer? He could still smell the room where the murder had occurred, and see the body of the woman with her blood-smeared pubis and the ligature around her neck. Nadia Mazurova still clearly thought he was a dangerous man. Strange. He hadn't eaten for twenty-four hours. Hunger was making him light-headed. He considered going out to find some food but decided against taking the risk. She had said nothing though he supposed that her hunger must be nearly as acute. Tell me you are hungry, he thought, allow me even so far into your world. He filled his belly with smoke and stared at their reflections in the window.

"Batumi," he mused aloud. Something stirred dimly in his memory. "You seemed surprised when I mentioned it."

"I thought we would go directly to Moscow," she responded dully.

284

"It wasn't that." Kirov pictured the look on her face. "Not that. Have you been here before? Was Viktor here?"

"Last year."

"How — why?"

"Georgi liked to come here for his health. He stayed at the sanatorium in Kobuleti."

"And Viktor?"

"Georgi invited us both to visit at his expense."

"That was when Georgi and Viktor were still friends?"

"They were always friends."

"No," Kirov reminded her. "Viktor changed, didn't he? After Zagranichny beat up your girlfriend, Vera, at Viktor's *dacha*, Viktor became unpredictable. He burst into tears one night at the Aragvi — you know because you were there. Georgi didn't like that. No more friendship after that. Strictly business — and business demanded that Viktor be thrown to the wolves."

"I had hoped — " she didn't finish. She buried her face in her hands and her body was racked by sobbing. Kirov found himself watching her and thinking that this was how it would look if he had struck her a blow in the face and that her body and the expression in her eyes were keyed for it, for the expectation of violence. He wanted to tell her that it was not like that, step across the room, take her in his arms and shake her until she understood.

"Batumi," he resumed to put his other thoughts away. "Did Viktor ever come here on business?"

"Sometimes," she answered, wiping her eyes.

"Why?"

"I don't know."

"What was Georgi's involvement with the Pharmprodsoyuz factory?"

"He provided transport."

"When they shipped the goods out of Tbilisi to put them on the black market?"

"Yes."

"But Batumi? What business could they have in Batumi?"

"I don't know. Georgi also supplied things which the plant needed. Perhaps they came from Batumi."

"Things?"

"Things — I don't know."

Kirov believed her. Behind her fear and distrust she was trying to cooperate with him. And if her answers were obscure it was

285

because the Great Jewish Antibiotics Ring was obscure. Conspiracies are not meant to be understood. He should not be surprised if this one yielded its truth slowly. It was enough that he had another piece of the puzzle. The plant at Tbilisi received supplies from Batumi, unrecorded deliveries: Kirov had seen one of the trucks at the factory. What were they? Why from Batumi?

She slept. In the darkness she curled up on the bed in a fetal position, and when he spoke she didn't answer. He covered her with the bedclothes and for a while watched over her. He went downstairs to the lobby and persuaded the desk clerk to allow him the use of the phone. He called Moscow, a safe number he had prearranged with Bogdanov. The old man was jumpy and swamped him with questions until Kirov calmed him and put his own question: "Have you managed to pull Craig's file?"

"No. I told you it can't be hurried. Krapotkin can't find the access code. He's waiting for a legitimate request for a closed file and he hopes to piggyback our business onto it. Maybe tomorrow, maybe not. Where's the rush?"

"Craig is in Tbilisi," Kirov answered, and waited through the long silence.

"Jesus! How?"

"Craig and Zagranichny are the same man. That was the point of the film. That's how Viktor hoped to save himself."

The line went dead again and Bogdanov came back slowly: "I'll speak to Krapotkin. I can't make promises . . . I . . . like I said, I'll speak to Krapotkin."

"Do that."

"Sure." Tentatively the old man asked: "Anything else?"

Kirov ignored the plea behind the words, which said: Don't tell me any more. He asked: "What do you know about Batumi that makes it special?"

"Batumi?"

"The plant at Tbilisi is bringing in secret supplies from there."

"Batumi," Bogdanov repeated, and lingered over the name, using it like a spade to lever up an ancient memory. "The gold fraud?" he said speculatively.

"I've never heard of it. How is it relevant?"

"It probably isn't," the other man answered cautiously, "except for the way it worked. Batumi is only a few kilometers from the Turkish border. The boys in the gold fraud case used to trade gold over the frontier for Western imports. What do you think? Is that it? Those guys down there could be running a smuggling operation."

27

"Ludmila Fillipovna," Kirov said with quiet humility. "Here, let me carry that for you." She gave up her shopping bag without question even as she was examining the stranger with surprise. "Pyotr Andreevitch Kirov — I work for your husband — I have visited your *dacha* — do you remember?"

"I remember," she answered peaceably, and in her distracted fashion glanced back at the village grocery store in case she had left something. "Yes, I remember," she repeated as though the memory were a fond one. "We don't receive many visitors, Mother and I. Rodion Mikhailovitch says that his work is too confidential to allow many friends. Is that right?" she added with a strange curiosity.

"Friends can be unreliable."

"Like Pasha Radek?" she replied unexpectedly shrewdly. "He brought me presents when he visited us. I didn't think it was necessary. It was showing off. He'd been somewhere — Kiev, I think — and was feeling very pleased with himself. I tried to warn my husband, but he wouldn't listen. He said he had to trust someone. I thought that he would have trusted you."

"I thought he did trust me. I was mistaken."

Nadia emerged from behind a car. Kirov took her gently by the arm and introduced her to Grishin's wife as a friend. Ludmila Fillipovna accepted this explanation. She looked down at the snow underfoot and her felt boots and the others' shoes and said: "You're not dressed for the weather."

"We've been away — in the South."

"That must be nice. The general is also away at the moment."

"At your flat in Moscow?"

"I think so. Things are very busy there."

"Is anyone staying with you other than your mother-in-law?"

"No—should there be?"

"Have you had many visitors lately, perhaps Radek or his friends?"

"No."

"Workmen at the *dacha?*"

"No." She laughed to suggest that that never happened.

"And neighbors?" he said with a receptive smile. "Still the same old neighbors?"

"Yes, of course."

"Of course."

"You think we're being spied on?" she asked with the same odd display of intelligence, so that Kirov concluded that Grishin's wife was not the rumored idiot. She was naïve, childlike even, a product of the purdah in which some of the KGB and Party chiefs kept their partners, but no fool.

They walked away from the village along the snowbound paths that serviced the secluded cottages behind their screens of birch and spruce. Ludmila Fillipovna talked gaily of life in winter out here in the countryside; she shared the general's intimate love and knowledge of their private territory. Kirov nodded and sympathized and watched the cars and the passersby, the shuttered houses and the fleeting figures chopping wood and clearing snow.

She opened the door of the *dacha* and called out: "Mother, we have visitors!"

"Who are they and what do they want?" The old woman emerged from the kitchen with flour on her hands and her face set in a sour grimace.

"What *do* you want?" Ludmila Fillipovna asked.

"Haven't you asked them?" interjected the mother. "Times like these, and you don't ask questions of strangers? Idiot!"

"I need to speak to Rodion Mikhailovitch."

"Go and see him in Moscow," said the mother.

"I'd like you to phone him," Kirov addressed the daughter. "Ask him to come here. But don't tell him that anyone is here with you—don't even hint it."

"You'll do no such thing!" said the mother. "We're in enough trouble as it is."

Ludmila Fillipovna regarded the older woman meekly, but she reached for the phone.

Under pressure Grishin agreed to come to the *dacha*, but not before evening. His time was occupied by another long session in front of the Rehabilitation Committee, justifying his role in the affair of Academician I. A. Yakovlevitch. Kirov passed the brief day watching the silent snow and the uneventful forest. Nadia sat with Grishin's wife while the latter took her through the children's stories that she spent her days writing; and the old woman rattled like a poltergeist in the kitchen. "Have you read these?" Nadia asked him, referring to the stories. "They're really good!" Kirov shook his head. He had noted the bond of sympathy building up between the women and felt excluded from it. "Is anyone out there?" she inquired. He told her nobody. There was no one out there, nobody to turn to: he had reduced all the world to strangers.

Grishin came bustling through the door at six thirty. He gave his eager wife a peck on the cheek and said testily: "What's this all about? Can't you see I have things to do?" Kirov emerged from the back room and put a finger to his lips to silence the other man. He moved to the window and studied the road. The general's Chaika was parked conspicuously, the driver lounging at the wheel. Behind it was a gray Volga with four occupants showing no interest in getting out of the warmth of the car.

"How are you, Rodion Mikhailovitch?" The general was across the room and it seemed to Kirov, watching them, Grishin small and open-mouthed clutching the hand of Ludmila Fillipovna, that they were refugees as he had seen them in films. "You weren't expecting me? You thought that Heltai had got me—or maybe Radek?"

"What are you doing here? My spouse—my parent . . ."

"Your wife recognizes a friend when she sees one," Kirov answered. Ludmila Fillipovna retreated at that suggestion of involvement; her lively eyes turned to glass buttons. Kirov put a hand under Nadia's arm and raised her out of the chair. "May I introduce Nadezhda Aleksandrovna Mazurova. I may have mentioned her. She was Viktor Gusev's girlfriend."

"You must be insane!" Grishin snapped. "I'm under investigation!"

"I don't have many choices. Like you I have to rely on my friends."

Grishin was not disposed to argue that proposition. With a

shrug he became calm and self-possessed and inquired: "What do you want?"

"Help. What do *you* want?"

Grishin shook his head and, finding a vacant chair, settled into it and composed himself with a what-happens-next? expression on his face. His wife squatted beside him. He looked sourly at her, but eased when he saw her look of luminous happiness. He stroked her hand. "I'm sorry," he said, addressing his visitor.

"For what?"

"You know for what."

"It doesn't matter."

"I was confused."

"You thought that I was responsible for provoking the investigation into the Yakovlevitch case?"

Grishin shied from the directness of the question. He confined himself to saying: "It was logical."

"It doesn't matter," Kirov reassured him. He had in mind his father's betrayals and in turn the betrayal of his father by Beria among Uncle Lavrenti's many betrayals. It was the way things were. You couldn't quarrel with it.

"Where do we go from here?" Grishin asked.

"Tell me about the Great Jewish Antibiotics Ring."

Grishin laughed. It was a bitter laugh. He let it flow out until it went on too long and became embarrassing. He squeezed his wife's hand and kissed her cheek then threw a long look of curiosity at Nadia Mazurova. And then he returned to Kirov, his face as sick as tallow beneath his round rosy cheeks. "Do you honestly believe I understand it?" he began with a long slow sarcasm. "It isn't a *thing* — at least, not a single thing. It's like" — he was searching for a word — "putty. All the children are allowed to play with it, and, as long as you have it, you can make what you want out of it. Do you follow me?"

"What's your version?"

"You know my version."

"Tell me again."

"It's the same story that Radek gave the Rehabilitation Committee. Andropov asked me to put together a scenario that implicated Yakovlevitch and a group of senior Jewish doctors in the illegal trade in antibiotics. That's all there is to it. You want to know if it's true? The answer is: No. It's a fabrication: no doctors, no Jews, no conspiracy. We made the whole thing up because at the time it was convenient."

"And Andropov's own version?" Kirov asked. "He had a different version, didn't he? What was it?"

"He didn't tell me. He took the KGB and he played with the bits like a musical instrument, one department doing one thing, one department doing another. He could do that because he ran the business."

Kirov nodded understandingly. He understood that Grishin was being evasive. Partly a matter of guilt, he supposed. Partly it was that there were some things that were not supposed to be talked about but merely hinted. The secret world had its own version of prudishness. "But you found out," he said, and Grishin admitted that was so.

"Later — when Andropov had died and the thing was unraveled. It was Stalin, Beria, the Doctors' Plot, all over again. This time Yakovlevitch and his friends became poisoners. They were plotting to kill Andropov and the beneficiary was going to be Chernenko. Andropov would unmask the plot and Chernenko and the rest of the old Brezhnev gang would be off the Politburo and into retirement if they cooperated — and something else if they didn't. Do we have to go into this? It didn't happen. Andropov died."

"Or was murdered."

"He died!" Grishin affirmed vehemently. "There was an investigation by GRU when Chernenko got wind of what was happening. Everyone was cleared. There was no murder!"

"If you say so," Kirov agreed.

"Damn right I do!"

The force of the reply puzzled Kirov. Then an idea came to him, which was obvious enough, or would have been if the Ring did not cloud everything. "Is the Committee moving to involve you in Andropov's death?" When he received no reply he knew it was true and that Grishin had been wrestling for his life to explain the ambiguous structure of fact that had been created. He glanced at Ludmila Fillipovna who was sitting on the floor with calmness wrapped around her. He looked to Nadia. She had abstracted herself as if the things that men did to each other in their violence and ambition did not concern her.

"And you?" Grishin snapped back almost jovially. "What's your version?" There was a note of scorn, an implication that Kirov had pursued a children's tale. "Did you solve the mystery of Viktor Gusev?"

"Most of it."

"Well?"

"Viktor was the Moscow distributor for a drugs racket operating out of Tbilisi. The boss is a local gangster called Georgi Gvishiani. The drugs are packaged to appear to come from Bulgaria, but they don't. Some of them are produced at a factory in Tbilisi; but, because demand is so high, the Ring smuggles in additional supplies from Turkey through Batumi. I don't know where these extra drugs originate but they are organized by an American by the name of William Craig—" Grishin stopped him.

"How did Craig become involved?"

"I'm not certain until I see his file. He has some expertise in pharmaceuticals production and was selling his company's secrets illegally. He helped to set up the factory in Tbilisi and defrauded his company of the license fees that should have been paid. While he was in Tbilisi he fell in with Gvishiani and the two of them devised the scheme—probably with some help from the local military, since there is a second installation on the same site that seems to be Army-run. The whole racket is tied to dealing in diamonds. Viktor bought them from a jeweler called Ostrowsky and the Ring used them to pay for the drugs it was importing—and it probably keeps some of the profits in the West. The diamonds have two advantages. They're easier to carry out of the country than the mass of small bills that the Ring gets from its customers. And secondly, the price the diamonds fetch in the West is substantially higher than their cost here, so the conversion makes the overall scheme more profitable."

"Clever."

Kirov felt that Grishin wasn't really interested. This interpretation of the Ring was as tawdry and shabby as the goods you could buy in the stores—but to Kirov it also had the same authentic Russian feel; it couldn't be dismissed. He said: "But there's still one more version, isn't there? What does Ferenc Heltai's version look like?"

Perhaps it was guilt; Grishin's face flickered with sadness and regret. Kirov thought calmly: I used to be his protégé and he sacrificed me to protect himself. He could understand why and it did not bother him. It was this fact of not caring that had become the mystery.

"I don't know Heltai's version," Grishin answered.

"But you knew he was dangerous."

"I knew he had killed Academician Yakovlevitch. After the collapse of the plot, I had to keep an eye on Yakovlevitch because he *knew,* and he could tell. So when he was given an exit visa, it was clear to me that it couldn't be the real thing. No one was going to allow him to start talking. I suppose Heltai was chosen for the killing because he had already become involved and because he knew something about poisons. Maybe that's all Heltai's version is. Maybe he simply has a brief to stop the stories surrounding Andropov's death from getting out."

"I thought Andropov wasn't murdered."

Grishin shugged. "That's the reality—but it's the appearances that count. Perhaps we're all a little crazy. We ran around making it look as though Andropov was murdered. It can amount to the same thing. Yakovlevitch was killed out of—embarrassment, I suppose."

"Heltai is still killing people."

"Yes, I know," Grishin acknowledged coolly. "I can't fully explain it. You can't expect complete answers to everything."

There was a noise outside. One of Grishin's watchers had got bored and come up to the house. He was rooting among the trash and the woodpiles like a stray dog. Kirov peered through a gap in the shutters and saw the man standing at the vegetable patch. A smoky stream of urine hit the earth. He found Grishin at his shoulder, examining the scene morosely.

"That's the dross we have to work with," Grishin observed philosophically. "Do you see us building our bright new world out of characters like that?" He felt no necessity of explaining that he was personally on the side of the angels and always had been notwithstanding certain conduct in the past and the convenient treasons of everyday life such as pushing Kirov in the direction of Heltai and the GRU killing machine because it had seemed expedient. "The changes have created uncertainties." He turned from the window and the dark world outside and was blinking at the lights. "Uncertainty creates opportunities. Perhaps GRU are doing no more than trying to exploit these for themselves and their masters in the Army."

"The Army is involved in the plant at Tbilisi," Kirov reminded him. "There is a second installation there producing—biological warfare agents? Poisons? Georgi Gvishiani can't have been running his operation without military involvement. They control the plant and they turn a blind eye to the cross-border smuggling. Heltai works indirectly for the Army. Perhaps that's the connection between the different stories. That and the American. What does the Army want?"

"It doesn't want to see the military budget cut as a result of *perestroika* and disarmament," Grishin said drily and in an almost jaunty mood now that he had recovered his nerve asked: "And what do you want? And what's in it for me?"

"Radek hasn't beaten you yet."

"You can stop him?" Grishin retorted skeptically.

"If you bring in a big coup."

"Like what?"

"Give them the Ring, the complete explanation that ties in Heltai, the Army, Yakovlevitch, the whole thing. It represents everything that *perestroika* is working against. Deliver it to the Committee and the past will be forgotten."

"You're guessing that there is some sort of total explanation." Grishin knocked any shred of enthusiasm out of Kirov's answer. Then he relented. "Maybe, maybe. Where else is there to go? OK — maybe there's something in what you say. But where are you going to get this answer?"

"From the American, Craig. He was involved in the Bulgarian plant and is up to his neck in the racket at Tbilisi. He's the link between the GRU investigation after Andropov's death and whatever the Army is up to in Georgia. Whatever the Ring is, Craig is the key."

Jack Melchior opened the door of his apartment.

"Hello, Peter — you'd better come in." The little man looked up and down the corridor nervously and left a crack in the doorway just wide enough to slide through. "The others are here as promised. Hush-hush, eh? Bog didn't say. 'Do me a favor, Jack,' that's all. Well, where would I be if I didn't do favors — where would we all be? That's what I say. Nothing untoward, though — right? You wouldn't drop me in the shit, would you, Peter?"

Two men were already in the room: Bogdanov and a second man that Kirov took to be Uncle Bog's friend, the computer wizard, Krapotkin. One of Jack Melchior's wives was in the kitchen fixing some snacks and another was in the bedroom drying her hair. Melchior had spruced himself up in a frogged velvet smoking jacket and a pair of brocade slippers. Bogdanov was in a dirty mismatched suit and still wearing his hat. Krapotkin was a short, white-haired man of fifty with hamster cheeks and a pallid complexion. He gave a look of recognition as Kirov came into the room and then fell back into his chair where he was nibbling at his thoughts.

Bogdanov opened up. "Tell your missus to hurry up with the snacks, Jack, and then bugger off, will you. Have you two met? Sergei Pavlovitch Krapotkin — Pyotr Andreevitch Kirov. Well, you've met now. Come on, Jack, get a move on. Jack's helping us out —"

"A favor," said Jack.

" — a favor."

Krapotkin was a man with something on his mind and was wrapping his expressive face around the problem.

"Sergei insisted on seeing you face to face," Bogdanov explained with a hint of contempt. He emphasized the point to Krapotkin: "Doesn't trust his uncle Bog to get the story straight. Doesn't want to commit his words to writing in case the Bad Men read them."

"Did you break into the file?" Kirov asked.

"Of course he broke into the bloody file!" snapped Bogdanov. He stared at Jack Melchior. "What — are you still here?"

"Sorry, Bog, just getting some things."

"Clear off. And you too," Bogdanov added, taking the plate of *zakuski* from Melchior's wife, a sullen, goggle-eyed woman, twenty years younger than Jack.

"Just a moment," Kirov interrupted. Melchior paused, pleased that he might be helpful.

"Yes?"

"You've traveled, Jack. Where do cigarettes that smell of clove oil come from?"

"Christ, you haven't been offered some of those, have you? I wouldn't wish them on my enemies. Coffin nails, real El Stinkos!"

"Where do they come from?" Kirov repeated.

"Indonesia mostly, but you can pick them up anywhere in the East."

"So, boss, any trouble getting here?" Bogdanov asked when Jack Melchior was gone and he could ease up a little.

"No."

"What? No spooks? No trailing cars? Men reading newspapers?

Maybe this profession isn't all it's cracked up to be."

"And you?"

"So, so. Radek is losing interest. He thinks you're finished, and his hands are full piling stones onto Grishin's grave so he doesn't rise from the dead. It seems that not everybody on the Rehabilitation Committee thinks this Yakovlevitch case is such a big deal. A yid doctor is killed—and, even these days, who cares? Heltai is trawling the streets with his goons—I had to shake off a couple—but he still doesn't have the resources for complete surveillance. I'm not sure he has the full GRU organization behind him. This business could be just a stunt to cover some game that Heltai and a few of his friends in the Army are playing—a piece of private enterprise. Does that make sense to you?"

"Perhaps." Kirov scrutinized the old man. Too cheerful—too prickly. He was fit to laugh to breaking point. Kirov turned to Krapotkin who was brooding morosely. As friendly as he could he asked: "Why didn't you bring me a printout?"

Krapotkin peered up and looked embarrassed. "I couldn't take the risk of the printout being found if . . . you know . . . *if* . . . Anyway it seemed safer to tell you myself. I memorized the file. I've got a good memory," he added proudly in case Kirov had his doubts.

"I'm sure you have," Kirov soothed him. "Well? Tell me. Who is our Mister William Craig?"

"He's CIA," said Krapotkin. He giggled.

At all events Craig had been CIA. Whether that was still the case was uncertain. According to Krapotkin, the American had been born in Boston in 1938 to a good family and had received an education at Cornell and MIT. He had degrees and postgraduate qualifications in human biology and biochemistry. For what it was worth, he had been married once and divorced in 1967. There were no children. He was currently the European Vice President of the Lee Foundation and had been since 1975.

The file said that Craig was recruited by the CIA in 1968. No authority was cited for this statement; so, said Krapotkin, the information must have been volunteered by Craig himself. The American had worked at the biological warfare research institute at Fort Detrick, Maryland, from 1968 to 1972 and was then posted to the Far East.

"What was a biochemist doing in Vietnam?" Bogdanov asked.

This biochemist, Krapotkin explained, was not in Vietnam. He was establishing a clandestine facility in Taiwan producing poisons and BW agents for CIA covert operations in Southeast Asia. He did this until 1975 when the war ended and the operation was terminated and the physical plant converted to civilian production.

"Who owns it now?"

"The Mimosa Drug Company. It's a small operation, owned by the Taiwanese."

"Does Craig have any continuing involvement?"

Krapotkin liked that question. "I did a check on the company. The Lee Foundation is trying to stop Mimosa's products from being circulated. It seems that Mimosa has some of the Lee Foundation's formulations. You might like to ask where they got them from."

After the Vietnam war, Craig was removed from the CIA's operational staff and took employment with the Lee Foundation in Europe. In 1980 he showed up in Bulgaria to negotiate a license with Pharmachim, the foreign-trade organization for the drugs industry. The result was the Bulpharma plant. That was when he came to the attention of KGB as a result of a violent sexual incident that occurred on one of his trips. "I can't get any more details on what happened," Krapotkin said in answer to the inevitable question.

"KGB," he said, "passed him over to GRU because of Craig's background in the military use of drugs and other pharmaceuticals. The Army used him to set up a plant in Tbilisi—partly to produce drugs based on the Lee Foundation's technology, and partly to use his experience at Fort Detrick to help out with their own military installation at the same plant."

And that, according to Krapotkin, was all there was, other than a suspicion that Craig still maintained some sort of contact with the CIA—it would be unusual if he didn't.

"Where's the woman?" Bogdanov asked. He was smoking a cigarette and examining Jack Melchior's framed certificates from bogus American universities and the faded photograph of Melchior and his buddies in the Palestine Police, grinning with glossy hair oil and sunburnt knees, glasses of beer clutched in their hands.

"I've left her at Grishin's place."

"With his wife? Is she really an idiot, the wife?"

From the bedroom came the laughter of Melchior and his women and a *breep-breep* as Melchior did his trimphone impression for their amusement.

"Not an idiot," Kirov answered distractedly. "Innocent, perhaps."

Krapotkin shuffled himself and said: "Well, I'll be going. I hope what I had to say was helpful."

"What? Oh, sure," said Bogdanov. "I'll be seeing you around."

"Thanks," said Kirov and offered a hand, which Krapotkin took gratefully. He bumbled after his hat and coat and then left. Melchior must have heard the door close; he came out of the bedroom.

"Everything all right here? You blokes finished?" He stared at Kirov seriously for a second. "I knew there was something bothering me. You've grown a mustache, haven't you?"

"No, he hasn't," Bogdanov retorted.

"No? Oh—well, if you say so. A nod's as good as a . . . yes, well, mum's the word."

"Bog and I still need to talk," Kirov told him.

"You heard. Sod off," said Bogdanov.

"Righty-ho," Melchior agreed apologetically. He returned to the bedroom where his wives were complaining.

Bogdanov took a leisurely bite at one of his nails. "Is Grishin going to help?" he asked.

"He's agreed to provide travel papers."

"Is he still in a position to fix that?"

"He says so. He has friends. They don't want to see the Committee come up with the wrong answers. Investigating the past makes them uncomfortable."

"It makes a lot of us uncomfortable. Nobody expected virtue to come back into fashion." Bogdanov took his hat off and started to pick the dirt from it. "What are you going to do with the Mazurova woman?"

"Take her with me."

"Abroad? After Craig?"

"It won't be expected," Kirov answered. He didn't know whether that was true or if it was the real reason for his decision, but he couldn't dissociate the woman from the solution to all the mysteries. She still bore herself as if she carried the clue deep inside her—as if there were another version of the Ring, shared only by Nadia Mazurova, the dead Vera and the rest of Viktor's women, a version that explained their loyalties and the tears at the Aragvi that no one claimed to understand. Kirov looked up to find Bogdanov studying him.

"It's your funeral."

"My funeral," Kirov agreed.

"You're crazy!" Bogdanov said with exasperation. "You don't even know where Craig is!"

Kirov shook his head. "I know," he answered. "Craig has gone back to the source. It's where he feels safe. He thinks he can sit events out there and watch the game."

"Where is 'there'?" Bogdanov asked.

"The plant that Craig set up to produce drugs using the formulations he stole from the Lee Foundation." Kirov glanced at the notes he had taken from Krapotkin's explanation. He remembered the smell of cloves from the oriental cigarette that Craig smoked as he killed the woman Vera. "Craig is in China," he said.

28

The road to Taiwan led through Budapest and Vienna. Grishin provided travel papers to Hungary and two Austrian passports bearing photographs with a passing resemblance to anyone who combed his hair a particular way and wore heavy spectacles. There are no visa requirements for Austrian citizens visiting Hungary, and the border can be crossed with a simple entry and exit stamp and no formality. Bogdanov obtained currency from Yuri the Bazaar. Hungarian forints are not officially convertible, but in practice can be exchanged for hard currency in Vienna, where Kirov and Nadia Mazurova stayed for two days waiting for clearance to travel to Taiwan. Visas are required for Taiwan, but, since the country has few foreign embassies, they are issued on entry at Taipei. All that is required is a letter of introduction from one of Taiwan's foreign liaison offices. In Vienna letters can be obtained from the Institut für Chinesische Kultur in the Stubenring. The office is concerned mainly with whether the applicant has connections in the Eastern bloc. Kirov told the diffident Chinese clerk that he had never been to a Communist country.

Taipei like other vigorous cities appears to lack a middle ground. The flashy towers that house the banks and the international hotels jostle for space with ramshackle workshops, spice emporiums and old wooden godowns, with no sense of transition. The present sits on the past like an army of occupation and the population act as collaborators, defrauding the occupier even as they smile and clean his boots.

Kirov and Nadia Mazurova checked in at the Howard Plaza in

301

Jen Ai Road. The clerk produced a message in an envelope along with the room key. Kirov opened the envelope and found a slip of paper printed in Chinese. He showed it to the clerk. "Chinese opera," said the clerk. "This is ticket for performance — seven thirty this evening. Opera is at Armed Forces Cultural Activities Center." He wrote some characters on a slip of paper. "Give to taxi man and he take you to Chung Hua Road. Stop at building seven of China Bazaar and cross street. OK?" Kirov pocketed the ticket and asked the bellboy to take up the bags.

"We're sharing a room?" Nadia asked when the bellboy was gone. The two cases lay on the bed. The room had the vacant look that affects all hotel rooms. The television was showing an English-language film. Nadia was sitting on the bed studying the folds of her dress.

"We spent too much money in Vienna," Kirov told her. "I don't have much left." In the film people were shooting each other. He turned from watching it and found the woman watching him. "I'll sleep in a chair," he said indifferently and returned to the tepid action on the screen.

The afternoon passed. A sharp fall of warm rain rattled off the window and then stopped. Kirov fended off the effects of travel with cigarettes. He had taken the opera ticket from his pocket and it lay on the table by the ashtray. Once he called the desk and asked if there were any more messages but there were none. Just the ticket with its unintelligible script.

"I have to go to sleep," Nadia told him. She searched for a nightdress in her case. "Is it possible to have some clothes washed?" He answered that he would see what could be arranged. Their cases were by now full of unwashed clothing, rumpled and sour. Finding no nightdress Nadia turned her back to him and stripped off her clothes so that he could see the fine curve of her naked back and buttocks, and the shallow play of light on her skin.

"Viktor was homosexual, wasn't he?" Kirov said. She froze, still not looking at him. Her hands clutched a scrap of underwear. "That's why you weren't his mistress, isn't it? That was the little secret between Viktor and all his women."

"He was kind to us," she responded distantly. She folded her clothes and stooped to place them on a chair. The fall of her breasts was in shadow, the nipples like darts emergent from the silhouette.

"He could afford to be."

"Other men can't?" she asked. The bedclothes were folded down. She slipped between the sheets and pulled them so that only her shoulders were exposed and her face with its expression that was not an accusation but a plea holding no hope of its being answered.

"I don't know," Kirov admitted. He lit another cigarette instead of giving in to tiredness. He put a couple of questions to her — what did she think of Taiwan? — as if she were a tourist. The smoke was making him sick. He extinguished the cigarette and poured a glass of mineral water from the bar and took this to the window where his reflection and hers and the view over Jen Ai Road to the distance and an unidentified Chinese monument confounded themselves. Her manner told him again that the relationship between men and women was a mystery, a conspiracy as fluid as the Ring, open-ended as the actors turned it to their needs, a question to which all answers were provisional.

When he turned from the window she was asleep. He placed his empty glass on the table and took a seat where he could keep watch over the woman. He checked his watch for the hours until the performance at the Chinese opera and his heavy-lidded eyes struggled to focus. What he needed was sleep. He began to remove his clothes.

Her sleep was restless. She made a fist of her right hand and clenched the pillow. Outside a brewing storm stained the sky purple and revealed a furtive moon in wracks of indigo cloud. Kirov stood naked by the window, with moonlight on his back and his dark impenetrable gaze lying upon her. His body was hard and still as a statue while her pliant form whimpered and writhed in her dreams. He stepped slowly across the room, leaned forward and drew back the sheets at one corner of the bed exposing the flesh of her spine and the soft swell of her contours. He sat on the edge of the bed and leaned over to touch her shoulder.

She shuddered. The pace of her breathing changed. He heard the irregular rhythm, the catching in the throat. She turned over slowly. Her face was shadowed by his except for a bar of light across her forehead and a single bright dot in her eyes. He knew he must be invisible to her, no more than outline of form, translatable into any man. He came no closer and withdrew his hand so that they did not touch and only their breathing, stirring the insubstantial air between them, formed a link. She said: "It's easy to love men." The words hurt her. She turned her head toward the pillow so that her expression was wholly in darkness. Kirov's hand was resting on the pillow and he could feel the tears that he could not see. Her muted voice went on: "But it's difficult to like them."

"You liked Viktor?"

"Yes."

"I see." He began to remove his hand but encountered her fingers splayed across the pillow. They touched his and halted there, hooked around his fingers like a question.

Kirov made love to her tenderly, although she was a stranger.

At six thirty Kirov rose and dressed. He told Nadia that he had to leave her for a while, warning her to close and lock the door behind him and not to answer any callers. He collected the opera ticket and went down to the hotel lobby where he checked again for messages. In the street he picked up a blue-shield cab and had the driver take him to the China Bazaar in Chung Hua Road.

In the mild night the pavements were crowded with pedestrians. Chung Hua Road was a chaotic stream of cars and motorcycles maneuvering between lanes. People were crowding around a new restaurant that displayed a series of red floral targets calling on good luck and the gods' blessings for the business. Kirov crossed the road and made his way through the crush of local fans into the theater. He displayed his ticket and was shown to a seat among the rows of black-haired Chinese. The side of the stage was occupied by the orchestra. There were few props. In due course the orchestra struck up, the hubbub of voices subsided and the performance began.

He first became aware of the Australian when the row started bobbing up and down to allow someone to get past and a friendly Australian voice said: "G'day, mate. Know all about this stuff or do you need a helping hand? The fella there with the purple on his face, that's Lo Hung-hsun, he's the good guy. Look out for the fella in the white paint job, he's a cunning bastard."

Kirov turned his head. The man next to him nodded good-naturedly and revealed a row of teeth with a gold incisor. "Watch the show, mate," he said pointedly. "Fella there, red face, that's Yu. He's Lo's servant. Real bloody hero! Lo's in the mountains—chair there equals mountains, get it? The other fellas are robbers or something." On his lap the Australian had a paper bag. He took a peanut from it and nibbled. "Here they go, singing their heads off. The female is Pi Lien. Nice face, eh? Shame about the tits. Noth-

304

ing up here, your Chinese—flat, if you take my meaning," he added delicately. "She's Lo's girlfriend—or maybe his sister, I forget." He offered the bag of peanuts. "Go on, take one. In this place us Round-Eyes have got to stick together."

"You understand Chinese?" Kirov asked.

"Not this lot. This is Mandarin. The locals speak Fukienese. I've picked up a few words—how much? too much, please, thanks and fuck off. The big guy is Pi Lien's dad. He gets his mates together and they take on the robbers and rescue the hero or something like that. Do you really want to watch this or shall we get a bite to eat?" The Australian got to his feet, a big man with a big belly restrained in a pair of green and blue striped trousers by a heavy leather belt with a brass Chinese medallion as a clasp. Over this he wore a brightly patterned cotton shirt and a red handkerchief tied about his neck. His head was heavy, with plenty of chins and folds of skin, a narrow lipless mouth, broad wide-pored nose and hyperthyroid eyes. What was left of his hair was gray and he wore it pasted and swept across a mottled scalp.

"I know a place," he said as they emerged into Chung Hua Road. "A beer and a bite, OK? Watch for the cars. Jesus these Chinese! How they can stand that opera stuff, Christ knows! Mongolian suit you? You eaten Mongolian before? Pete, isn't it? That's what they told me."

"Pete will do."

"Harry—pleased to meet you, Pete—Harry Korn. There's a gap in the traffic, c'mon!" He took Kirov's arm in a powerful grip and together they dodged through the cars. Once on the other side Korn halted breathless. "Those bastards are going to be the end of me, I swear it. Where are we? Sure, this way." He took a side road past a *pachinko* parlor and a hotel that let rooms by the hour, and bumped his way through the crowds of Chinese bunching around the open shops and the small food stalls. "You notice," he said as they walked along, "that I don't keep an eye out for tails. There's no point. In this place a Round-Eye sticks out like a sore thumb. If someone wants to find you, he'll find you. The normal rules don't apply and you've just got to get used to it, so relax."

"Ko'tory 'chas?"

Korn laughed. "Sorry, mate, I don't speak the lingo too good."

"You're Russian?"

"As they come, but I left the old country when I was twelve and there isn't much call for the mother tongue in Sydney. It's something else you've got to get used to, I'll tell you about it sometime. Looks like we're here." They were outside a restaurant with a picture of a Mongolian horseman on the window and a sign in Chinese. Harry Korn led the way inside, dealt with the manager, found a table and ordered a couple of beers. "We serve ourselves," he explained. He took a plate from a stack and began helping himself to thin slivers of meat and chopped vegetables. He took them to the cook who fast-fried them on a hotplate and passed them back. When he returned to the table he found Kirov still there. "Not eating, huh? Too much tucker on the plane? You can try the other stuff if you like." He pointed out another table where the diners were picking morsels of food from a copper steamer. "No? I guess travel has screwed your guts up. Me, I'm a growing boy." He took a pair of wooden chopsticks, snapped them apart and prodded at his dish. A few seconds of this and he put the chopsticks down and put on a miserable face. "You're fair putting me off, Pete, that's the truth. Something getting at you? Spit it out."

"What were you told?" Kirov asked.

"You don't trust me, eh? I can understand that. But I'm loyal, believe me. I may have spent most of my life in Oz, but my dad was a good union and Party man and I took in Marx and Lenin with my mother's milk."

"That wasn't my question."

"No? Suit yourself. What was I told? The answer is — not a lot. I got a request to give you whatever help you needed but strictly off the record, something to do with a fight among the grown-ups back at Moscow Center. OK, so I don't care, I'm a soldier and I do what I'm told."

"What help can you give me?"

"That depends on what you want. But not much." Korn shrugged and looked serious. He was a big man and the other customers were small people. Kirov was conscious of their visibility. Harry wanted to confide. "I've been trying to tell you something, Pete. This place isn't like other countries — different rules apply. The fact that I'm from Australia should have told you that." He leaned forward. "Do you have any idea how difficult it is to place a Russian here, in a country that's paranoid about Communism and has no business with the Soviet Union? You were thinking maybe that there's an organization here — that somewhere there's the usual gang of KGB-issue hoods and pimps backing me up? If that's your idea, you can forget it. Harry Korn is *it!* And even getting me installed, up and running was like landing a man on Mars." Korn fell back in his chair, his belly resting on his lap. At the next table the diners were leaving. Korn checked his watch, mopped his brow and called for another beer.

"What sort of support do you have? Do you have a local network?"

"Oh, sure!" Korn answered ironically. "I have a local network, and so does the CIA. The trouble is that they're the same network!" He laughed and sank his face in his tankard of beer. When he had finished he gave Kirov a goggle-eyed stare. "Let me tell you something about your Chinee," he said slowly in the way that people do when they're about to tell you they've been in the business for forty years man and boy. "Your Chinee doesn't give a fuck for ideology!" This was wisdom, so he paused to let it sink in. "He cares about the members of his family — all five hundred of them — his clan and his secret society. You've heard of the Kuomintang that's supposed to be the government? Well, you can forget about that too. It's just window dressing. Political parties are strictly for Round-Eyes. The real power in this country is a secret society — the Bamboo Society. Anyone who's anyone is a paid-up member."

"What does that have to do with your network?"

"The Bamboo Society supplies it — where else am I going to get one from? They supply me, they supply the CIA, and they supply every other Round-Eye intelligence agency that tries to get a foothold here. They do things for me if they feel like it, and they tell me what they want to tell me. Same goes for everyone else."

Kirov looked about the restaurant again. Another table had cleared. No new customers had come in. Harry Korn was checking his watch again. Seeing Kirov watching him, he grinned and tapped the watch glass. "Rolex," he said. "Do you want me to get one for you?"

"Like the one you gave Scherbatsky?"

"Who told you that? I never gave Scherbatsky a watch," he said crossly. "Let me tell you about that bastard. He came here and he gave me a load of shit about being a big shot back in Moscow so that I was running around and spending a fortune on him. And then he tried to sell me this piece of junk that he'd bought in Singapore one time, not even a genuine Taiwan Rolex."

"What about your genuine Taiwan network? Is it any more genuine than your watch?"

Horn looked shocked, then thought about it and nodded: "Perhaps you've got a point."

"Then who are you really working for?"

"It beats me. The Chinese? I used to worry about it but now I don't. Like you, Pete, I'm just a policeman. Once upon a time I thought that policemen were loyal to something, you know, something outside of themselves. But then I realized that the blokes who were giving the orders told me lies, and I could never understand what the point of it all was. So then I became loyal to the idea of just being a policeman—and, you know, *it was all right!*"

In the silence the waiters haunted the doors of the almost empty room. A fan whirred and stirred the muddy air.

"Let's get pissed," said Harry Korn.

"Do people normally go home this early?"

A waiter was relaying a table. The others were just standing around. Harry Korn said: "I don't know what the Chinese normally do. Maybe it's a saint's day or something." He tried a fat smile. "Relax, Pete."

Kirov looked down at his glass where the beer was losing its sparkle. He thought that the big man might be right: travel had screwed up his guts and everything else. He was tired. The walls of the restaurant were closing in. A Chinese box—was he inside or outside? When he cast his eyes in Harry's direction again, the Australian was still holding his dopey smile and his goggle eyes were as loose as beads.

"What do you know of the Mimosa Drug Company?"

"Why do you want that information?" Korn asked.

"You don't want to tell me?"

The other man flashed his gold incisor. "Did I say that, Pete?"

"Who are you expecting? Why do you keep looking at your watch and the door?"

Korn came over as if he would cry. "Hey, Pete, is that any way to carry on? I'm just nervous. Aren't I allowed to be nervous—here, on my own, with all these Chinks forever spying on me? You're not an easy bloke to get on with," he added reproachfully.

"The Mimosa Drug Company."

"Mimosa—OK," Korn said hastily, then paused to think. "It dates from the early seventies. There's one factory, some place in Kaohsiung. They make medicines, antibiotics a whole range of stuff." He halted. "I could bore you with the details, what do you want to know?"

"What's the involvement of the CIA?"

"You pick your questions." Korn let out a laugh. It was all air and no enjoyment. "Seriously — you haven't been listening to what I've been telling you. Sure, the CIA set the factory up so that they could play nasty games away from prying eyes; then they sold out in 'seventy-five or around then to the Chen brothers. But it's all a front. The CIA couldn't have operated in the first place without the Bamboo Society taking a piece. And who do you think provided the Chen brothers with the money to buy? You see what I'm getting at? Out here the boundaries aren't too clear. Maybe Mimosa is still working for the CIA."

"Or maybe for us?" Kirov inquired calmly. He caught sight of his hand lying still on the table, a remote object flickering distantly. He went on: "Or maybe for both of us — KGB and CIA? You just said it, Harry: out here the boundaries aren't too clear. And we're all policemen doing policemen's work, aren't we, so we don't care who we work for? If Ferenc Heltai gives you orders and a bit of money to soothe your problems, then you don't mind carrying the orders out, do you? What did he ask you to do, Harry? Organize shipments of antibiotics so that he and his friends in the Army could make money on the black market? And then perhaps arrange some fancy poisons that the CIA have been producing over here? Who does Heltai want to poison, Harry?"

The last question was final like a door slamming. Korn's fingers tightened and snapped one of the wooden chopsticks.

"Well, Harry?" Kirov asked reasonably.

"You bastard!" Korn whispered in a dry weepy voice. His hand began to move toward his jacket. "You're a dead man," he added and probably meant the words to be scary but they sounded as though he wanted his ball back. The steps to the restaurant rattled with feet.

As Korn pulled his gun, Kirov glanced to the side. Three Chinese, taut as springs, appeared at the entrance to the room. Kirov kicked under the table at the fat man's shin and tipped the table forward. Korn was too slow to avoid it. He went down in the crash. Kirov dived low to avoid a shot from the direction of his three new assailants, and, as they came at him, sprang up, grabbed the copper steamer from the closest table and threw the whole boiling mess into the face of the nearest man. The other two hesitated, frozen by the scream that issued from the injured Chinese. Kirov used that split second to scoop up a tablecloth and fling it over the head of a second man before heading for the nearest door. A couple of shots followed him.

The door led into the kitchen. A gaggle of cooks and waiters cowered at the far end by the exit. By the near wall was a trolley. Kirov grabbed it and pushed it against the entrance door. For a second he held the door closed, then the wood shivered as bullets came through it. He released the trolley, backed down the space between the stoves and seized a pan of vegetables from one of the burners as the door from the restaurant burst open. He let fly with the pan at the intruder's head and looked around for another weapon.

And then silence.

The door stood open and empty. The wreck of the trolley lay on its side in the gangway. The pan was on the floor in a pool of water and vegetables. Water dripped from a corner of the stove. A faint hiss of steam came from somewhere and a low jabber of voices from the terrified cooks. A digital clock dropped a number like a brick. All that noise and silence. Then an Australian voice said: "Go in and get him, you slant-eyed prick!" And a man appeared in the doorway firing.

He fired wildly. One of the cooks went down with a whimper. The others yelled murder and scattered. The shots ricocheted from the cast-iron stoves and the tiled walls and blasted pans from the burners. The burst lasted a couple of seconds and stopped. The door to the restaurant swung open and empty as before.

Kirov found himself on the floor in a gap between racks of plates and vegetables where some reflex had thrown him. The stillness was like death. The Chinese cooks, in their white cottons, were stacked like mummies. From the direction of the door came the click of bullets being fed into a magazine and of a magazine being jammed into the position and a bolt action doing whatever bolt actions do. A foot crashed into the door, which flew back and smacked the wall. One of the cooks let out a wail and was drowned in hushes from the others. Slow footsteps echoed on the tiled floor.

Kirov slid a few feet to a gap in the racks with a view of the main gangway and a glimpse of feet in soft rubber-soled slippers and legs in black trousers and, over the stove, a sallow expressionless face. His assailant picked up a spatula and drummed it on the cast iron — clack — clack — rhythmically, each hit as sharp as a firecracker. Another couple of steps and he was invisible.

"Where is he?" Harry Korn yelled from his shelter in the restaurant. Then, feebly, he tried: "Hey, Pete, let's talk about this! What do you say? Come on, Pete, you're a professional, you know when you're beat!" A pan was knocked from the stove and crashed to the ground. After a pause, a plate followed, then another. Stacks of crockery were swept from every surface and smashed on the tiles. The kitchen resounded to a crescendo of breaking plates, and, as suddenly, the noise stopped and there was nothing but cautious footfalls.

Kirov edged again into shelter from the direct view of the other man. Across the gangway, on a table in a mound of vegetable rind, was a cleaver and by the cleaver a glass bowl holding a black sauce. The distance was only a few meters, but the open gangway was between and he had only an approximate idea where the man with the gun was located. But the cleaver was the only visible weapon. He could not stay put. He had to take what chance he had and use it. He moved into a crouching position ready for a leap into the open.

He sprang to his feet and threw his body across the gap. No one in the gangway. He reached the table and his hand stretched out to grasp the cleaver. A yell from nowhere shattered the silence. A figure appeared suddenly from the same nowhere on the other side of the table. The gun swept down and smashed his fingers and another hand reached for the cleaver. Two shots rang out. Kirov's injured hand rested on the blade and the other hand grasped his and fought for it. His wrist was yanked and forced back. The face grinned. His fingers lost the cool feel of the cleaver blade and he was flung backward against the stove. The yell again and a nightmare vision of the Chinese cooks dancing a mad gibbering dance. His eyes rolled in pain and his attacker was there again, close against him, his face flat and pale as the moon. Kirov thrust out his hand to grasp at the gun, but already he had lost the cleaver and it was held by his enemy and swinging through the air toward his head. In desperation he released the other man's gun hand, took up the bowl of black liquid and dashed it into his face. There was an unearthly scream as the salt and acid in the sauce burned the other man's eyes. He let fall the cleaver and rolled forward with his face in his hands.

For a moment Kirov stood back in a state of paralysis. His adrenaline was spent and he could feel shock closing down his body systems. The Chinese was on the floor, bundled in pain and clutching his gun somewhere underneath him. Then Harry Korn was in the doorway. But the fat man had his eyes tight-closed and was pumping bullets in every direction except the one that counted. Kirov glanced at him almost casually and then stepped to the kitchen exit and out into the alleyway and the cool night air. No one followed him.

He walked the length of the alley and then some more alleys that might have been streets since they were full of people and small storefronts selling clothing and recording cassettes, and the occasional food stall with a couple of stools and a display of cooked chicken feet. He hit a main thoroughfare but he didn't know which one it was. The pavements were still packed and the people stared at him, perhaps because he was a tall Round-Eye or because his clothes were a mess with spatters of the black sauce and somebody's blood. He kept his left hand shoved inside his jacket and didn't want to look at it. The pain told him he was alive and that seemed like a good idea. All the while he was conscious of the eyes watching him, the neutral gazes of the placid old men sitting at the food stalls and storefronts and timid women with their children in tow, watching him and avoiding him when he returned their looks, now you see me now you don't, a meaningless espionage that unnerved him as if he were naked. And then he was opposite a large railway terminus which registered dimly and he guessed this was Chunghsiao West Road.

He crossed the road and went into the station. He joined a queue at the public telephones and when one was free fed it a dollar and called the hotel. The ringing tone to his extension lasted a half minute and then the receiver was picked up. Nobody spoke but some faint English dialogue from the television set came through. Kirov said: "Nadia," and waited for a reply.

"Hi there, Peter," said an American voice. "This is Bill Craig. I've got some news for you. Billie-Boy has got the girl!"

29

Craig's instructions were short. "Go to the Lungshan Temple."
He wasn't interested in questions. "You'll just have to trust me,
Peter. Remember that I've got the girl. I guess that by now you
know all about my funny ways." The telephone couldn't disguise
his excitement or his massive self-satisfaction.

Kirov left the station and picked up a cab. The driver didn't understand English but was used to taking Westerners to the Wanhua
section of the city. The vehicle slipped into the traffic along
Chungking Road South and then cut west by Kwangchow Street
where things livened up, the small stores were doing a roaring trade
and the press of people was thick. The cabbie dropped Kirov on
the south side of the street and pointed at a large building with a
pagoda roof that stood in an open compound across the way.
Crowds came and went through the portal. Kirov was the only European in a sea of Chinese.

He pushed his way into a large hall where in chaotic fashion the
tourists mingled with the worshippers and it was difficult to tell
which was which. A booth dispensing wooden chips for telling for-
tunes was doing brisk business and a group of Buddhist monks
floated through the crowd as if it didn't exist. The hall gave onto
an open courtyard opposite the main shrine. The latter was a clut-
ter of statues and offerings, a mix of dusty gold and bright patches
of fruit; at other times Kirov might have been interested but he
could only remember that Craig had got Nadia and that the American was capable of anything once the mood was on him; and the
mood was on him if the mad excitement on the phone was a guide.

Why here? What was he to look for? His appearance was at-

313

tracting attention as before, but it was the same mix of visible invisibility that the Chinese paid to all foreigners. Or maybe, as Harry Korn implied, it was that he couldn't tell the difference. He skirted the courtyard, watching for any sign of recognition and found himself at the back of the temple caught in a throng of students praying for their exams at a row of brightly colored idols. As he scanned them, Harry Korn appeared.

The Australian had cleaned himself up, straightened his clothes and combed his sweaty hair. He ignored Kirov and concentrated on nodding and mumbling in the direction of the nearest idol, a grimacing red-faced character. He had taken his jacket off and slung it over his shoulder. Whether it was his intention or not, it showed that he wasn't carrying a gun.

"Hello again, Harry."

The fat man flicked a glance in Kirov's direction and returned to contemplation of the statue. He said: "This fella is Kuan Kung. Don't be put off by the face, he's a good bloke, famous for loyalty and bravery. We could all do with a bit of that, don't you think, Pete, loyalty and bravery?" He made a small obeisance to the idol and turned his fat sad face to Kirov. "Look, mate," he said with difficulty, "I'm sorry about the business earlier."

"About trying to kill me?"

Harry kicked his heel. "Yes — well. The fact is I was a bit emotional and you got me going. Killing you wasn't the general idea. People want to talk to you, straighten things out." He gave an honest-Joe smile. "I screwed up, didn't I? Truth is I'm not much used to this violent stuff — I never had the training. Not much inclined that way either. Too fat and slow."

"Why am I here, Harry?"

"Like I said: people want to talk to you."

"Craig?"

"For example."

"Craig has got Nadia."

Korn bit his lip and shrugged. "Well, I admit, he can be a bit frightening at times. But," he added with a false show of optimism, "he's a fella who listens to reason. He doesn't mix business with . . ."

"Pleasure? Is that what you meant to say?"

"Christ, Pete, you're not making this easy! Can't a bloke apologize? I'm trying to help the pair of us, don't you see that? I don't have to like Craig — in fact he's a vicious bastard — but I'm under orders."

"Heltai's orders?"

"Bloody hell, you want everything up front and spelled out!" Korn took a damp handkerchief from one of his pockets and mopped his damp face. The nearest of the students broke off his prayers and turned his expressionless moon-shaped face in the fat man's direction. Korn barked something at him in Chinese. "Bloody Chinks," he said to Kirov, "you can never tell how much they understand."

"Who is the GRU station chief?" Kirov asked.

"What station chief? I told you, this is a shoestring operation: I'm *it*."

"So you report to Aquarium as well as Moscow Center?"

"If you like. I send them the occasional love letter. There's not much goes on here on the military side; you couldn't justify the cost let alone the difficulty of putting a second bloke into Taiwan." In frustration he went on: "What are you asking me? Is that how Heltai got at me? Yes, it's how Heltai got at me. Am I bought and paid for? Too bloody right I'm bought and paid for! There! Satisfied?"

"Craig is working for the CIA," Kirov answered. His companion waved his hand limply as if saying goodbye to everything. He looked around for a place and then squatted heavily on the ground.

"Who cares?" he said wearily. "What does it bloody matter?" He looked up like a fat schoolboy looking for guidance. "Were you ever on a foreign posting?" he asked.

"Once."

"Where?"

"Washington."

"Ever talk to the CIA? You know what I mean, on a friendly basis."

"Sometimes."

"I'll bet you did!" Korn moved uncomfortably on the paving. He spread his buttocks like a suction cup. "Our political lords and masters," he resumed in a quiet, thoughtful tone, "don't give a toss about us. We're expendable. It's the same on the American side. They'd have us at each other's throats and blood all over the place just so long as we came up with the goods. And good luck to them! But what about us? Don't us poor dumb animals who don't know what's going on—don't we have a say?"

"Come to the point."

"The point is we talk to each other — to the other side. We reach agreements, we negotiate, we do deals. It helps to keep the body count down. So I'm cooperating with the CIA? Looked at the other way, the CIA is cooperating with me! So who's the traitor, eh?"

"You tell me, Harry."

Korn gave an acid laugh. "You don't catch me so easily, Pete. Ask Heltai when you see him next. He says I'm to work with Craig, so I'm working with Craig."

"What for? What's the purpose?"

"Search me. All I know is that, as long as I'm cooperating, Craig isn't trying to kill me. And from my point of view that's a bloody good idea." Korn struggled to his feet, leaving a damp patch on the paving the shape of a heart. He studied his hands, his shoes, his rumpled seersucker pants. "What do you say?" he added almost affectionately. "Let's go, huh?"

On their way from the temple Harry Korn bought a couple of fortune chips. He cast them on the ground and checked his fate against a paper slip. He murmured: "Shit!" and stuffed the paper in his pocket, then took Kirov's arm and pushed him through the crowd.

A narrow lane ran at right angles to the other side of the road. It was lit by lanterns from the open fronts of the shops, and heaving with a chattering crowd. The corner spot was occupied by a pox doctor's clinic in a wooden shack decorated with poster-sized photographs of diseased genitalia. Next to it was a food stall, a couple of boards, a couple of stools, a griddle with some prawns on it, a rack of chicken feet. The lane smelled of food, hot fish and stir-fried greens, pungent sauces and sometimes a whiff of spice from a herbalist. The traders pushed their lines of imported cigarettes, fake Rolexes, perfumes, audio cassettes, just-like-gold jewelry, ginseng, elixir of life, love potions, charms, toys, idols as colorful as dolls, brassware, leatherware, bits of stick and feather with scrolls of Chinese calligraphy. People haggled, sat and ate, scratched their backsides, cuffed their children, made great raucous spits. By the shops sat grave merchants and wrinkled old men, aloof from the crowd, waiting for the mug or the connoisseur. Young crooks in T-shirts and tight jeans assembled customers and harangued them. In the alley that ran off the main lane, children with come-on eyes

316

peered through the flimsy bamboo screens of the brothels. "Four thousand years of civilization," said Harry Korn. Then: "Where the hell am I? Hang on a minute while I take my bearings."

They had stopped by one of the shops. The counter gave straight onto the street and was stacked with cases holding live terrapins. A young orangutan with bright dreamy eyes was sitting on the counter chained by one foot. In his spare foot he clutched one of the terrapins and, in an acrobatic movement, brought it to the level of his pouting lips and studied it with ancient wisdom. The shopholder sat behind the counter watching a video of a dogfight. The struggle was over and the winning cur had its head buried to the ears in the entrails of the loser.

"Got it—that one. C'mon, Pete." The fat man grabbed Kirov by the arm again and, brushing the Chinese aside, forced his way through the crowd. They reached another shop where a press of people had gathered and a young Chinese was making a vigorous pitch for their attention. He stood at a trestle table; behind him was an open room with a few more tables and chairs laid out like a cheap cafeteria. Over his head was a steel bar and hanging from it a row of dead snakes like a rack of ties. There were more snakes in cages stacked on the ground. On the counter was a live cobra.

Korn checked his watch. He took out his handkerchief and mopped his face again. The armpits of his jacket, his crotch and the pockets of his seersucker pants were damp with sweat. He had a bright new Band-aid plaster on his cheek which he fingered as he spoke. "Watch the show, Pete," he said. "This is something you've got to see." For his part he was on tiptoe and looking up and down the lane over the seething mass of people. He turned to Kirov. "Watch—watch," he urged with a thin-lipped grin. Behind his counter the Chinese was making passes at the mesmerized cobra.

The youth had an insistent, jabbering voice. His eyes were fixed on the crowd and he seemed indifferent to the snake except to wave his hand generally to indicate its finer points. Then, without interrupting the low of banter, he grabbed the beast and stuffed it into one of the cases. From a back room somewhere a skinny kid scuttled out, lifted another case and placed it on the table. The older Chinese pushed a stick into the box followed by his hand. It emerged gripping a snake firmly behind the head. He brandished it with a flourish to the crowd. The reptile was a meter or more long and thrashing furiously.

317

"A blue *krait*," said Harry Korn.

Kirov's eyes were fixed on the reptile, its flickering tongue and impotent flailing. He felt its cold fear.

"Is it poisonous?"

The Chinese continued speaking, a high-pitched yammer-yammer.

"Fucking deadly," Korn answered evenly. "But this young bloke knows what he's doing. You and me on the other hand, we should stay away from snakes." He returned to the show. The Chinese, in one sharp movement, impaled the snake on a pair of scissors, slit along its length and tore out its heart.

The snake continued to thrash. Its eyes continued to glitter coldly. Its heart, the size of a man's thumb, lay on the table and continued its regular beat. The skinny kid dashed out from the wings bringing a dirty beer glass. Without taking his eyes from the crowd, the Chinese grabbed the snake and wrung out its blood into the glass. The blood squirted and filled the glass a dark venous red with a crimson foam. The Chinese held it up and his voice grew louder and more emphatic. The snake's heart went thump-thump on the table and showed no signs of slackening.

The skinny kid, like a conjuror's apprentice, produced a smaller glass tumbler with two fingers of murky liquor at the bottom. The Chinese gestured at it and at the snake, which now hung limply though its detached heart was still beating. He took the scissors again and slit further along the animal. His fingers plucked out the gall bladder. He held it between finger and thumb and squeezed until a dark jet of fluid shot out and turned the liquor in the glass a sickly green. He held up the glass and explained its virtues in the same hypnotic tone. Then the skinny kid came out again and placed a small spirit glass on the table. This glass was full.

"Snake venom," said Harry Korn. He checked his watch again. "Show's over and Craig is late." Kirov was still watching the Chinese. The boy was ordering the three glasses on a tray. He finished then disappeared into the wings again and returned with a bowl and spoon. The contents of the bowl steamed. He placed it on the tray. Harry Korn said idly: "Chicken soup."

"Why soup?" Kirov asked.

The fat man paused. His eyes were looking at something over Kirov's shoulder. Then he remembered as if prompted and said: "Didn't I explain? That little piece of butchery is a meal."

"And I'll take it," said Craig.

Craig was wearing Levis, cuban-heeled boots with medallions stitched into the pointed toes, and a tough-guy leather jacket. The zipper of the jacket was partly down and showed a yellow silk scarf wrapped around the American's throat; above this was some chicken skin where his age showed, and then the firm jawline and taut tanned skin drawn over the bones of that monumental head. The hair was all in place and the face freshly shaved even though it was evening when the stubble normally shows through tired skin. Kirov had never before given thought to the American's vanity, but here it was; you could literally touch it, and somehow it was part of the engine that drove the other man's violence.

"Let's go inside," Craig said with a handsome toothy smile and nice-as-pie voice. "Shall we?" His arm was around the waist of Nadia Mazurova. Kirov had so far paid no attention to her because Craig was claiming it all for himself with his piece of theatricality. Now that Kirov was looking at her he thought how calm she was, how assured. And it disturbed him: there was too much martyred calmness in that steady gaze, so that for a moment he had the idea that she and the American were complementing each other, finding meaning for themselves in the posture of the other. It chilled him because it meant that she was adopting the madness of Craig as representing something wider, and, if that was so, then she was as crazy as the American.

Recognizing a hesitation Craig said pleasantly: "I've got a knife to Nadia's back. Does that shock you? Don't think that I wouldn't use it. I know this place and you don't. I could kill her now and walk away and no one would stop me. You've seen the way they treat animals here — and we *gweilos,* we're just animals. Ask Harry."

"He's right," Harry Korn said cautiously. "I've seen it before. The Chinks don't get too excited when the Round-Eyes start killing each other."

"So we're not going to start any trouble, right?" said Craig. "We're going to sit down and talk all of this through like adults."

"You'd be wise to agree," said the fat man. "Definitely a good idea."

Craig snapped his fingers at the skinny kid and threw some bank notes on the table. The kid picked up the tray and took it to one of the tables at the back of the shop and beckoned them through. "You first," said the American, and he followed with the girl. They took positions at the table, Kirov and Harry Korn on one side, Craig with the woman to his right on the other. The kid came up with more cutlery and a paper napkin; he addressed a few words to Harry Korn. Harry asked: "Want a beer? If you don't want to eat the goodies, the boy will get you a beer."

"No beer," said Kirov.

"Well, I need one. And you, whatsyourname — Nadia — for you a beer, a Coke? One beer, one Coke, nothing for you, Pete, not even a Coke? And, Bill, you want something to take the taste away? Beer? *Mao tai?* No?" Harry placed the order and then sat forward and looked pleased that something was accomplished. "OK — fire away," he said.

Craig studied the other men in a leisurely, relishing fashion and then examined the tray in front of him. With his free left hand he picked up the porcelain spoon and tasted the soup and pronounced it good. He looked away and Kirov followed his eyes beyond the confines of the eating house into the mild night. The lanterns strung across the lane gave a sea-green cast to the deep blue of the sky. In the booth directly across, four men, ranged like a tug-of-war team, were skinning a python. Craig seemed satisfied by this and returned to his meal.

"Have you been to the Orient before?" he asked. "I don't recall anything in your record that said you have — but records can be incomplete."

"I haven't been to the East."

"No, I thought not. No doubt Harry has given you some local color on this place. And I could probably give you more; I spent a longish time here in the seventies — but I guess you know about that."

"Yes."

"Yes," Craig repeated thoughtfully. He picked up the glass containing the snake's blood and took a small sip.

"Christ!" groaned Harry Korn. "Do you have to, Bill? It fair makes me want to heave."

"Shut up," Craig retorted. He faced Kirov and dabbed away the rim of blood from around his lips. "Am I disturbing you, Peter?"

"No."

"Do you want to try some? Whatever Harry may feel, it really isn't disgusting; his feelings have more to do with culture shock than with taste, as to which he is entirely ignorant. I recommend

320

you to try. The purpose of this concoction is to enhance virility, masculinity. I can vouch for its powerful effect."

Kirov could see the powerful effect too, and wondered what stimulant the other man was using. He suspected cocaine or an amphetamine. Cocaine was associated with flashes of paranoia. Cocaine, probably. Where did the knowledge get him?

"Why have you come after me?" Craig said sorrowfully. He pulled Nadia closer to him as though he could derive some comfort from her. Kirov caught the glint of light from the knife blade that he had pressed against her. "Is it because of your Great Jewish — what's the name?" He seemed distracted; he passed a hand across his eyes to screen out the light, and took another drink of the blood. "Why *Jewish?*" he asked, this time wiping his lips imperfectly so that a circle of blood remained to emphasize the redness of his lips.

"A sort of joke — a piece of irony."

"And is that why you came after me?" Craig turned to Harry Korn and said with amusement: "Listen to this, Harry. Peter is going to tell you of a conspiracy I'm supposed to be involved in."

"This Jewish thing?" Harry asked in some confusion.

"It's their invention, not mine," Craig explained. "As far as I'm concerned, I didn't regard it in those terms at all. *Conspiracy* is a pretty big word for something that was just a little piece of business. What do you think, Peter? Did George Gvishiani and me get together with the rest of the bad guys and work out a plan to sell antibiotics in the Soviet Union? I like the idea. Where did we meet? What were we wearing — black cloaks and big black hats?" Craig paused and considered Kirov with a cold hostility, then, abruptly, he picked up the glass of gall and threw it back in one gulp. He said: "Did you know you're a goddamn joke, Peter? A pathetic small-time operator!"

"Tell me about it."

"Starting where? You're so damned ignorant you couldn't understand the explanation."

"Tell me about Viktor Gusev," Kirov answered.

The American remained silent. The silence lasted long enough for Harry Korn to start looking concerned, as if Craig had died on him. Kirov knew the truth that the silence arose from the conflict between the other man's massive arrogance and his uncertainty and self-doubt. He turned his eyes away to avoid the threat posed to Craig's dangerous mood by a direct gaze. Instead he looked beyond the other man's shoulder into a small room where an old couple were dining placidly with the skinny kid. They seemed to sense him: the old man placed his chopsticks by his bowl and stared blankly back. Then Craig was saying: "Viktor? Would you believe I met Viktor three times in my life? The first time, I was with George Gvishiani in Moscow and we ran into Viktor in a restaurant. George tells Viktor that I'm called Smirnov, but Viktor has this thing about names and he calls me Zagranichny because he figures I'm a foreigner. We talk about this and that—you wouldn't think we had any business together. Only afterward does George tell me that Viktor is his Moscow distributor."

"And?"

"And? Nothing! Viktor Gusev was an insignificant little faggot and the antibiotics game was just something played for peanuts. You want to know how it started? I was helping the guys in Tbilisi to build their pharmaceuticals plant, and some of the soldier boys said that there was a market for antibiotics and why don't we all make some money out of it. And that was it. George arranged transport and distribution and I organized production. And then, when demand outstripped supply, I brought in stuff from this place with the cooperation of a couple of generals who don't mind taking a bribe. The pay-out was all arranged in diamonds from some jeweler in Moscow."

So Kirov's first version of the Ring had been right, though now it did not seem important. Kirov realized why he had attracted the old man's attention. The old man was talking to the skinny kid. The boy had forgotten to bring the drinks and was rushing to put the order together from the bottles and crates that also occupied the small living quarters. Craig meanwhile applied himself to his meal—a mouthful of chicken and a mouthful of blood—and Harry Korn watched as primly as a middle-aged woman observing a sexual peccadillo. Craig was still at his game of playing out pieces of sexual theater to fascinate others and master the world and himself. When he was in control his voice had a caressing tone; his lips were stamped large, dark and vaginally red. Kirov looked to Nadia Mazurova to see what she saw.

"What happened?" he asked her.

"He had a key to our room," she answered. "I don't know where he got it from. I suppose that here he can do things like that."

"Are you all right?"

She nodded. Kirov watched her hands. They lay flat and shivering before her on the table. Her body was held erect and rigid, her face gray and composed. By an effort of will she had stripped herself of her sexual identity to avoid any dangerous cues, knowing that in the American's frightening mood the slightest thing could prove fatal. He saw Craig's arm wrapped around her body in a secure embrace, the hand holding a sharply pointed blade to the woman's kidneys. In his tension Craig had pricked her with the knife. A scarlet stain, the size of a coin, marked her cotton dress. A drop of blood shimmered on the blade.

"Why am I here?" Kirov asked. "What do we have to talk about?"

"A deal."

"What sort of deal?"

"You stay out of our business."

"Is that your idea?"

"Of course it's Bill's idea!" Harry Korn interrupted. His voice was too loud. At the front of the shop the Chinese youth halted his slaughter of another snake and spared them his empty gaze. Harry whispered: "Bill's a reasonable man."

"No, I'm not," Craig said evenly. "I'd prefer you dead. But there are other interests."

"Bill!"

"Keep your mouth buttoned, Harry."

"Whose interests?" Kirov asked. "Ferenc Heltai's?"

"Could be," Craig assented. He had finished with the glass of blood; it stood on the table, opaque with red foam; his fingers played on it. "How come you know Frank?" he asked. "He seems to have a personal interest in you."

"He tried to kill me."

"Did he?" Craig said skeptically. "You're still here. I get the impression Frank wants to save you from yourself. He seems to see himself as a father figure. What is he, a friend of the family?"

Kirov thought of the encounter in the snow at the Darvitsky Reserve. Heltai hadn't pressed the chance to kill him. He thought of Riga.

"I met him years ago," he answered.

"Years? How many years?"

"A long time ago."

Craig picked up the words, looking for weapons. "Cream cakes and small boys — I figured that was Frank's style." His lips parted, cruel as a sickle. "Your style too, Pete?"

"Not mine," Kirov replied slowly and his eyes took up the other man's and forced them away.

Bouncing in his seat, Harry Korn chimed in: "Let's stop the sparring, shall we, fellas?" He gave a tearful grin. "We could have an aggression situation here, if we're not careful. That wouldn't be a good idea, now would it?" A loud splash marked the blood of another snake being squeezed into a glass and a groan went up from part of the crowd. On the knife blade pressed against Nadia Mazurova, the drop of blood had become a small dark flow, and Harry was laughing.

"Let's all relax, eh? All this tension . . ." Craig's forefinger, hooked around the ricasso of the blade, was stained with blood. "All this tension . . ." said Harry.

"What deal am I buying?" Kirov let the words snap out. They would all be as mad as the American if they didn't seize some shred of sanity. "Tell me, Bill — what deal is it that puts GRU and CIA together?"

"That's what you'll never know," Craig answered. "Think of that, Peter! You'll never know!"

Kirov recognized the power play. Give in and he was lost.

"It's not enough," he said and got to his feet. Nadia looked up from her hands.

Craig said: "Walk away and I'll kill the girl."

"Go ahead. Kill her."

"You don't mean that."

"In a couple of seconds you'll find out." Kirov pushed his chair back. It scraped along the floor and broke the thread of patter from the front of the shop. Craig looked sharply to the street. The crowd of Chinese were ignoring the snake handler and staring silently at him. He hesitated, then waved a hand at Kirov.

"Sit down, Peter," he said. Kirov took his place again.

"It looks as though Heltai has a hold over you too," he suggested. He looked away in order to emphasize his indifference. "I suppose he must have. These last few years he's been supplying you with your own private madhouse. How many girls have you got through, Bill?" Kirov's voice made it clear that he didn't care. As long as he didn't look at Nadia he didn't care. Instead he let his eyes focus on the stack of cages piled near them against the wall, and the condemned snakes moving sluggishly and flickering their tongues. "Well?" he asked. "What's the deal? What are you and Heltai really up to?"

"Tell him, for God's sake!" Harry Korn urged. Good old Harry, oozing fear—spraying fear everywhere so that everyone got his share. Kirov could have thanked him for it since Craig was also affected; the American's confidence was cracking. Reality was leaking into his fantasies. When he opened his mouth it was a smaller voice that spoke.

"Do you want to know what your people and my people both want?"

"Not my people. Heltai maybe."

Craig contradicted him quietly: "Yes, your people too. *They want things to continue like they've always been!*" He fell silent. Only a snake moved with a dry rustle of scales.

"And that's it?" Harry Korn asked. He looked from one man to the other with incomprehension. "So what happens now? We all go home?"

"Be quiet, Harry," Kirov told him. He could see the knife tip buried into Nadia Mazurova's side. How deep? How could she hold back the pain? There was blood all down the blade; it was smeared all over Craig's hand; the crimson stain on her dress was weeping a long hanging tail. "Go on," he said to Craig. His voice sounded gentle as the warm air.

"Who wants all this change?" Craig's eyes glazed over as he began. Nobody there. Talking to himself. "Whose idea was it? Mine? Yours? Do you think that dumb bastard Grishin wants it—having the past dragged out and raked over? Believe me, Peter, nobody wants it!"

"Persuade me, Bill."

"We had something," the other man went on, "and it worked. It wasn't clean, it wasn't beautiful, but it worked. For damn near fifty years America and the Soviet Union have been facing each other, hating each other, suspecting each other. You don't have to like it, but at least you know where the other guy is coming from— and because you know that, it's safe. You think we want the Soviet Union to disarm? The hell we do! We've got generals and armies and industries and jobs that don't exist if that happens and we don't have any idea how to structure the alternatives. Do you think the Russian people want to change the economy? Not a chance! Maybe they want the other guy to change and work harder so they get more — but they don't want to change themselves. Even the black-market capitalists love Communism. It creates opportunities for guys like Viktor Gusev to get ahead. That's how it is. It's corrupt and it stinks, and we all wish the other guy would do something about it. But good or bad, that's how we've made the world — and that's how the world has made us. You can't change it and take it apart without remaking the people."

"You can try," Kirov answered. But he didn't believe it. He thought of his father. In all the changes and betrayals — Yezhov, Yagoda, Beria — he had never changed himself. He was always a policeman.

The tray still lay in front of the American. It held two empty glasses and a soup bowl surrounded by spills. The third glass held snake venom; Craig showed no sign of drinking it. Kirov wondered what the effect was. Perhaps it wasn't poisonous in the gut, as long as it didn't enter the bloodstream. With his background Craig would know. Heltai too, who had made a living murdering with poison.

"You can't murder change," he said.

Craig laughed. It was an unearthly and uncontrolled laughter. His body shook with it; his eyes glittered moistly; his face shone with sweat; his hand trembled on the knife. Whether the other man was drunk, drugged or insane, Kirov had never seen such a wild display of suppressed violence and malice or experienced a personality so terrifying and destructive, so that for a moment he was paralyzed by it and could hear only that Craig was yelling at him: "You don't know Frank! Frank can do it — you hear me, Peter?"

And at that point Kirov understood. *Heltai could murder change.* But he had no time to consider the point because, as the other man's hand wavered with the knife, Nadia Mazurova swept his arm away and, her face a mask of terror, screamed: "Help me, Petya!"

For a second all three men were frozen, their eyes locked on the woman. She was falling away from them, her face shut with pain, her hands pressed to her side to stem the blood that leaked through her fingers. Pathetic Harry Korn leapt to his feet with his own fat version of terror hanging like a leech from his sweating skin. Then he recoiled as Craig struck out crazily with the knife and the flimsy table upturned.

Kirov grabbed a chair and flung it in Craig's direction. The American sidestepped and the chair went crashing into the stack of cages. The stack tumbled over, the catches on some of the cages burst and the snakes spilled onto the floor. Craig stooped and seized one of the animals behind the head before it could recover. He lifted it triumphantly into the air and threw it at Kirov. The snake's dry scales whipped across Kirov's face and the reptile fell somewhere behind him.

A bedlam roar went up from the crowd. Harry Korn was dancing and stamping as if putting out a fire. The room seemed to be full of Chinese—the skinny kid, the two old people, the stallholder—running about with sticks and chairs and yelling their heads off. Nadia was on the floor somewhere where she had fallen. Kirov could see them all, but between himself and the American there seemed to be a cone of stillness.

About Craig there was now an eerie calm. He had got hold of another of the dazed reptiles. It was gripped firmly and held in an outstretched hand with the jeweled eyes pointed at Kirov and its long body thrashing rhythmically. "Come and get it," he was saying but only with his lips; no sound came out. In his other hand the knife, smeared and bloody, flickered like the snake's tongue. Craig came forward and Kirov retreated before him, his feet feeling their way through the debris. The floor seemed alive with skittering snakes.

Step by step they crossed the room.

And then, slowly, Craig's mouth opened—a big soundless hole—and his pace faltered and his eyes started from their sockets. The features of that great leonine head locked themselves rigid in a paroxysm of agony and with every step that he advanced he seemed to become smaller until suddenly he tumbled and pitched forward onto the ground. Then he was weeping: "Help me, Peter—I've been bitten." A snake writhed from underneath him.

They stepped from the shambles of the eating house into the lane with its shadows and lanterns and its smells of spice and cooking. As Harry Korn had said, they were invisible to the Chinese. The whores and the hawkers, the snake butchers and the peddlers opened a path for them, the tall Round-Eye holding up the frail woman in the bloodied dress and, behind them, the bobbing fat man. A voice could still be heard crying faintly: "Help me, Peter," and in the eating house a skinny kid, two old people and a youth in T-shirt and denims were standing around a lying figure, counting money and righting the fallen chairs.

They reached the end of the lane. Now there was traffic and lights to break the tropical darkness. Across the road the Lungshan Temple lay in shadow and smoldering color. They walked in no particular direction, the man with his arm around the woman holding her upright and close to him as if there were a bond of tenderness between them. The fat man called plaintively "What's it all about? What were Craig and Heltai up to? A conspiracy, yes? To do what? Tell me, for Christ's sake!" He stopped and breathlessly took a rag from his pocket to mop his face. He yelled after the departing figures: "What was all that stuff about murdering change? Who's going to be murdered?" His final words were: "Why *Jewish?* At least tell me that!"

Among the street-front stores and godowns, a colorful bazaar sold electrical goods and a crowd stood outside it, blocking the pavement. Kirov and the woman struggled to make headway through the clamoring people. A child tugged at his sleeve and pointed to the interior of the store where a television was playing its picture into the night.

The picture was a still shot of Mikhail Gorbachev standing calmly in an entourage of wary security men at some airport or other. Close by him was a second man, this one in late middle age, with thin red hair and eyes that appeared to have neither brows nor lashes.

The commentator was talking with furious urgency. But his words were in Chinese.